S. J. MAKIELSKI, JR.

BELEAGUERED MINORITIES

CULTURAL POLITICS IN AMERICA

BELEAGUERED MINORITIES

BELEAGUERED

MINORITIES

Cultural Politics In America

J. Makielski, Jr.

ola University, New Orleans

∃

H. Freeman and Company
Francisco

Library of Congress Cataloging in Publication Data

Makielski, Stanislaw J.
  Beleaguered minorities.

  Includes bibliographies.
  1. Minorities–United States. 2. Political
participation–United States. I. Title.
E184.A1M26 1973   323.4'0973   73-12290
ISBN 0-7167-0789-6
ISBN 0-7167-0788-8 (pbk.)

CONTENTS

Part Two   *Minority Politics*

PREFACE

"The study of politics," Harold D. Lasswell wrote in 1936, "is the study of influence and the influential."* Although the validity of his precept remains unchanged after nearly forty years, students of politics today have come to realize that "the influential" are not always those who occupy the obvious seats of power.

The events of the 1960s drove home the lesson that the powerless can, under certain conditions, exert influence in ways that were previously overlooked or underestimated. By challenging the political system, minority groups forced it to respond. A response was not always tangible; often it took the form of a painful reappraisal of what America is, where it is headed, and what are to be the purposes of its political life. But, significantly, every reappraisal had to take into consideration the goals, strategies, and tactics of those who formerly had had no influence.

This study is an attempt to come to grips with the roots, directions, and methods of the search for power by the powerless. It is concerned with those who make a conscious effort to overcome the disadvantages associated with "minority status."

In time, historians may decide that the effort was fruitless or that, for all the energy expended, the political system absorbed every challenge without seriously modifying itself. From the perspective of the early 1970s, however, it appears that minority politics will persist separate from the mainstream of conventional American politics. In the winter of 1972-73, black students rebelled at Southern University, Louisiana, two of them dying in the confrontation; American Indians "liberated" the Bureau of Indian Affairs and attempted to withstand a siege at

*Harold D. Lasswell, *Politics: Who Gets What, When, How* (New York: McGraw-Hill, 1936), p. 13.

Wounded Knee, South Dakota; and women held their first full-scale political convention. Events like these deserve explanation in a context larger than a single, brief period in the nation's history.

It is hoped that the framework offered here—a politics of culture—will be a step toward providing the needed explanation. It is further hoped that this study will help to advance our understanding of what "influence" is, how it works, and how political man attempts to gain it and use it to his purposes.

A book like this inevitably rests on the work, thought, and efforts of others. The large body of research that has been drawn on in these pages defies adequate acknowledgment. Those who read in the field will understand how dependent this book is on prior scholarship.

In addition, over 150 men and women, who are members of minorities, volunteered their thoughts and experiences in conversations and in correspondence. Few are prominent in the conventional sense of the word, but all are serious thinkers and were sensitive to the needs of my research and eager to be helpful. I cannot thank them enough, and only hope that I have done justice to their kindness.

Finally, but by no means least, I must thank Valerie Jean Conner, who read and criticized the entire manuscript. Her understanding of America's history saved me from many serious errors. Those that remain are entirely my own fault.

May 1973

S. J. Makielski, Jr.

Part One
THE MINORITY CONDITION

One
The Beleaguered Minorities:
An Overview

The importance of minorities to the political structure of the United States is incontestable. Practically every person is a member of some minority, that is, some collection of individuals who do not and cannot have their wills prevail all the time. There is a double dilemma in the concept of a minority. First, in our society identifiable and separate groupings are regarded as both politically and sociologically unhealthy. Yet, somehow these groupings are essential to our sense of community, personal identity, and perhaps even the functioning of the political system itself. Second, minority groupings are almost always associated with positions of subordination, perhaps of exploitation, and certainly of disadvantage. We simultaneously concede, however, the necessity for elite minorities—not everyone can earn a Ph.D., nor can everyone serve in high political office or achieve a position of great power in the corporate structure. Those who do are certainly members of minorities, at least in the numerical sense. The 100 members of the United States Senate are such a tiny percentage of the population that it would be useless to compute it, yet they wield a power individually and collectively so great that many men sweat blood and money to attain membership. Thus in the public mind it seems that minorities combine that which is good and that which is bad—that which is politically essential and that which is politically pathological.

Three Political Questions

The confusion inherent in attitudes toward minorities is not limited to the United States. Nigeria, the Sudan, Bangladesh, and Northern Ireland are names that are now painfully familiar. Although the problems of these nations cannot be viewed entirely as minority politics, an important part of their anguish must be understood in just those terms.

In this respect, the United States is not alone in the modern world, even though it is undeniably the wealthiest of the great nations of the world. As a democracy, it can claim one of the longest histories of stability, continuity, and consensus. But, in the 1960s this country was plagued by the threat of domestic revolution, widespread rioting, individual acts of violence, bitterness, distrust, and alienation.

The roots of the difficulty lie in unresolved conflicts of belief, behavior, and assumptions about our political order. Since the turn of the century, American scholars and public figures have rejoiced in the "pluralism" of our society. Within the context of a universal acceptance of the nature of society, individuals, groups, and organizations were seen as free to struggle to attain their own special interests. In practice, however, there were unpleasant aspects of pluralism. Even in the early 1900s, the condition of the cities, the "Negro Question" (as it was then called), and the persistence of urban and rural poverty indicated that the American system worked imperfectly. But it can be safely said that most Americans assumed that "progress" was taking place: today's poor would be tomorrow's affluent; slums would be converted into garden cities; the family farm would once again become the sturdy backbone of society. Even the Negroes could hope to attain eventually the same economic and social status that others, such as the Jews and the Irish, had attained before them.

The widespread belief was that the United States could solve its problems without having to change fundamentally its political processes or economic order. Even more, it was assumed that its political and economic institutions would solve the problems. There were, of course, doubters. The hardy band of socialists and progressives, the much smaller band of communists, a sprinkling of anarchists, and simply skeptical intellectuals dissented noisily, but these were, truly, a handful.

In retrospect, what seems difficult to understand is how tenacious the dream was. The Depression of the 1930s shook many of the faithful badly; but surges of patriotism caused by war seemed to heal temporarily most of the scars of the Depression years. Well into the 1960s, the number of doubters remained small. Those who struggled against "the system" usually said, and quite evidently believed, that their goal was not to change it, but simply to make it work a little better by distributing its benefits to everyone.

It would be easy to say that the burning of the cities in the mid-1960s also burned out a great part of the faith in the American system. The war in Vietnam and the bitter confrontations on college campuses only underscored a disillusionment that had already set in. As the following chapters will show, however, the seeds of fundamental conflict were sown long before the 1960s; they have, in fact, been the history of America's beleaguered minorities.

The 1960s marked the arrival of a critical point of grievance, neglect, and, ironically, concern. America's Negroes, Indians, and Mexican-Americans had been groping toward a mode of self-expression for decades. In the 1950s they found their voices; in the 1960s they established new political vehicles. Moreover, two other segments of society also began to consider seriously their position in the American scheme. Women, although numerically more than a majority of the population, began to see their status as that of a minority (like the blacks of South Africa or Rhodesia who have numerical superiority but minority status). Students in colleges and universities (and high schools) also began to think of themselves as a minority. Both women and students based their minority status on their inability to control the forces shaping their lives. Many felt that at best they were treated with indifference; at worst, as objects to be oppressed and exploited.

What occurred in the 1960s was akin to a revolution of rising expectations in underdeveloped nations. Self-consciousness arises; it is realized that nothing is immutable and change can be brought about by deliberate action. But, and the qualifier is important, often the hope for change outstrips the progress that actually occurs. The disparity between expectation and reality is painful enough if it is between economic capacity and human wants, as in so many developing nations; it is even more agonizing if it is between segments of a population, such as a minority and a dominant set of interests.

The disparity raises three serious political questions for the United States. The first is, What is the source of the division between "dominant" and "minority" segments of society? In other words, why are some people privileged and in control and others underprivileged and controlled? The most general answer is that the distinction is a product of the tension between a desire for social stability and a desire for social change. In theory, the two are compatible. In practice, however, one man's social stability is another's social discrimination, especially if such stability freezes into law and political behavior a historical pattern of deprivation, prejudice, and isolation.

A minority, in examining the political, economic, and social landscape, can begin to perceive that life consists of misery, poverty, dependence, and dehumanization. Stability in society, in these circumstances, is no more than the preservation of the intolerable. As a consequence, the minority, or significant parts of it, chooses to upset the stability of the system in order to improve its own lot. The feminists cry out for a radicalization of the family system; the Black Panthers insist on revolution now; some members of the Chicano movement contemplate total separation from the United States. These battle cries are shorthand statements of the failure of the political order to find a means of meeting new expectations. They are also, however, expressions of the effects of discrimination, which in turn are rooted in deep-seated cultural values.

The second question is whether a minority has the capacity to undertake political action in any successful fashion. Is the modern, corporate, postindustrial, bureaucratic state a promising arena in which to work out minority aspirations? The answer will not be known until well into the future. It is clear, however, that the kind of political styles, goals, strategies, and tactics that minorities adopt will have an effect on the answer. They can choose to play by the established rules of the political game or can attempt to create a new game that they believe is better suited to their handicaps and aspirations. Many of America's "new minorities" feel impelled to think in terms of a different game because the political system as they understand it is too resistant to change.

The third, and equally difficult, question concerns the overall effect of the new minority politics on the American political system. There is no doubt that there has already been an effect and that there will continue to be far-reaching ramifications. Is America to become more open to all or to move towards greater repressiveness, even conceivably to a form of crypto-fascism? There are those who look at the evidence and see one answer; others who view the same data come up with an entirely different conclusion.

These broad questions cannot be completely answered today. But, we can see clearly that the efforts of a minority to express its needs create a new set of political conditions. These conditions are not new in the sense that they never existed before, but in the sense that our society has reached a point at which differences between minorities and the dominant segment are so extreme as to produce intense political activity. We are facing a situation in which the role of minorities in the political system poses questions that we have done little to answer in the past and that we are ill-equipped to answer now.

Old Minorities and New

The "beleaguered minorities" in American society consist of those who feel themselves to be surrounded by a hostile environment, who have a long history of being subjected to discrimination and deprivation, and who are relatively powerless in making any change in their condition. As minorities, they feel themselves to be alone, even though other minorities have existed in this country for a long time. In that they sense that they are beleaguered, they are "new."

The "old minorities," the ethnic groupings composed of Jews, Italians, Irish, Germans, Slavs, or Scandinavians, have previously faced hostility, prejudice, and maltreatment. As a consequence, it is always tempting to compare the old minorities with the new, arguing that a society that has fairly comfortably accommodated one minority will eventually in the same way make room for another.

There are, however, some differences. One difference is the nature of the "mark" that the new minorities wear. They are labelled by society in a fashion that is clear to that society. Whereas the members of ethnic groups may choose to join the majority by changing their names, religion, and language, and by adopting mores, values, and an appearance that will make them acceptable, blacks, women, and American Indians do not have such a choice.

Second, the historical pattern cannot be ignored. Blacks have been in American society since 1619–longer than any of the ethnic groupings of significant number by almost two centuries. Yet, that advantage in time has not produced the degree of assimilation that exists for any of the ethnic groupings. Even in the North where slavery was terminated before the advent of ethnic groupings, blacks are the targets of prejudice and deprivation. The same, of course, is true of the American Indian and of the Mexican-American.

Aside from the cultural determinations, the reasons for the differences in the degree to which minorities are assimilated are no doubt partly historical. The great waves of immigrants came to America at times when manpower was desperately needed to exploit the new technologies for using the nation's natural resources. Although many people were abused in the most brutal manner, many found economic opportunities available. Immigrant labor was the basis for the development of corporations and unions.

Moreover, immigrants chose to come to America and to come on terms that were in harmony with American values, that is, the achievement of economic well-being and liberal democracy. Although shared aspirations did not prevent anger, resistance, and resentment on the part of the old-line Protestant groupings, there were fewer cultural clashes between immigrant and older inhabitant than either might have originally expected. Although expressing it in different tongues and different ways, both shared the same general set of values.

The immigrants gathered at strategic locations. In cities, the political organizations either had to absorb them (and be absorbed by them) or collapse. They were able to grasp fairly quickly the levers of local and state political power and thereby gain access to national political power. Although they were constitutionally denied the choicest plum of the political process (the presidency of the United States), they did gain other, often equally rewarding, offices.

Most, and possibly all, immigrants felt a powerful need to change the circumstances of their lives. They were aggressive enough, daring enough, and skillful enough to undertake a major uprooting of their families and traditional patterns of life. Although many were undoubtedly disappointed by the actual results, their ambitions and aspirations died hard, being transmitted to their children and their children's children. If America did not turn out to be the land of opportunity in every case, it continued to be the land of hope.

Some would argue, too, that American society has since become quite different. In the twentieth century this country has shifted from a rural to an industrial and postindustrial society; from a nation dominated by the small and local businessman and farmer to one in which giant and complex corporations are the characteristic institutions; from a highly fragmented, largely unspecialized governmental system to one in which bureaucratization and interlocking relationships are the important processes. It is undoubtedly true that the immigrant who came before the changes took place found the situation more fluid than he would today.

Circumstances are quite different for the new minorities. Blacks were brought to America involuntarily; Indians were here in the first place and had their land taken away from them; women came as dependents of men. Given these circumstances, there was little hope for individual development or achievement.

What follows, then, rotates around three closely intertwined themes. First, America's new minorities are made up of those who have a special mark, and because of that mark they suffer from a sense of powerlessness. Minority status is not just numerical or statistical. Women, for example, are more than 51 percent of the nation's population, but can be thought of as a minority because of their status rather than their numbers. And, minority status includes economic, social, and legal deprivation as well as subtle forms of psychological discrimination.

Second, the cutting edge of minority politics has been and continues to be group politics. Efforts to overcome the consequences of minority status place a high premium on organization, cohesion, and a sense of unified purpose. America's new minorities have responded to this need with varying degrees of success, but respond they have. Third, the politics of powerlessness is a different kind of politics. It has led to new ways of thinking about the political system, which in turn has produced new sets of goals, strategies, and tactics.

Bibliography

Banton, Michael. *Race Relations.* New York: Basic Books, 1967. An exhaustive study of the topic on a cross-national basis.

Cole, Steward, and Mildred W. Cole. *Minorities and the American Promise: The Conflict of Principle and Practice.* New York: Harper, 1954.

Gordon, Milton M. *Assimilation in American Life.* New York: Oxford University Press, 1964. The standard work and an invaluable sociological examination of assimilative processes.

Handlin, Oscar. *Race and Nationality in American Life.* Boston: Little, Brown, 1957.

Marden, Charles F., and Gladys Meyer. *Minorities in American Society.* New York: American Book, 1968.

Myrdal, Gunnar. *An American Dilemma.* New York: Harper, 1944. One of the few books that is an absolute "must" in readings on minority relations.

Rose, Peter I. *We and They: Racial and Ethnic Relations in the United States.* New York: Random House, 1964.

Simpson, George E., and J. Milton Yinger. *Racial and Cultural Minorities: An Analysis of Prejudice and Discrimination.* New York: Harper, 1965.

Vanden Zanden, James W. *American Minority Relations.* New York: Ronald Press, 1966.

Two
Differentiation and Discrimination

All men are alike; each man is unique. Around this paradox rotate many of the political, social, and economic problems that both primitive and modern societies confront. Any full appreciation of the bases of minority group politics and the place of groups in a society must begin with these fundamental premises, which in their turn are rooted in the biological and cultural circumstances of the human species.

Cultural Bases

In biological terms, people are both similar and different. Their similarities never become identicalities, and their differences have thus far not become so extreme that they are incapable of interacting with each other on a biological basis. However, a visitor from a foreign planet would be struck by the sharp distinctions among groups of people. African tribesmen and white urban Americans would seem quite different in behavior, interests, social structure, and appearance. On a comparative basis, the differences between these people seem to be far greater than those between, say, a horse and a zebra.

Many of the differences among humans can be explained in terms of their respective "societies," that is, the institutions that people have created through time to govern themselves and to fulfill economic, educational, and religious requirements, and the patterns of relationships established among such institutions. Included within, and underlying, every society, however, is a more significant basis of differentiation: culture. Every society is a reflection of at least one culture; in the United States and all other large nations, the society includes more than one culture.

Culture is such a significant basis of differentiation among groupings of people because it establishes the differences in their life-styles, adjustments, behaviors, and attitudes. For our purposes, it is highly satisfactory to think of culture as an intermediary between man and his environment (remembering that environment includes other men as well).

Biologically an individual human is incapable of ordering all of the reality that impinges on his consciousness. Culture enables him to select those things which are important to him, which he needs to know in order to eat, drink, avoid threats to his life or his psyche, mate, or protect his children. He can learn which things to accept and which to ignore by trial and error, sometimes at a terrible cost. He can also learn from other members of the culture, especially those who have a common interest in his survival. They, through language, training, and other signals, help him in the process of ordering his universe so that he is able to cope with it. In short, this is culture: a group of people order the world as they know it so that each of its members can relate to that world in a manner that contributes to the survival of the individual and the group.

Like evolution, the process is not perfect. Not all features of a culture are necessarily "functional" at any given point in time, just as not all evolutionary adaptations are advantageous. Culture may dictate that a primitive people, in large spear-wielding masses, attack a colonialist power equipped with machine guns. What would have been "functional" against an equally equipped enemy is "dys-functional" against a more sophisticated one.

Nonetheless, culture does serve basic functions for the survival of groupings of people and for the individual. First, it provides a general way in which to comprehend the world. It explains phenomena that we experience directly but cannot explain ourselves. Philosophy, theology, science, art, and literature are "cultural" in this sense; they tell us how to understand the strange world in which we live.

Second, culture provides us with a means of ordering priorities in our minds and behavior. It tells us what is important and what is not, at least in a general way. In effect, members of a culture have a set of categories to which experiences can be assigned, ranking them according to importance and immediacy.

Third, and obviously related to the second function, culture does provide a means of communication: a language, including vocabulary, syntax, inflection, gestures, and facial expressions. Although there may well be universal signs, such as a frown or a smile, that all men share in common, the greater refinements required to transmit experience from one individual to another are a cultural phenomenon. Language becomes even more vital because it is one of the most important means by which one human transmits his culture to another. It therefore reinforces and preserves the other functions served by culture.

Perhaps most critical for our purposes, however, is that in combination these functions provide a means by which a cultural grouping can identify its own members as well as persons outside of it. That is, in helping people to explain and understand their environment, culture also helps to define their relationships to other people—a very important part of that environment. Thus, because a man speaks a different language, or has different mating habits, or has different religious beliefs, he can be recognized as an outsider, a stranger, a "foreigner."

Even within a culture, human cultural standards make distinctions between people: between the old and the young, between men and women, between the sick and the well, between the "insane" and the "sane." These distinctions may have biological roots in many cases. Rites of passage perhaps were originally intended to mark the dividing line between a person too young to mate and one capable of mating and thus available for it. One of the important characteristics of such cultural distinctions, however, is that they are transmitted through generation after generation, and their sources may no longer be recognizable.

Biology, then, produces certain objective differences among human beings. Skin color, stages of development (age), and sex are all obvious ones. Cultures react to these distinctions and add new categories as well: behavior, beliefs, and languages, categories of explanation and thought. Taken together, these distinctions begin to take on social and political significance, because they provide a means by which men discriminate among each other and act on the basis of that discrimination.

Discrimination

A culture provides a set of signals or cues that tells its members many things about their environment, including members of the culture itself and people who belong to different cultures. In effect, a human being, as a member of both a society and his culture, is provided with a set of categories by which to order his universe in a way that he has learned to do from early childhood. And it seems universal that one of the sets of categories that everyone learns quickly is to make the distinction between "them" and "us," between "insiders" and outsiders."

It is easier to grasp the concept of insiders and outsiders if it is applied to relatively small groupings than if it is applied to a larger population: a "community," a "race," a nation, a class, or any of the other numerous convenient categories of "us" that people have invented over the years. Further, the leap from a we-ness that is close and protective to a general we-ness that is superior to "them" is even more difficult to grasp. Yet, both seem to be fairly common phenomena. Mankind differentiates among large groupings of people on an insider-outsider basis, and assigns additional sets of categories to that basic one, such as good or bad, trusted or feared, loved or hated, superior or inferior.

Once the label is attached, it continues through time, since successive generations absorb the categories as they acquire the prevailing cultural values of the society. And the labels themselves become a basis for behavior, a set of categories by which members of the society act toward each other. That is, used in a very strict sense of the word, discrimination is a means of differentiating among human beings, either within a society or culture or toward those of different societies and cultures. It may be positive discrimination, in which the people who are the targets of discrimination are regarded as generally superior, are rewarded for their superiority, and perhaps possess special social and political power and privileges. People who have fair skin, for example, are often the beneficiaries of positive discrimination. Discrimination may, however, be negative. The person who is marked for differentiation is controlled, deprived, isolated, or otherwise excluded from full we-ness by those in a position to act on the basis of the category. In this book we are concerned with negative discrimination, although it must be kept in mind that negative and positive discrimination exist together: discrimination against someone means that there is discrimination in favor of someone else.

Because biological "marks" provide a convenient and commonly used means for establishing differences among human beings, they also are persistent sources of discrimination. The most obvious quickly spring to mind: skin color and sex. In addition, however, it is necessary to take note of another essential biological difference, age. And, there is an important distinction between skin color on the one hand and age and sex on the other. The first, at some point in time, earmarked different cultures. Cultural groupings having different skin colors also spoke different languages, probably ate different foods, and had different family structures and codes of ethics. Age and sex, however, are intracultural, which adds a new dimension to discrimination. Discrimination is not just the "clash of cultures," but the *product* of internal cultural determinations, categories that say that some people are different and better (or worse) than other people.

The intracultural implications are important, because it is often assumed, as it was for the "old minorities," that acculturation, the acquisition of the values of a larger culture, should bring an end to discrimination. But, discrimination is itself built into cultures. Even though skin color, or dialect, or ancestry may become diluted in the larger culture, no longer representing very important variations in behavior or values, cultural marks persist through generations as a basis for intracultural discrimination.

Skin color, sex, and age differences are perhaps the most conspicuous marks in the United States, carrying as they do certain burdens. In addition, deviance in terms of the use of the language, in religious preferences, in name, in family structure—all have an impact, although it would seem to a lesser degree.

As already noted, America's pluralism seems capable of absorbing certain cultural and intracultural differences with a fair degree of "success," if by success it is meant that those considered to be different manage to be accepted by the society. However, when the deeper cultural marks are examined, it seems less true. Blacks, American Indians, Orientals, women, and the young, among others who are clearly bio-culturally marked, have had a less easy time of it and still face ranges of discrimination, or minority status.

Dominant and Minority

The term "minority" implies a majority. It is wise to avoid its numerical connotation and use the term "dominant" instead of majority, since it is by no means certain that the United States is ruled by a "majority will." Yet, even the term dominant has its difficulties. What are, precisely, the dominant elements of American society? What values hold sway over the greater portion, or at least the most powerful portion, of the nation's population? Who really runs things?

Just as it is difficult to be honest and objective about one's own conscience, it is difficult to appraise objectively one's own society. By being a part of it, it is almost impossible to evaluate what it is, because having been raised in that society means that the observer has absorbed its values and categories almost always unconsciously.

Yet certain elementary points can be made. The "dominant culture" of America stresses the importance of the male (the white male in particular). He is expected to be a primary economic and political figure, although not necessarily an important "social" figure in the narrow sense of the word. The dominant American culture also seems to stress what are called "middle class" values: economic success, education, cleanliness, the acquisition of private possessions and property, and what may be called a modicum of respect for public institutions and authority. It would also seem that the dominant culture places a high value on Anglo-Saxon or Germanic patterns of behavior that stress orderliness, a sense of the appropriateness of Western cultural traditions, and the associated skin tones.

It can be said that the dominant groups and institutions of American society are those which play the most important roles in forming and transmitting these values. Those institutions are, aside from the family, the major corporations, labor unions, universities, federal, state, and local governments, mass media, and, to a lesser extent, the major denominational churches. Each plays a more or less specialized role in preserving and presenting the dominant values of the society. Although in 1970, for example, there were approximately 1.5 million corporations in the United States, the five hundred largest of these employed 20 percent of all nonfarm workers; these corporations, then, in large measure set the standard for economic success. The churches, the mass media, and the educational institutions "socialize" the population by communicating in many different ways what is "good" behavior and what is "bad," what the individual should expect of himself and his friends and family, and what his relationship to society ought to be. Governments play a similar role through the public educational institutions, but also are responsible for resolving conflicts within the society in a way that meshes with prevailing values.

What then is the relationship of minorities to dominant groups and institutions? The rest of this book is devoted to answering that question. In a preliminary fashion, it can be said that the difference is that minorities exercise little control over the decisions made by the institutions that shape the society. Minorities may or may not subscribe to the values embodied in the dominant culture, but they suffer from one serious liability: whether they subscribe to those values or not, they do not directly benefit from their application and sometimes they suffer from them.

Stated in another way, the working out of cultural differences—who is to receive jobs, whose income is to grow or to decrease, who is to own a home and who is not, who is to hold high office and who is to be denied—is settled through social institutions. The beleaguered minorities are those individuals and collectivities who only sporadically or never participate in the decisions made within these institutions. Minorities are, for cultural reasons, outsiders, and as outsiders they have little or no chance to shape the content of the culture that defines them as outsiders. If this condition were benign, if minorities were full beneficiaries of the distribution of the benefits of the cultural system of values, their status might be less painful.

Bibliography

Benedict, Ruth. *Patterns of Culture*. Boston: Houghton Mifflin, 1934. A classic study of how cultures function and are distinguished from each other.

Boughby, Arthur S. *Man and the Environment*. New York: Macmillan, 1971.

Dubos, Rene. *Man Adapting*. New Haven: Yale University Press, 1965.

Henry, Jules. *Culture Against Man*. New York: Vintage, 1963. A critical, but valuable, study of the nature of modern American cultural patterns.

Hofstadter, Richard. *Social Darwinism in American Thought*. Boston: Beacon Press, 1955. A study of one aspect of the cult of success and individual "superiority."

Kimball, Solon T., and James E. McClellan. *Education and the New America*. New York: Random House, 1962. Perhaps the most valuable single analysis of the main facets of American culture and the forces for change and stability within that culture.

Lipson, Leslie. *The Democratic Civilization*. New York: Oxford University Press, 1964.

Potter, David. *People of Plenty: Economic Abundance and the American Character*. Chicago: University of Chicago Press, 1959.

Three
Minority Status

A culture establishes categories of "we-ness" and "they-ness" and attaches these categories to individuals or collectivities. In a fairly heterogeneous society, nearly everyone at some time or other is an outsider, whether a wealthy socialite in a workingman's bar or a Protestant attending a Roman Catholic religious service. People in such situations are apt to feel vaguely uncomfortable or defensive; they know that somehow they are out of place, even though their presence may be overtly ignored. They know, in fact, that they are violating or challenging some socially determined category of where they belong and when, and in this sense are targets of discrimination.

Such situations are often no more than trivial experiences, the stuff of cocktail party conversation. No one feels severely damaged, and if the insiders feel that the "invader" does not belong there, they may be annoyed, they may even eject him more or less violently, but the incident passes as one of the thousands of human relationships in a complicated society. There is a point, however, at which the categories of we-ness and they-ness begin to take on greater social significance. When the distinctions are patterned and are related to a specific collectivity of people, and when the pattern is one in which the outsiders become the objects of persistent differential treatment, then a minority exists. There are two other elements that go into the making of a "minority." One is that the differential treatment includes discrimination or deprivation. The second is that because of deprivation minority members themselves must be conscious of their status and the effects of that status.

Deprivation

All humans are to some degree deprived. To complicate matters, deprivation is itself a relative condition. Assuredly, there is a maximum deprivation, a point at which enforced starvation, ill health, exposure to the elements, physical abuse, and mental anguish threaten existence to the extent that deprivation is obvious. But, below this maximum, the varying degrees of deprivation defy easy comparison or even definition. Is a housewife living in a $40,000 home, surrounded by labor-saving devices, with the best medical care on call, whose primary nutritional problem is one of losing weight, by any standard deprived? A Navajo Indian living on a reservation might emphatically say no. A member of an organization dedicated to the liberation of women would say, as emphatically, yes. What, then, constitutes "deprivation"?

Deprivation can be either "objective" or "subjective." Objective deprivation can be observed by someone who is not actually experiencing the deprivation. Subjective deprivation is known only to the individual experiencing the deprivation, which is not readily observable to an outsider except by some concrete indication. The two are related, but the relationship, as will be seen, is not a simple one. The basic elements of objective deprivation must be examined first. They are legal, economic, and social.

Legal Deprivation

It is a cliché of modern political science that the laws of a society impose burdens and costs on some people and provide rewards and benefits to others, whatever the intent of the laws may be. In itself, the process of burdening and benefiting is not necessarily discrimination in the specific sense used here. A real-estate agent may feel that zoning laws discriminate against him in favor of individual homeowners, for example, and he may actually suffer a measure of deprivation of economic opportunity as a consequence. Yet, generally speaking, such laws do not usually make a deprived minority of the people involved. The real-estate agent is deprived of an opportunity to make money in certain geographic areas, but he is not denied the chance to earn a living in a general way.

In other cases, however, legal standards have been applied to perpetuate and reinforce cultural discrimination. The most notorious of such instances are the Jim Crow laws in the American South and the apartheid policy in South Africa. The primary characteristic of such laws is that *culturally marked* people are selected by law for differential treatment and the treatment is backed by the power of the state.

In the United States, the Jim Crow laws are now gone, although the spirit that motivated them still exists in some areas. A cursory survey of American laws would indicate, however, that legal standards that have the primary characteristic of Jim Crow and apartheid laws are still in existence; that is, they are based on cultural distinctions. Some of these are:

Minimum voting age for citizens.

Minimum age for holding public office.

Minimum age for legal "responsibility and competence."

Abortion laws.

Selective service laws.

Differential standards of employment for women.

Differential marriage and divorce standards.

Laws against homosexuality.

The *in loco parentis* doctrine for students at high schools, colleges, and universities.

Federal laws and regulations governing activities of reservation Indians.

One of the effects of such laws is to shift the burden of change from those seeking to restrict the deprived minority to those who are marked for special treatment. And, in many instances, the burden is such that change is made difficult. For example, 18-year-olds were ineligible to vote on the proposition that gave them the power to vote. Homosexuals, in campaigning against laws imposing criminal penalties on homosexuality, risk making themselves known to law enforcement agencies for surveillance.

The pattern in the United States, however, and in most industrial societies has been toward a gradual diminution and elimination of the effects or even existence of special treatment laws. Those that still exist are enforced less rigorously, and almost all are subject to change through the conscious efforts of those who oppose them. As a consequence, the important criteria of minority status can be found in other aspects of the society.

Economic Deprivation

In popular thinking, minority status is associated with being poor. However, poverty in the economic sense is a relative condition. Below some minimum, the poor starve, live in ill health, and are unable to improve their lot because the bitter biological necessity of moment-to-moment survival prevents any other activity, assuming that the opportunity to improve their lot exists. Above that minimum, however, the shadings become more complicated. Poverty becomes a comparative standard, to be contrasted with a regional or national average, a "quality of life" standard, or some other measure. Some of the possible standards are shown in Table 1.

There are other measures available, almost as many as there are ingenious people to devise them; but as Table 1 indicates, there is more than enough room for disagreement about what constitutes "real" poverty once past the level of minimum sustenance. Not only are the basic concepts relative, but they incorporate a number of explosive underlying assumptions.

First, is any level of poverty below that of the "developmental life-style" self-perpetuating? Some argue that by tolerating a lower level of poverty, society

Table 1   Criteria for Levels of Poverty

Standard	Components
Minimum sustenance	Sufficient food, clothing, and shelter to prevent death
Minimum basic needs	Healthy foods, safe and sanitary housing, physical health care, warm clothing
Decent life-style	The above plus transportation, public recreational opportunities, minimal amenities
Developmental life-style	The above plus educational opportunities, exposure to the media, freedom of physical mobility

imposes on future generations a "culture of poverty." When parents are poor and unable to escape poverty, they transmit to their children the same sense of hopelessness and despair, and thus their children are almost certain to be poor as well. The implications of such a position are that society has an obligation to bring everyone to a level of developmental life-style, to break the effects of the culture of poverty, and thus to relieve both the poor of their misery and society of the costs of that misery.

Others take an almost diametrically opposite viewpoint. Although, they argue, no one should be in the position of facing starvation, any level above the sustenance level ought to be individually determined, by personal enterprise, determination, and ability. If someone chooses to remain at a particular level of poverty, that is his or her right. Further, for government to intervene is to create in place of a culture of poverty a "culture of dependence" on the largesse of government.

Second, conditions of poverty are subject to interpretation. One man's poverty may be another's comfort. Hippies, for example, even choose to move from affluence to poverty in order to escape the shackles of material possessions. The argument is infuriating to many because it implies that the poor ought to be content with their lot, and social pressure is brought to bear on them to make them content. For others, it is a political opportunity; there are always those sufficiently better off than someone else that the affluent can be used as handy targets for rhetoric; even middle-income people can be whipped into a state of anger against the "very, very rich."

Sorting out all the arguments and feelings about poverty, especially the poverty of others, often seems a hopeless task. More to the point is the simple recognition

Table 2   Economic Status of Selected Groupings in the United States, 1969-70

Group	Median Family Income	Percent below Poverty Line	Percent Unemployed
Blacks	$6,500	33	8.2
Mexican-Americans	7,200	35	8.0
Indians	3,600	75	40.0
Women as heads of household	4,500	40	43.0
Total U.S. population	8,600	23	5.0

SOURCE: Computed from data obtained from the U.S. Bureau of the Census and the U.S. Office of Economic Opportunity.
   Note: All figures are approximate.

that degrees of economic deprivation do exist and that certain categories of people tend to be closer to the minimum economic level than to the developmental level. In the United States, these groupings are often (but not always) marked by skin color and language—blacks, Mexican-Americans, Indians, and Puerto Ricans—and marked by age and sex—widows, the elderly, and the young (see Table 2).

Because deprivation is a relative condition, general societal improvement may only mean that those who have been relatively deprived before continue to be relatively deprived, even though their condition has improved absolutely. The average income of blacks has increased since 1960, but it has continued to lag behind the general income level of the society. The minority member may experience better conditions but may still find that his status compares very unfavorably with dominant groupings.

Three additional and closely related aspects of economic deprivation serve as both consequences and causes of differential poverty in America. They are initial opportunity, continuing opportunity, and the concept of the "opportunity structure" created by economic deprivation.

Initial Opportunity. Although, as one wit has put it, the major cause of poverty is a lack of money, the primary cause for the lack of money is the inability to find employment that pays adequately. A minority person has three basic disadvantages in seeking initial employment: his minority status; his past deprivations, which may have left him without marketable skills or experience; and his lack of mobility, which can reduce his capacity to seek jobs at other locations. Furthermore, his willingness to look for work can be eroded as he is repeatedly rebuffed in his efforts, and he may reject those opportunities which require him to make an effort to take advantage of.

It is difficult to single out which of these is the most important contributing cause. Discrimination is vital, partly because an employer can rationalize his discrimination on the basis of an applicant's lack of education, arrest record, distasteful appearance and manner, or any number of other apparent deficiencies. What has been called "institutional racism," as applied to blacks, may also be at work. The pattern is one in which the demands of the job are such that they imply qualifications that only a middle-class, white male would have. Even though these qualifications may not be necessary for the tasks to be performed, personnel specialists have brought their own training and cultural values to the task of defining the job and the qualifications of those who might hold it. The result is that "fair and objective standards" often exclude perfectly well qualified persons from employment. A survey of city personnel practices in one city revealed this tendency toward institutional barriers. A high school education was required for every job. The city manager, when asked whether the high school requirement was really necessary answered, "No, not for all jobs, but we've fought so long and so hard for an upgraded employee system we can't let go now." He admitted that one effect was to exclude a large number of otherwise qualified blacks.

In urban areas, especially, the shift of new jobs to the suburbs and the nearly complete breakdown of transportation systems make jobs simply out of reach for urban-based minority members. Conceivably, they could move to where the jobs are, but often housing costs and discriminatory land-control policies prohibit that alternative. A similar mechanism is at work in the insistence on higher and higher educational standards for all jobs. Education is expensive, either in time and energy or in the loss of immediate, earned dollars, which a minority family may need to make ends meet. A member of a minority with an inadequate education faces an institutional barrier that he lacks the resources to overcome.

What happens, then, is that the minority member may find that he cannot break into the economic system, except in menial jobs or temporary ones. Consequently, many minority members, even when employed, are "subemployed," that is, working at jobs that provide them with only small incomes. Many of the subemployed do not have the benefit of employer-provided medical and life insurance plans, do not build up pension benefits, have too little income to save for the future or even to meet current expenses such as dental or health costs, and lack the funds for major investments such as better housing.

Continuing Opportunity. Even if a minority member succeeds in obtaining an initial opportunity, he can be faced with limits on future opportunities. Most careers begin with a low- or middle-range entry into a job, followed by steady promotion with consequent income growth, including chances to move to other more desirable jobs; they peak when a person is in his late forties or early fifties. Salaries or wages cease at retirement, but a reasonable income is obtained from pensions, investments, and social security, and the major expenditures (except for medical care) are now well behind. Therefore the assumption most people make as they begin their careers is a powerful motivating force: *this* job is going to lead to even better ones in the future.

Many minority members, however, cannot make this assumption. Few blacks, women, Mexican-Americans, Puerto Ricans, American Indians, or American Orientals rise to major executive posts or supervisory positions; few become full professors, deans, or academic department chairmen; few become union leaders or generals in the armed services. They may experience modest growth opportunities, but these rarely include the prospect of competing for the upper positions in their occupations. In short, the initial opportunities available lead only to limited continuing opportunities.

Like the lack of initial opportunity, the absence of continuing opportunity can frequently be a result of rational considerations, that is, a lack of appropriate educational background or necessary skills and experience. However, discrimination itself plays a major role. The dead-end job confronts all but the most exceptional and fortunate members of the new minorities, and there is evidence that many members of the old minorities face the same problem.

The lack of continuing opportunity has ramifications, although they are perhaps not as serious as those of being unable to find any job at all. Where continuing opportunities are missing, an employee not only reaches a peak in his career sooner, thus losing the economic benefits of a higher income level, but may be subject to the "last hired, first fired" effect. Because he has risen so slowly and so little, because he may in fact be discontented and disenchanted, and because he does belong to a minority, he is easier to let go in times of economic stress.

As a result, opportunities that lead to other opportunities may be inaccessible to an employee who is a member of a minority. Apprenticeships, in-house training, management-development seminars, and firm-supported higher-education programs will be tendered only reluctantly to an employee about whom doubts exist. Such an employee may thus be denied the chance to gain the qualifications he lacks.

The Opportunity Structure. At any given point in time, every person is confronted with what can be called his "opportunity structure," which is the set of alternatives available to him—in other words, his options. Each person's opportunity structure is shaped by a number of limitations, such as psychological predisposition, physical assets or handicaps, social status, economic standing, geographic location, range of social contacts, age, and sex. Generally, opportunity structures change through time, the number of choices available increasing as one passes from infancy into childhood and adulthood and then usually decreasing at the onset of old age.

Much of the foregoing discussion has been addressed to the limitations on the economic opportunity structures of members of minorities. Other considerations, such as how income is spent, further limit these opportunities.

It has often been pointed out that the "poor pay more." They do so in part because they lack the knowledge to shop comparatively. But economic deprivation creates its own imperatives: the poor find it hard to travel to places where better bargains are available because they lack the transportation to get there. The well-to-do can afford the initial cost of a new automobile, thereby saving themselves the heavy burden of maintaining an old one; the poor cannot, or if they attempt to, they may face repossession and the total loss of their investment.

Economic deprivation affects the way in which the poor allocate their disposable income for other purposes as well. It is less expensive to invest in immediate and continuous medical care than to wait for an illness to reach critical or disabling proportions; but such steady allocations, to savings accounts, medical insurance plans, or periodic medical examinations, may be beyond the means of those whose incomes fall at or below "minimum basic needs" on the scale of relative poverty. The freedom to set priorities is limited because priorities are determined by the amount of money available. And, of course, to the extent that unwise decisions can be made in the use of available funds, freedom to make choices is even further curtailed. Although it is popular to criticize the poor for the unwise decisions they make in spending their money, the same is true of the more affluent. The difference is that those who are better off have a wider margin for error; their irrational spending habits do not necessarily deprive them of the chance to spend money on other necessities as well.

Even those who have overcome the lower levels of poverty and the initial limitations on economic opportunity may still find themselves restricted in their economic opportunity structures. The jobs that they do have may seem to be too secure to permit them to accept new and more rewarding positions in which their status as members of minorities is unknown to them. Each must consider the proposition: "I am accepted here; the new job pays more money, but how do I know I won't run into real discrimination with those new people." It may seem to be, and perhaps actually is, safer to stay in a dead-end job than to gamble everything on a seemingly better opportunity. A member of a minority is forced to be prudent, if not actually cautious, about taking risks that to dominant members of the society seem to be routine changes of status.

Patterned economic deprivation, then, sets limits on a minority's opportunities, to say nothing of imposing physical and psychological burdens on its members. Aside from the consequences that have already been mentioned, the following stem from economic deprivation:

Limits on geographic, economic, and psychological mobility.

Inability to save money and thereby enlarge the opportunity structure for one's children.

Vulnerability to economic and technological change.

Impetus (for some) toward crime as a means of enlarging the economic opportunity structure.

Impetus (for some) toward escape from frustration and humiliation through drugs, alcohol, superstition, and messianic religious sects.

Impetus (for some) toward exploitative economic activities, often an exploitation focused on other members of the minority.

Impetus (for some) toward economically marginal or unsound businesses in an effort to create one's own economic opportunity structure.

It should be mentioned that what is statistically true is not individually true. Many members of minorities have escaped and will continue to escape from economic deprivation. Others have never been deprived, except in very mild, and perhaps to them unnoticeable, forms. The exceptions are exceptions, however, and do not eliminate the generality. In the United States, certain culturally marked groupings suffer from patterned economic deprivation.

Social Deprivation

In America, there is a close relationship between economic status and social status, although the relationship is by no means perfect. Yet, for members of minorities, economic success does not guarantee social acceptance by economic peers. The poorer members of minorities are caught in a double bind: they are neither accepted as social peers nor benefited by tangible economic rewards. For the very poor, the economic problem is more pressing than that of social status, but for those who have attained some degree of economic success to find that it does not open the doors of society is demoralizing, especially in a society in which money seems to be the key to success.

The range of social deprivation is as great or greater than that of economic deprivation, but some of the more significant manifestations are as follows:

The first is ghettoization, in the sense that a member of a minority is limited in his social contacts primarily to other members of the minority. Ghettoization includes limitations not only to specific geographic areas (e.g., slums, Indian reservations), but also to general social contact, such as exclusion from clubs and informal associations.

The second is denial of recognition. A member of a minority is reminded of his status as an outsider in a large variety of small ways, ranging from the omission of an engagement or marriage announcement in the social column of the local newspaper to patronizing remarks and actions. He is treated as if he were invisible, or, if his presence is acknowledged, or forced upon the consciousness of others, it will be disregarded.

The third is stereotyping or labelling. Stereotyping is actually just another form of denying recognition, by lumping individuals into an abstract collectivity and ascribing characteristics to that collectivity that have no relation to an individual.

As Gordon Allport has pointed out, stereotypes are difficult if not impossible to destroy because individuals who fail to fit the stereotype are either regarded as extraordinary exceptions or ignored. Stereotyping, as a form of deprivation, robs a person of his individuality, his personal achievements (and faults), and, more basically, his humanity.

Other, more concrete social deprivations are outgrowths of these general ones, including exclusion from schools, housing areas, social interchange, recreational opportunities, and service in public places. Like economic deprivation, social deprivation has cumulative and diverse effects, including a sense of anxiety and insecurity, frustration, self-hatred or self-rejection, and, if encountered often enough, reliance on withdrawal and escape mechanisms. A member of a minority is accordingly deprived of a large part of the richness and diversity of life. There are places he cannot go or is afraid to go because he may be subjected to humiliation. There are people whose companionship he is denied but whose knowledge, ideas, and personalities could enrich his life (and for whom he might provide enrichment). Through ghettoization, he may be forced to associate with people who share no other interest or characteristic with him than minority status.

Subjective Deprivation

The "objective" aspects of deprivation – legal, economic, and social – are closely related to subjective deprivation, the feeling that a member of a minority has about his own status. As a factor in politics, the subjective aspect is more important, because how people see themselves in relation to the world forms the basis for their political actions. The crucial point is that whether objective deprivation exists or not, if a *sense* of deprivation is there, a basis for minority political action exists. Conversely, if there is no subjective dimension to the deprivation, people are not motivated to act, because they do not recognize their deprivation.

Subjective deprivation is, then, awareness of deprivation. Those who are subjectively deprived can deal with it in one of two ways. They can either withdraw into themselves, isolating themselves from a society that forces them to be aware of such a miserable condition, or recognize deprivation as a characteristic of minority status, turning to others who share that recognition in an effort to eliminate it.

For our purposes, the single most important characteristic of subjective deprivation is the accompanying sense of powerlessness. The term "power," although commonly used, has no single, standard, accepted definition. Perhaps the most useful concept of power is that it is *the ability to impose one's will upon the environment*. An environment includes not only nonhuman elements, but other humans and their creations. Under these terms, of course, no one has absolute power and no one is without some trace of power.

Another way of expressing the sense of powerlessness that is characteristic of minorities is in terms of a limited opportunity structure. Some minorities have few opportunities; those that they have do not always lead to significantly greater ones. Moreover, they realize that their capacity to change the opportunity structure is itself limited. The powerlessness of a member of a minority is one of the most distressing characteristics of his subjective deprivation. Even though he has the money, he cannot purchase a home in a location of his own choosing; even though he has an education, he cannot persuade an employer to give him the job that he wants and is qualified to do. Finally, he knows that as an individual he has no control over what it is that makes these rejections possible, that is, his cultural category. He may know his abilities, the contributions he could make, his needs and aspirations, but there seems to be no way in which he can convince the people who make the decisions that affect him. The only way out of this objective deprivation, of which he is subjectively aware, is to seek power, at least enough power to broaden his opportunity structure to a tolerable level.

Bibliography

Allport, Gordon W. *The Nature of Prejudice.* Garden City, N.Y.: Anchor, 1958. The most famous, and still the most useful, study of prejudice, its causes and behaviors.

Bettelheim, Bruno, and Morris Janowitz. *Social Change and Prejudice.* New York: Free Press, 1964.

Blau, Peter. *Exchange and Power in Social Life.* New York: Wiley, 1964. One of the most systematic and thorough efforts to produce a "general theory" of power relationships.

Ferman, Louis A., Joyce L. Kornbluh, and Alan Haber, eds. *Poverty in America.* Ann Arbor: University of Michigan Press, 1965.

Ginsberg, Eli. *The Middle Class Negro in the White Man's World.* New York: Columbia University Press, 1967.

Gladwin, Thomas. *Poverty USA.* Boston: Little Brown, 1967. A useful study of the profile of the economically deprived in the nation.

Kain, John F. *Race and Poverty: The Economics of Discrimination.* Englewood Cliffs, N.J.: Prentice-Hall, 1969.

Lewis, Oscar. "The Culture of Poverty." *Scientific American,* October 1966, pp. 19-25. Available as Offprint No. 631 from W.H. Freeman and Company, 660 Market St., San Francisco, Calif. 94104, and 58 Kings Road, Reading, England RG1 #3AA. The viewpoint that formulated the concept of the culture of poverty.

Valentine, Charles A. *Culture and Poverty: Critique and Counter-Proposals.* Chicago: University of Chicago Press, 1969. Especially useful for the analysis of varying theories and approaches toward the whole concept of poverty.

Washington, Joseph R. *Marriage in Black and White.* Boston: Beacon Press, 1970. A study of attitudes toward interracial marriage and the effects of ghettoization.

Wilcox, Clair. *Toward Social Welfare.* Homewood, Ill.: Irwin, 1969.

Woodward, C. Vann. *The Strange Career of Jim Crow.* New York: Oxford University Press, 1966. The most famous study of the effects of legal deprivation.

Four
Minority groups

Objective and subjective deprivation alone are not enough to produce minority group politics. Although some members of minorities attempt to improve their condition and relieve their sense of subjective deprivation by individual activity, they quickly find something more is required to exert power in the political system. In the United States, the something more has usually been organized group action, which, although never including all the members of a minority, nonetheless acts as the political spearhead, rallying point, and often self-designated spokesman for minority interests.

Because of the importance of group action to minority politics, it is necessary to examine the nature of groups and groupings with special reference to the nature of minority groups.

Groupings and Groups

It is possible to describe collectivities of human beings in perhaps an infinite number of ways, ranging from physical characteristics ("tall people" or people over fifty years of age) to imputed psychological characteristics (the "alienated," the "silent majority"). These descriptions are useful for a variety of purposes, including the classification of people by the U.S. Bureau of the Census, public-opinion sampling, and political rhetoric and journalism, but the descriptions are often no more than statistical abstractions. The people included in a given category may have nothing more in common than one characteristic. They may even be unaware of others in their category and indifferent to the characteristic itself. For example, blue-eyed people apparently do not have a strong fellow feeling for other blue-eyed people.

Something more, then, is required to convert a "grouping" of people into a collection of people who are aware of the characteristic they have in common and act on it. The commonly accepted conditions are: first, an awareness of a characteristic shared by others; second, sufficient importance or "salience" of that characteristic so that the people having it feel it does or should influence their lives; and, third, interaction among at least some of the people sharing the characteristic. The product of these three conditions is what social scientists call a "group."

A group, then, is a collectivity of people who share a characteristic that is sufficiently salient for them to interact on the basis of it. Stated in another way, if the people concerned did not share the characteristic, they would probably never have any reason to get together, and, if they did, it would be because of some other characteristic, which seemed more important to them. Obviously, an enormous variety of characteristics would have to be included, such as role (student, parent), activity (work, chess-playing), occupation (doctors, cab drivers), proximity (neighbors, adjoining offices), cultural category (Mexican-Americans, blacks), and others. A glance at this list shows that none of the categories are necessarily mutually exclusive. An individual could, and often does, belong to a variety of groups, some of which may even share membership—an example being a bridge club whose members also belong to the same social organization of a church. Belonging to more than one group can lead to what is called "cross-pressuring," which happens when group memberships conflict. Cross-pressures are common enough; a housewife might find that her luncheon group is scheduled to meet at the same time as the executive board of the Parent-Teacher Association.

Because people have multifaceted interests, personalities, and commitments, almost everyone is subject to cross-pressuring. This is, in part, because belonging to a group involves two sets of demands. One set of demands consists of those made by other members of the group, in the form of basic expectations. First, the group expects that each member will act in a way that is supportive of the group, contributing to the group's good functioning and helping to make it worth belonging to; second, each member is expected to conform to group standards or "rules"; and, third, each member is expected to share the attitude of the other members toward the characteristic that brought them together in the first place. These are really "membership criteria," for they assume that an individual who wants to belong to a group is willing to make some concessions to it in an effort to insure the group's continuation. The demands may be no greater than that each member conform to group rituals or rules (for example, members of a coffee-break club taking turns in providing the doughnuts); or they may have larger implications, such as the insistence that every loyal party member vote a straight ticket and make an annual contribution to the party campaign chest.

In general, a new member finds himself entering a web of already-established expectations, sometimes represented by formal rules and standards, but probably more often by unspoken rules ("that's just the way we do it"). Later, he may find that those expectations run counter to his own, and he may rebel, or be expelled, or drop out. He will find that continuing comfortable relations with members of the group depends on his conforming to group expectations. And, of course, his own expectations become part of the demands made on other members of the group.

The other set of demands are those brought to a group by an individual member. They are crucial to the functioning of the group and do much to explain why groups come into being in the first place. In a broad sense, groups can perform two functions for their members. One function is *instrumental* and refers to a group's providing its members with practical benefits that they could not otherwise attain, or could not attain as easily. To play bridge, there must be other bridge players; to run a business, there must be other businessmen; to protect doctors' interests, it seems to be more efficient to have a pressure group. A group in performing instrumental functions is not much more than a means to achieve the goals of its members. Were another and seemingly better means available, a member would probably turn to that alternative. There are the elements of a bargain in the relationship between a group and an individual member. He is willing to conform to group expectations in return for having his own expectations of goal-attainment met through the group.

The other major function can be labelled the *identification* function. Identification functions meet an individual's need to have a relationship with other people that incorporates affection, "positive ego reinforcement," comfort, security, self-esteem, and the knowledge that other people care about one's existence. Although identification is a goal that the group helps to attain, the function performed is much more intrinsic to the group. There is *no* way in which an individual can achieve the values of associating with other people except by associating with them.

A self-employed person may be able to achieve his instrumental goals without belonging to a group. If an artist sells his work through an agent or a dealer, he must interact with that person, but he may not feel that he shares any salient characteristic with him. If, however, he desires to satisfy his "normal" hunger for affection, comfort, human development, and respect, it must be done in a group context, whether that group is the most basic of all groups, a family, or whether it is a group of friends, a social club, or an association of his colleagues. In our terms, we could say that the opportunity structure for instrumental functions or goals is much more diverse than that for identification goals; the former does not necessarily require group participation (although as a practical matter in modern society it usually does); the latter, however, does.

These two functions are not inseparable. Any group combines both functions, although it may perform one to a greater degree than the other. A social group may be a source of useful business contacts, but it is likely that the other members of the group would become quite angry if they felt that a member was "using" them for the sole purpose of advancing his business interests. Conversely, in a corporation in which most group activities (committee meetings, consultations, relations between supervisors and those supervised) are primarily instrumental, identification groups will emerge.

Few people can distinguish the functions performed by any given group or set of groups to which they belong. It must be kept in mind that groups, like the people who belong to them, are fluid: they are formed and dissolved; they evolve as members' expectations change. A friendly neighborhood group may suddenly become a pressure group fighting the incursion of a filling station or apartment house; a work committee may evolve into an after-hours drinking club. It is also probably true that any group at any given time is predominantly serving one function rather than the other.

As a general proposition, the hold of predominantly instrumental groups on their members is less strong than that of identification-oriented groups. Certainly, as an individual develops, he will move from one identification group to another, but at any stage of his life, he is apt to feel more dependent on his identification group or groups than he does on his instrumental groups. The reason for this is rooted in human psychological needs: we *must* have the comfort and affection of human companionship to maintain our mental health and sense of self-worth.

It must be stressed, however, that the combination of instrumental and identification functions—a combination that can amount to a virtual merging of the two functions in the minds of the members—operates to reduce group tolerance of individual restiveness, rebellion, and deviance. To question the performance of a union, a political party, a firm, or a church may not only suggest that the group is failing to perform its instrumental functions for all its members, but also challenge the group's identification functions, therefore threatening the emotional comfort and security of its members.

Group Interaction

As the definition of group indicates, the key ingredient separating a group from a grouping is interaction on the basis of a shared characteristic: those who are members of a group communicate with each other, cooperate or compete, and organize themselves because they share that characteristic. They may not even be conscious of the characteristic all the time, but it is what has brought them together and keeps them together. And they will arrange their interactions with each other on the basis of their shared characteristic and the functions the group serves, whether the interactions consist of playing chess, holding briefings, sharing gossip, or singing in quartets.

Interaction occurs in a number of ways. Besides interacting face-to-face, members of a group interact by means of letters, memoranda, rule books, the telephone, the mass media, specialized media, or even indirectly through a third party. Through modern technology, a group is able to span large geographic distances in maintaining fairly effective patterns of interaction. These methods are certainly less efficient than face-to-face communication because they often cost more and probably have less impact, but they are of major significance, especially since they expand the possible membership of any one group enormously.

Furthermore, these methods of interaction mean that a group can have an "invisible membership"; that is, people who are aware of the group's aims and actions and share its characteristic, regarding it as salient to their lives, but because of circumstances do not or cannot formally participate in direct interaction. The invisible membership of a group can be largely discounted by group members in the on-going workings of the group, but it is an important constituency of the group in many respects. The invisible members are a potential pool of new members, a possible source of public support in times of stress and crisis, and, to the extent that members are aware of the invisible membership, an influence on group decision-making. The invisible members may have their expectations, or what group members think are their expectations, incorporated into the group's life. The boundaries of a group, in psychological terms, are hard to determine, since "interaction" can occur in a variety of ways, over long periods of time, and at great distances. Even those groups with formal organizations and formal membership criteria only in part solve the problem, because they may well have a large number of invisible members who are committed to the group's goals and who strongly identify with the group. Political pressure groups, for example, are apt to depend heavily on their invisible members. Medical associations know that there are people outside the profession who nonetheless will rally against "socialized medicine." Labor unions know that many people who do not belong to a union sympathize with the workingman's causes and will contribute money, time, and political pressure to support their campaigns.

The core of any group consists of those persons who interact frequently and at least occasionally face-to-face. On the basis of behavior, these are the people who have made the most serious commitment to the group and who hope to have their needs most directly satisfied by group membership. Those members who interact less frequently and those who are invisible members have an impact on the group, without question, if for no other reason than they are a potential resource for the group in times of stress.

The Minority Context

Because minority groups are a subset of other groups, many of the previous generalizations apply to the formal and informal groups drawn from minorities. There are significant variations, however, which are a product of the influences that shape minority groups, the opportunity structures of members and of the groups themselves, and the resources available to them.

The common characteristics shared by minority members are not necessarily any different from those shared by members of society who are not members of minorities. Occupation, activity, geographic proximity, and so forth, can lead to groups composed primarily or entirely of minority members who interact on the basis of that characteristic. There is an additional factor, however, that can play a major role: minority identity.

Imposed Identity

All other things being equal, a large number of black professionals might prefer to associate with other members of their profession regardless of race; women might choose to join and participate in male societies; homosexuals might prefer to draw their friends from the "straight" as well as the "gay" world. But often the choice is unavailable to them. In a variety of ways, ranging from overt exclusion to slights, humiliations, and oversights, a minority person finds that he is not welcome. He is an "outsider." He may be permitted formal membership, especially now that federal laws against overt discrimination make refusing membership legally risky, but he is not granted a full position in the pattern of interaction. Because he knows or senses his "they-ness," he can never relax or allow himself to become vulnerable to the spoken or implied accusation, "Well, what are *you* doing here?"

A minority member can find it useful from an instrumental perspective to become a member of a group composed primarily of dominant members of the society, but he is constantly confronted with an identification problem. He must either mimic the other members of the group and hope that they will become less aware of his differentness or forego full acceptance. The former course of action is theoretically possible, but it assumes that the minority member carries no expectations or experiences from outside the group into it. Except in rare cases, he is reminded of his status when he is away from the group. Is he to forget those reminders so easily? As a simple example, a working housewife can join a group of men engaged in shop-talk, but other matters that are of interest to her, such as marketing and childcare, are not subjects that she can bring into the discussion, although the men in the group can introduce their masculine domestic interests. A black can associate with his coworkers on the job, but when they discuss their golf scores at the (segregated) country club or their new homes in the (lily-white) suburbs, he is an outsider.

Because discrimination is not a simple denial of membership in a given group at a given time but is pervasive, affecting roles, living arrangements, and social patterns, even a group totally receptive to a minority member does not protect him from discrimination and deprivation in other areas of his life. In short, his hope of having his identification needs satisfied by a group that consists mostly of people who are not members of a minority is sharply limited.

The effect is one of social deprivation at a personal level. The full range of close-knit ties, mutual and comparative experiences, ego-reinforcement, security, and assurance of affection that are essential to the group identification process are limited or even totally denied. The minority person is told in effect, "We can work together, but we are not really friends." Or, "We can be friends only as long as you don't remind me of who and what you are." The bonds of identification are always qualified, and by virtue of the qualification, the group itself has a limited capacity to satisfy the expectations of its minority members.

A minority member must continue to turn to those who share his minority status for any full satisfaction of his needs. As a black man who worked in the white world put it: "I may be white when I'm on the job, but I go to my brothers when I want to be black, and, man, there are times when I *need* to be black." When such a choice is voluntary, there can be no complaint; rather it is a tribute to the pluralistic opportunities in American society. But if a black person must be with other blacks because the color of his skin overrides all the other characteristics he may possess, he is in effect having an identity imposed upon him. He is not just a chess-player, he is a *black* chess-player. Thus groups composed of minority members take on an added dimension; whether their function is predominantly instrumental or that of identification, they are also defined by their minority status. Group membership then tends to be forged by two links: the common characteristic, such as occupation or desire for friendship, and the awareness of minority identity.

Where exclusion by dominant groups is overt, the pattern is similar, but less subtle. Minority members are forced by deprivation to turn to those sharing their minority status, for both instrumental and identification needs. A minority group is built out of minority status by an enforced recognition of that status.

In sum, a minority member faces three potential dynamics in attempting to win inclusion into dominant groups.

1. Direct exclusion, by which he is denied membership per se because of his minority status.

2. Inclusion with exclusion, by which he is granted formal membership but is excluded from any real interaction with the other members of the group.

3. Exclusion by inclusion, by which he is granted membership, is nominally a member of the group, and is included in interactive patterns but is constantly reminded of his minority status, of his "they-ness."

In the last two situations, instrumental goals may be fulfilled, but identification expectations are stifled, and a minority member must turn to a group or groups composed of fellow minority members for a fuller group life.

Ghettoization

One feature of social deprivation is what was called ghettoization. Obviously, one product of ghettoization is to set limits on the opportunities for group life. A Mexican-American confined to a barrio, a black to a slum, or a housewife to a suburb devoid of anyone but other housewives and children is intrinsically limited in the range of groups available for membership. Because ghettoization springs from minority status, any group joined must carry that status as an important characteristic. Yet the subjective awareness of minority status may not be present in these groups. That is, unlike minority groups that spring from an imposed identity, groups that are the product of ghettoization seem more "natural." These groups are the result of the social opportunity structure. Proximity is the common characteristic that serves as a basis for interaction. Often these groups attain minority awareness only after some outside influence intervenes. Police harassment of a street-corner group, discussion and reading about women's liberation, or the impact of mass media can make members of such groups begin to see their relationship to each other and to the world around them in a different light. New members can have the same effect, especially if their expectations are based on an awareness of minority status. The new awareness may create stresses within a group, if it converts a group whose predominant function is identification into an instrumental one, that is, a political-action group. Some members, most likely the older ones, will resent the changed focus (level of expectations) and will feel that their own expectations are being ignored.

Because ghettoization throws minority members together, it provides the physical opportunity for interaction. Some of the communicated expectations and experiences will stress minority awareness. Ghettoization is, consequently, a form of social deprivation but at the same time a form of group opportunity.

Catalysts

The raw materials of a minority grouping can be converted into interaction and thereby a group by precipitating events. Common characteristics must exist, and these must have a degree of salience before a catalyst can be effective; but in the chain of events that converts a grouping into a group, the catalyst often is fundamental. A list of catalysts might include:

First, repression, at least as subjectively defined. Students, for example, who are confronted with a drastic change of rules, a police raid of the campus, or collective criticism, may become profoundly aware of their status. They may convert their awareness into a sense of deprivation and begin to create groups that interact on the basis of that deprivation.

Second, the organizer. A skilled and perceptive organizer, who is able to heighten a hitherto latent minority awareness, can have a catalytic effect. An organizer may be an "outsider" or a member of the group who has had a frustrating personal experience and turns to the group to reinforce his sense of grievance and to find in it a means of release from his frustration.

Third, abrupt rejection. A group conducting its affairs in a relatively serene fashion, if suddenly rejected or frustrated by the environment, can become acutely aware of the sources of its powerlessness and thus its minority status. A homeowners' group composed of blacks, for example, if faced with a critical homeowners' problem, such as the location of a highway, a delay in street improvements, or a zoning change, can abruptly become a *black* homeowners' group if they feel that they cannot reach the city fathers because of their status.

Fourth, the media, especially television. The media equalizes a sense of minority status across the country, especially if it focuses on that status in connection with some dramatic event, such as a protest, a strike, or a riot. The degree to which minority members are given a collective sense by watching a black riot, a student revolt, or a women's liberation demonstration is difficult to determine, but one of the effects of television is to make common an experience that is directly felt by only a few. A cynic might argue that the new awareness is purely imitative, but from the standpoint of behavior, it makes little difference whether a newly formed group is trying to gain some of the publicity enjoyed by others or whether it is pursuing its own aims because it has been given a new consciousness of those aims.

Social Preference

Minority members may turn to minority groups out of simple preference. The life experiences of members of minorities are different from those of members of the dominant culture. Even a minority member who has achieved success in terms of the dominant culture has had to achieve it under circumstances that are usually far different from those of under which members of the dominant culture achieve success. Because of these differences, blacks, women, students, Mexican-Americans, Indians, or homosexuals may prefer to associate with those who have shared their unique experiences—with those who have what blacks call "soul."

Social preferences, in this sense, is part of the "American tradition," a tradition that ties Irish-Americans, Jewish-Americans, German-Americans, and other "old minority" groups together and contributes to the diversity of American political and social life. However, if the interaction takes place not only because of preference but because of feelings of deprivation and isolation, a group will develop a sense of being beleaguered. Frustration and powerlessness motivate a group to take action to do something about its status.

General Influences

The influences mentioned so far encourage the formation of minority groups. There are others, however, that operate either to aid or to discourage group formation, depending on the conditions prevailing at any given time. These influences have a role in structuring the opportunities available for group formation and for influencing the pattern of interaction that emerges from the group. The most important of these are geographic distribution, social position, mobility, and generational differences. In attempting to understand any group, an observer would be well advised to be sensitive to these nuances, because they help to explain the variety of minority groups that come into being.

Density of population is a physical fact that affects the opportunities for interaction. A grouping that is thinly dispersed over a large area faces a serious problem in terms of forming groups and preserving group interaction. Conversely, concentration in numbers means that the probability of like-minded people finding each other is increased, or at least of sharing experiences that can produce like-mindedness.

As Edgar Litt has pointed out, this may be one reason why cities have been important settings for the "accommodation" of minorities in the past; they are ideally suited for organization, development of interaction, and rapid communication among members of the group.

A minority, such as blacks or Indians, that is spread over a large geographic area, is a grouping of individuals who have very different personal experiences. A black raised in an urban slum has experienced a life substantially different from that of a sharecropper of the Mississippi delta. Although the two may well be able to find a common bond in their blackness, they also live in extraordinarily different worlds.

If members of a grouping are constantly shifting their places of work or residence, groups have little chance to form or to achieve permanence. Demographic stability increases group opportunities, and certainly one of the effects of slum-clearance programs and the high physical mobility of urban dwellers has been to discourage group formation and interaction, especially among Puerto Ricans and blacks.

Class, status, and occupation can also work to influence a minority group's chances of forming or the form it will ultimately take. A woman who is a housewife and mother and a woman who is single and self-supporting come from the same minority grouping, but they may have very different life-styles and perceptions of their conditions, therefore bringing very different expectations to group life. The same is true of a black professional and a black day laborer, even though they might be neighbors. Minority status can and does override these differences and bring varied people together within one group, but the group will suffer the potential for internal stresses, problems in communication, and divergent perspectives on the nature of minority status.

Often the underlying differences in occupation or activity are simple age differences. People of different ages have basic biological differences that might affect their impressions of themselves and of the world. That the young are willing to dare more and the older are more prudent means that even if individuals of different ages agree on the nature of a problem, they may have very different ideas about how to solve it. Further, people of different ages necessarily have had different experiences. A man fifty years old in 1970 would have lived through the Great Depression and World War II, events important enough to color his understanding of life and the world. A person half his age would have experienced those events only by word of mouth, in the classroom, or through the media. Finally, the experiences that are a product of time – raising children, grief, repeated successes or defeats, an awareness of impending death – all give an older person a sense of time and the nature of the human experience different from that of a younger person. Whether this different perspective is "wisdom," as older people sometimes refer to it, or weariness and fear, as younger people are apt to see it, is beside the point: the difference exists. In a minority member, a sufficient number of years can produce a kind of adjustment, whether of despair, indifference, or accommodation, that to a younger person amounts to "copping out."

In sum, these influences must inevitably give any minority group (and any other group) its own individual style of operation. Minority status may well override any of the particular influences, especially under the pressures of imposed identity and a catalyst. But as immediate pressures are relieved or become digested by the group, some or all of the other influences will begin to reassert themselves, often producing tension and stress within the original group. One of the implications of all these influences is that it is unlikely that any one group can embrace all the members of a minority, either as active members or even as invisible members. Inevitably there will be competing groups, especially in the political arena, claiming to speak for or to represent the "real" attitudes of the minority. Another implication is that minority groups, like other groups, are not fully assured of the hold they have over their members, for minority status must also be seen in the context of other characteristics. A minority group must combine minority status plus some other characteristic or characteristics as the basis for interaction and group life.

Frustrating Influences

Thus far, we have seen that minority groups contrast with other groups mainly because of the roles of imposed identity and ghettoization as agents that give a minority member a sharply heightened awareness of his "they-ness" and thereby provide a basis for group formation and interaction. There is, however, an additional set of factors that are generally more associated with minority groups than others because they have their origins in the patterns of deprivation that affect minorities. The effects of these influences on minorities are deleterious: they frustrate group life, stifle expectations, and may ultimately destroy the group itself. In part, they help to explain the rise and disappearance of various groups, but more important, they stress the nature of deprivation in the political life of the country.

Field notes from a community organizer (who prefers to remain anonymous) in a southern rural area help to illustrate the frustrating influences at work on minorities. In this case he was attempting to organize black political leagues:

> Things are not off to a good start. Meeting Tuesday and Thursday. Tuesday meeting was with already established voters' league. Only six people came. Was counting on Mrs. M. to show, since she's a natural leader. Found out yesterday she feels no point in the whole thing. Tired of sitting around feeling sorry for herself. Besides, too far for her to travel, with eight kids to look after. Mr. and Mrs. S. no show too. Think he's worried about his job at lumberyard.
>
> Thursday meeting some better. Set up Young People's Action Council. Ten came, which is pretty good, considering. Got organized, but problem: (a) want to put out a newsletter, and no money (only $40.00 in the kitty right now); (b) where can we meet regularly? Minister J. is not happy about our meeting here after tonight, or so he told me. Just one damn thing after another. . . .

Lack of Resources

For a group to satisfy either the instrumental or identification needs of its members, it must have some kind of "resources." These may be the direct benefits of an instrumental group: jobs, salaries, and economic opportunities; or the political opportunities of a pressure group. They may be the more intangible rewards of an identification group: an aura of good feeling and fellowship; stability; security; and a sense of identity with other human beings. Table 3 suggests some of the resources associated with each prototypical group. These "resources" are the benefits that are expected to be derived from group membership. They are resources insofar as a group can offer them to its members in order to bind the members to the group.

Although the resources (benefits of membership) are almost invariably distributed unequally, the lowliest, least popular, or least committed member nonetheless can expect to derive some small portion as long as he is a member. At the very least, he is held to the group in the hope of eventually sharing the benefits he sees others enjoying. The members who are most committed and who participate the most actively expect to be and usually are rewarded a large share of the benefits available to the group. Such expectations, however, can be met only if the group as a collectivity actually has them to provide.

Almost by definition any group in existence provides some benefits to all members, but the problem focuses on three relationships:

1. Whether benefits match expectations most, if not all, of the time.

2. Whether the group has a monopoly of benefits for its particular membership.

3. Whether benefits are appropriate to the "costs" of commitment required by membership.

Table 3   Group Resources and Benefits

Type of Group	Resource/Benefit
Instrumental	Money
	Jobs
	Useful information; inside information
	Useful contacts (economic)
	Social status
	Useful contacts (social)
	Political leverage
	Preferential treatment
Identification	Compatible associations
	Security and stability
	Ego reinforcement
	Numbers of friends
	Praise and recognition
	Protection from hostile environment

Obviously, all groups face the same set of key relationships, and all face the same problem of fulfilling the requirements implicit in each relationship. The essential difference between minority groups and dominant groups is that minorities usually feel the pinch of a lack of resources more acutely than dominant groups do.

As a consequence, members of a minority group are apt to feel that their needs are being frustrated. Either a group is asking more than it is giving, and has promised more than it can deliver, or members may feel that some other alternative is a better course to pursue. The problem is intensified because of minority inadequacy in comparison with dominant groups. The instrumental values that a minority group can provide pale in comparison with the enormous economic, opportunity, and other resources available to dominant groups.

An individual member can handle this contrast in one of several ways. He can, if given the chance, join a dominant group at the cost of losing identification values. This is the origin of "Uncle Tomism." At some point, an individual must ask himself if minority identification is worth the loss of all the benefits that the dominant society has at its command, and, if not, why should he cling to that minority identity unless forced to? Since benefits tend to be unequally distributed within a group, those at the outer fringes of the group (and therefore the least committed) can be tempted away from it. Even if they cannot break into the dominant society, they may unconsciously continue to struggle to do so, by imitation, by eschewing alignment with minority groups, and by denying the difference that the dominant society continues to maintain. From the standpoint of a minority group, these people will resist recruitment and will create divisiveness within the minority grouping by insisting that the minority group is no spokesman for their interests.

An individual can also handle the contrast by progressively seeking out more promising groups within a minority grouping. With each disappointment, he may turn to another group that seems to hold the key to fulfillment of his aspirations, or he may attempt to change the style, direction, and performance of his own group. In this evolutionary process, the seeds of radicalism are sown, as members come to feel that the only way to overcome the differential between minority and dominant groups is to drastically redistribute the benefits available to each.

Its restive member is a chronic problem for a minority group and its leadership. In the struggle to hold and benefit its members, then, a minority group suffers severe liabilities. It is limited in its own resources, and there are threats of competition from other minority groups and dominant groups who offer alternatives to frustrated members. Ironically, protracted deprivation and imposed identity may be the best guarantee of the continued strength of some minority groups. By continually rejecting minority members who would willingly give up their identity, dominant groups insure that identity will be preserved and encourage the rejected people to adopt more militant or radical postures toward the imposed self-awareness.

Self-Contempt and Powerlessness

Frustrations due to a lack of resources tend to be more related to instrumental goals and functions than those of identification. But, minority members may find that minority groups are incapable of serving identification needs as well. Subjective deprivation often causes a pervasive lack of self-esteem among minority members. In a group context, lack of self-esteem, even self-contempt, can be intensified rather than relieved. Group identification processes become negative; instead of bolstering the ego, they tear it down. In some religious cults, members may focus on their unworthiness in this world; in other groups they may resort to self-destructive behavior, such as addiction to narcotics.

The degree to which a lack of self-esteem exists in group life is difficult to assess, because the natural assumption is that people do not choose to fulfill identification needs by self-destructive interaction. The argument, simply, is that few psychologically healthy individuals would expose themselves for any great length of time to such a group context. But psychological health is usually defined in middle-class terms, without reference to the emotional damage inflicted by patterned deprivation and frustration. Self-contempt is a means of adjustment, a rationalization for conditions that would otherwise be inexplicable and intolerable, and for which there are no apparent outlets for the tensions they produce.

The reinforcement of self-contempt does not have to be a conscious process by which group members sit around and point out how pitifully inadequate each is.

The same thing is accomplished in a variety of subtle and unspoken ways; that is, by encouragement to stay in "one's place," to defer to "one's betters," or to avoid causing trouble. The pain of individual futility is made more comprehensible, if not more tolerable, by the mutual proof of group futility.

Coupled with self-contempt is a sense of powerlessness—an inability to impose the will of a group on its environment, to preserve its own integrity, to be free from incursions by the outside world. This powerlessness is in part an extension of its members' own perceptions and expectations about their individual status, but it is also a recognition of the position of the group itself in relation to the massive power conglomerations that are in the control of dominant members of society.

For those who turn to group life in order to overcome their own sense of isolation and ineffectiveness, finding that their group suffers from the same malaise is disappointing and frustrating. They may come to believe in power as an end in itself. Power thus becomes another potential resource and benefit that the group can and should offer, and power can combine both instrumental and identification functions of group life. Since power produces (or is assumed to produce) instrumental benefits, but is also shared with other members of the group, a lack of power becomes an explanation for group frustration and the quest for it a goal for participation. And, minority group power is derived from the action it takes with regard to its environment, which includes dominant groups.

Friction Between Minority and Dominant Groups

Individuals make claims on society with greater or lesser degrees of success, but individual claims, unless aggregated in some fashion, tend to have little impact on society; many are mutually self-cancelling, and others are "lost" in the structure and institutions of a mass society, or are so modest as to limit their impact. Many of the major institutions of contemporary America are, in fact, means of aggregating individual claims. In economic terms, brand names, advertising, and corporations can be viewed as aggregating institutions or devices. In politics, political parties and pressure groups perform the same functions.

However, when individual claims are aggregated into group expectations and when group survival is dependent on the satisfaction of these expectations, a fairly complex social dynamic is set into motion. There is, of necessity, intergroup friction. Either two or more groups lay claim to a limited resource, or the actions of some groups in seeking an entirely different goal frustrate the expectations of others. Even if the goals of several groups may be congruent, the groups may have divergent opinions about the proper means to achieve the goals.

Many groups, however, make virtually no claim on society; they demand only a small amount of time and energy of their members. Probably a census of groups, were it possible, would show that the vast majority of groups in American society would fall into this category. But there are enough groups in competition with each other to result in muted or open conflict and to warrant the generalization that group processes produce intergroup conflict.

It is not surprising, then, that the claims made by minority groups on society are a source of tension. In the first place, the dominant groups have indicated that minorities have a limited right to assert a claim on society, particularly if that claim involves economic or social "costs" as defined by the dominant groups. The very "they-ness" of minority groups means that as outsiders they should accept outsider status, that is, some degree of deprivation. Efforts to enlarge minority opportunity structures and to overcome economic and social deprivation are direct affronts to dominant interests, especially if the claims are made in the name of minority status rather than on individual bases.

Second, even those members of dominant groups who tolerate or applaud the assertion of minority expectations are often taken aback when those claims are actually applied. The amelioration of deprivation requires a transfer of some resources from the dominant groups to minority groups, or a modification of long-standing dominant practices. It may mean increasing taxes, competing for a limited number of jobs, opening hitherto exclusive neighborhoods or clubs, or sharing economic and political power. Again, members of dominant groups tolerate such demands on an individual basis, but when they become collective—when they in fact become power assertions—dominant members of the society are apt to flinch at the changes implied.

Third, minority group claims are change-producing and, as such, tend to be anxiety-producing. The sense of deprivation that haunts activist minority groups can be relieved only by some kind of change: economic, social, political, cultural, and individual. Most minority groups, in addressing dominant groups and institutions, insist that the changes must take place within the dominant culture. Although many dominant members are not satisfied with conditions as they are, they prefer that change occur in a direction that is rewarding, psychologically and otherwise, to themselves as well as to the minority. That is, it is again a question of power: Who is to determine what changes take place? Who is to benefit from them? How rapid are they to be? and What is the final changed state to look like?

And, finally, there are those who benefit from minority deprivation.

In short, friction comes from a clash of pragmatic interests or of perceptions of the world. The tension is not reduced when minorities come to realize that dominant groups expect them to accommodate themselves to dominant cultural norms and to tolerate affronts, neglect, and humiliation as the price of sharing in the system.

Bibliography

Argyris, Chris. *Personality and Organization.* New York: Harper & Row, 1957. A valuable examination of the relationship of the individual to formal and informal groups.

Blalock, H.M. *Toward a Theory of Minority Group Relations*. New York: Wiley, 1967. An exhaustive examination of minority-dominant relations, sources of stress and tension, and the forces at work within each party to conflicts.

Castles, Francis. *Pressure Groups and Political Culture*. New York: Humanities Press, 1967.

Deutsch, M., A. Jensen, and I. Katz, eds. *Race, Class, and Personality*. New York: Holt, 1967. A valuble collection of readings.

Glazer, Nathan, and Daniel P. Moynihan. *Beyond the Melting Pot*. Cambridge, Mass.: M.I.T. Press, 1963.

Guetzkow, Harold S., ed. *Groups, Leadership, and Men: Research in Human Relations*. Pittsburgh: Carnegie Press, 1951. A still valuable collection of findings about group dynamics.

Killiam, Lewis, and Charles Grigg. *Racial Crisis in America: Leadership in Conflict*. Englewood Cliffs, N.J.: Prentice-Hall, 1964.

Litt, Edgar. *Ethnic Politics in America*. Glenview, Ill.: Scott Foresman, 1970.

Mahood, H.R., ed. *Pressure Groups in American Politics*. New York: Scribner, 1967. An excellent collection of readings covering most aspects of "group theory," including criticisms.

Parsons, Talcott, and Robert F. Bales. *Family, Socialization, and Interaction Process*. New York: Free Press, 1955.

Truman, David B. *The Governmental Process*. New York: Knopf, 1960.

Five
The Black American

Race, or more accurately, skin color, has carried a pattern of deprivation that has been explained in countless ways. Literary comparisons of "good" to whiteness and "evil" to blackness are persistent in the Western world. But Latin Americans do not accept the simple "white-nonwhite" dichotomy that satisfies the U.S. Bureau of the Census, nor are Latin Americans even clear on what in the United States is obviously meant by "black," that is, non-Caucasian, non-Indian, and non-Oriental. Yet, in the United States, dark skin color triggers enormous economic and social deprivation. In part, the process has been historical. Africans presented a large, economical, and available pool of exploitable manpower. The profit motive, coupled with the ruthless skill of the Europeans and the European-Americans turned blacks into slaves. To rationalize the inhuman use of other human beings, Americans adopted the concept of racial inferiority.

The destructiveness of slavery produced confusion, fear, and, for both black and white, a heritage of structured relationships. With the demise of slavery as an institution, subtle forms of slavery continued. Not only did it have psychological utility for whites, justifying as it did exclusion, personal violence, and differential treatment, but it had practical benefits for whites, such as economic exploitation, sexual abuse, and political scapegoating.

Once the category was created, like all perceptual categories, it provided its own proof. That blacks competed with whites for jobs or for land, were used in the days of the industrial wars as scabs, were, for the South, the nominal reason for a humiliating defeat and an even more humiliating reconstruction, and emerged as an expensive social burden for the North during the twentieth century could only strengthen an already implanted set of attitudes.

The Impact of Slavery

Viewed from a historical perspective, then, slavery was the precipitating if not the causal event of the present status of the black American. It accounts for his presence in the United States. It made him a regional person for almost 300 years, forcibly confining him to the South where economic development lagged behind the rest of the nation. It marked him in the minds of many whites both in the North and in the South as the principal source of a wide range of problems that whites would prefer not to be forced to deal with.

What was the precise impact of slavery on the black American? Its most obvious short-term brutalities are clear: humans torn from their homes, families, and countries; a large part of a continent pillaged of its human resources; and the imposition of bondage on people accustomed to freedom. The long-run ramifications are still subjects of controversy. It has been argued that the black was "deculturated," deprived of his ancestral legacy. At least some blacks, however, deny total deculturation and argue that African culture has been transmitted through music, the dance, religion, and oral history. Some sociologists have asserted that slavery destroyed the black family as an institution; "revisionist" black sociologists have asserted that the black family is not nearly so fragile an institution as their white colleagues would have it. These and other debates about the impact of slavery will no doubt continue and perhaps defy resolution. But certain fairly significant products of slavery can be presented.

Most notably and most obviously, black enslavement set in motion a cycle of economic and social deprivation for a large portion of the country's population. The slave was held in a state of suspended animation while society changed around him. True, some slaves had limited opportunities to learn to read, and certainly there were some who were no more illiterate than their masters, but technical literacy—the ability to read and write—is not the only kind. While other Americans were acquiring skills and experience, accumulating land and capital, and benefiting from physical mobility, a slave was deprived of all of these opportunities either as rewards for his labor or as a part of his opportunity structure.

Many slaves learned useful skills and became in fact accomplished artisans without whom the plantation economy would have been unable to function, but they were not given the chance to acquire the peripheral skills of conducting a trade; that is, the business and commercial experience. Those who were agricultural laborers learned the same agronomy practiced by their masters: a soil-destroying, wasteful, and not especially competent art.

The impact of slavery on the primary identification and instrumental group, the family, was brutal. Although many slaves did have a family life, it was neither socially sanctioned nor protected by the society that had the means to control it. Slave-breeding practices weakened even the informal bonds that could be built. A child born into slavery was loved and had the chance to love, but his world soon became one in which he could see himself only as inferior in the eyes of those who held power over him—a world in which, even if treated with kindness, he was still little more than livestock, with the only hope of redemption being in a life after death. The psychological consequences of such a pattern of deprivation are difficult to measure and appalling to contemplate. No doubt at least some slaves had "happy" lives in the conventional sense of the word, but they probably achieved their happiness by adopting defense mechanisms of subservience, by flattering and entertaining their masters, and by having faith in a life after death. A child, then, grew up in a condition that was a mixture of subservient security and powerless insecurity—a condition over which he had no control.

A further effect of slavery, unintended in part, was the destruction of tribalism a-mong those brought to America. Although the blacks taken from their homelands primarily came from nine major tribes (Hausa, Mandingo, Yoruba, Ibo, Efiks, Krus, Ashantis, Dahomeans, Bimis, and Senegalese), all based on the western coast of Africa, there were significant cultural differences among these tribes. If tribalism had continued in this country, black Americans would to some measure be divided on this basis today. Instead, slavery had a "melting pot" effect. Although blacks from certain tribes were preferred to those from others, successive generations under slavery meant that such distinctions could not persist. Languages, religious rites, traditions, and memories were merged, blended, and intermixed. Although life in America brought a loss of culture and roots, it also created a potential for unity that could not have existed had tribal identities continued. A black American reached a point at which he could not describe himself as Mandingo or Yoruba; the imposition of slavery meant that he could only describe himself as black.

Slavery also created a black political style. Although slaves were denied direct access to the formal instruments of government, they created a politics of their own, focused primarily on the agencies of the state closest to them, the plantations and farms on which they were held captive. For lack of a better rubric, the politics that emerged could be called a "politics of revolt." At one extreme were the great slave uprisings; at the other were the symbolic protests contained in the words and music of the spirituals. In between were actual flights from slavery, barn-burning, petty theft, sabotage, and obedience of a grudging, slow, and awkward nature—an early form of "bugging whitey." Often, this political style accomplished no concrete benefits for the slaves themselves. Burning a master's corncrib brought no tangible gain to the man who applied the torch, but it did result in grief and expense for the master and it provided an outlet for the slave's frustration. It was thus in part a politics of release, an expression of anger and an assertion of manhood and independent action. Individual flights and attempts to create mass uprisings did require the search for a tangible benefit. But, in either case, blacks, by virtue of their exclusion from legally sanctioned political expression, turned to what was then termed (by whites) "criminal" political actions—in short, a politics of revolt.

It is dangerous to assume historical continuities, especially for more than a century, but one is forced to speculate whether the similarities between the early 1800s and the mid-1900s were purely coincidental. Slavery trained blacks to resist white domination and taught them that this resistance need not be "legal" according to the standards set by the dominant powers.

Slavery, without necessarily intending to, substituted a "culture" or "subculture" for the native culture of the blacks. A slave learned to speak English, but he added his own vocabulary, nuances, and syntax. His songs were in English, but their rhythms and meanings were of his own making. He was christianized but then modified the forms and expression of that religion. He was forced to learn a new basic cultural category of "we" and "they."

The extent to which the black life-style was and is a true culture is best left to anthropologists to decide. Without question, however, what the blacks found imposed upon them and how they handled it created a distinctive mode of life that was reinforced and perpetuated in the post-Reconstruction era and in urban centers.

Blacks lived in bondage in America for a longer period of time than they have been free. Despite the importance of the impact of slavery, other events have had an impact as well. It is useful to sketch very briefly those events in historical order.

Historical Sketch

For a brief time, what could be called a "preslave" era existed in America. In Virginia especially, for about twenty years the status of many blacks was equal to that of indentured servants. They had property rights, and some even had white servants. As the black population increased, as racial doctrines were developed, and as slavery became a profitable economic institution, colonial governments moved to nip in the bud the possibility that there might be equality of blacks and whites. Thus, during the 1630s, 1640s, and 1650s, slave status became legally defined and enforced. This was followed by two hundred years of slavery. Black slaves were forced to develop a *modus vivendi* with whites. For many, perhaps for most, this required cultivating a style of deference towards whites, simplicity, humility, ignorance, and unbelievable patience. Beneath the surface, were acts of petty revolt: minimum compliance with the master's wishes, theft, barn-burning, and escape. Acts of escape were a part of the politics of revolt. During the period 1830-1860, an estimated 40,000 slaves escaped to the North; how many fled to the mountains, the swamps, or the West is unknown.

The Prosser Rebellion in Virginia in 1800 was the first major uprising. Gabriel Prosser's goal was the conquest of Richmond and then the creation of an all-black kingdom. The plan was well organized militarily and tactically. At the height of the revolt, Prosser commanded an army of 1,000 blacks and an additional 2,000-5,000 were believed to be standing ready to join once the conquest of Richmond was accomplished. At the moment of the attack, however, Prosser's movements were betrayed and he was foiled by a storm that flooded stream crossings, washed out bridges, and rendered roads impassable. He and twenty-four others were tried and hanged.

Twenty years later, Denmark Vesey, a Charleston, South Carolina, freedman, built an elaborate communications network throughout the state. His goal was the capture of Charleston. It is estimated that he had as many as 9,000 blacks ready to participate in his plan. In 1822, within hours of the beginning of the assault, he too was betrayed.

Finally, one hundred blacks in Virginia took part in Nat Turner's Revolt in 1831. It was significant because white lives were lost, and it occurred at a time when the South was beginning to feel beleaguered by abolitionist criticism of its peculiar institution. As a result, the white reaction was violent, leading to the enactment of increasingly repressive black codes.

The significance of these attempts to revolt is that they required the knowledge that one could make the attempt, the active or at least passive participation of others, and contact with the outside world, through which communications reached other slaves. Despite the awesome power of their masters and their governments, black slaves found a wide variety of means to express their frustration and to search for a solution.

During the same period, in the states in which there was no slavery, two developments were taking place. Black-white coalitions developed into an active, pressure-group, political system. The most famous coalition, which temporarily allied Frederick Douglass and William Lloyd Garrison, was the Anti-Slavery Society. The Society of Friends also allied with black freedmen in efforts to influence Congress and state legislatures to abolish slavery.

The black-white coalition initially had substantial victories. Slavery was abolished in all the northern states shortly after the United States came into being, and after a grace period, slave trade was prohibited by the new Constitution. During the 1800s, however, blacks became increasingly uncertain about their relationship with white "radicals." Although the white radicals were sympathetic to the abolition of slavery, often it seemed that they were more anti-South than pro-black.

As a result, blacks began to develop their own black-power movement. In the 1820s, Donald Walker advocated a radical attack on slavery, postulating that the basic condition for the black was "to kill or be killed." In 1830, the first all-black convention was held in Philadelphia. During the 1840s, Martin R. Delany advocated black nationalism, with blacks controlling their own territory and having their own political, economic, and social institutions, free of white control.

In the years preceding the Civil War, these two streams developed side by side. Many blacks recognized that they were dependent on whites for any kind of political action or resource, yet they were constantly frustrated by the priorities that whites set on black aspirations. Little was done to give blacks the full franchise in the North, to recruit them into political parties, or to give them real resources beyond minimal financing for newspapers, pamphlets, schools, and churches.

Black-white coalitions seemed to operate on the assumption that whites of necessity would set the agenda, make the basic decisions, and be the primary intermediaries between blacks and the institutions of political power.

The purely black movement suffered from similar frustrations. It had no real political leverage—even its most vigorous spokesmen continued to be dependent to some degree on white financing—and it was dependent on lily-white political institutions for making the final decisions.

Underlying these frustrations was the perennial problem of white attitudes. Even the most sympathetic whites had a tendency to submerge the black movement in other issues. To blacks, the objective was clear: liberation. Whites, however, often considered the issue of black liberation to be dependent on other issues: North versus South, the nature of the Republic, the nature of federal power under the Constitution, and people versus property. Slavery was often only incidental to the struggle between white sectional and economic interests.

Many whites had little or no sympathy toward the black cause. The North was by no means completely hospitable to blacks. During the years 1832-1849, there were five major anti-black riots in northern cities. White artisans and working-class people were apt to be hostile toward blacks, but even more liberal and economically secure whites were uncertain about the "Negro Question"; whether blacks were not inherently inferior and whether they could be absorbed into American society were debated seriously and endlessly.

Yet, blacks made significant gains in the antebellum years. They established lines of communication among themselves and with the white political world. Some blacks were politicized; they gained insight into politics and acquired political skills. Finally, the period raised without equivocation the question of the relationship of blacks to white society and politics (and vice versa) in a way that could not be ignored.

From the beginning of the Civil War until the end of Reconstruction, blacks were accepted into the fold of the Republican party and gained in the South what had been denied in the North: real political power. Blacks elected their own representatives to the United States Congress, to state legislatures, and to offices of local government. Their votes were sought, and economic benefits were promised, although not always delivered. Black progressives, such as P. S. Pinchback, also made lasting contributions to their states and to the South by improving the structure of southern government through universal public education and modernized tax systems.

Despite these strides, blacks were able to elect only two United States senators. They never elected a governor, and they gained only a tiny foothold in the judiciary. It became clear that black political power was dependent on federal troops and white support. The end of Reconstruction vividly demonstrated that the national parties would use the blacks as long as they were useful, but once they could serve no purpose, they would be rejected. And, black loyalty to the Republican party was costly. Few benefits were gained by blacks, and white Southerners, both Republicans and Democrats, could ignore the black voter with impunity, since there was no evidence that blacks would become a "swing vote," casting their strength to one side or the other.

The Reconstruction era, however, did demonstrate that black political power existed and could be exercised, and the knowledge never quite died in places like Memphis and New Orleans. Rudimentary political forms continued, often centered on the churches, which also served as quasi-political clubs.

The period from the end of Reconstruction to the 1920s has been accurately labelled the nadir of the black experience in America. Blacks were systematically disfranchised in the South; they were segregated by law. In the North, they encountered persistent discrimination. In a society that was becoming urbanized, technology-oriented, and industrialized, they lived in a backward part of rural America, were deprived of any useful education, and worked primarily as farm or day laborers under near-slave conditions. When blacks came to the North as industrial workers, they were frequently brought there by industrialists who used them as strike-breakers in order to fight the growing power of the unions, and thus they became objects of intense hostility to northern labor organizers and union members.

Simultaneously, this was an era of political ferment. Booker T. Washington and W. E. B. DuBois held two very different strategic viewpoints about the role of the black American and the approach to his problems. Washington argued that the black needed to adapt himself to a predominantly white society by emulating white standards and goals. He should gain skills that were marketable in a white society, and he should remain as invisible as possible. DuBois, after a period of cooperation with Washington, took a militant stance, advocating black awareness and consciousness. With the cooperation of liberal whites, the National Association for the Advancement of Colored People (NAACP) was set into motion in the first decade of the twentieth century, with DuBois being one of the main organizing and intellectual forces behind it.

Four basic patterns came out of the post-Reconstruction era. The first was a hardening and institutionalization of anti-black attitudes. Expressed in the Jim Crow laws, in *Plessy* v. *Ferguson* in which the United States Supreme Court upheld the "separate but equal doctrine," in the purge of blacks from the Republican party, in the conversion of southern populism to race-baiting, and in the racialism inherent in social Darwinism and the new American imperialism, racism seemed to have gained the status of virtual respectability in the United States.

Second, both Washington and the NAACP represented a conscious effort on the part of blacks to align themselves with the wealthier, liberal classes of white society. Based upon an estimate of where any hoped-for access to the white world would lie, this alignment aimed at winning the support of the well-to-do, educated, northern white man, who with his philanthropic organizations, reformist tendencies, and political acumen could provide financial and moral support to the black. The white also could be a "legitimizing" influence, in the sense that his high-status whiteness might ameliorate some of the blackness of his constituency. White attorneys could argue for black clients, white money could fuel black schools, white magazines and journals could find their way into white homes to speak for black needs.

Third, however, the gap between black and white working and lower classes seemed to widen even further. The union movement for all practical purposes renounced any interest in blacks; southern populism played on white fears and prejudice and made it almost inevitable that the white politician run for office as an arch-segregationist.

Finally, there was the resurgence of a black separatist movement. In 1900 the National Negro Business League was founded, its primary aim being the creation of "black capitalism." In 1914, Marcus Garvey's movement began, which was to urge, variously, a return to Africa, religious mysticism, and full separatism within the United States.

The next major period in the history of the black American is that of the "great migration," which took place from the end of World War I into the mid-1950s. Blacks in vast numbers began to move into the urban areas of the North and West. The population shift was virtually unparalleled in United States history, in terms of the massive transfer of a deprived minority from one geographic region to another. With the migration came an increase in the industrialization and urbanization of the black. Larger and larger numbers of blacks benefited from the better educational systems of the North, acquired employment skills, and found themselves living in a world far more complex than one consisting of a crossroad gas station or a patch of cotton land. The sociological implications were staggering: a rural population marked with minority status and the legatees of centuries of deprivation moved into a world that had, true enough, "absorbed" the immigration of Jews, Irish, Germans, Italians, Slavs, and others, but rarely without strife, anguish, and bitterness. The reaction was violent: anti-black riots broke out in Chicago, Detroit, and elsewhere throughout the period. The Great Depression, although encouraging black migration, did not help the cities to accommodate the newcomers. There were too few economic benefits to pass out to anyone, much less to an obvious minority. Ghettoization became a mark of the time.

Efforts to absorb blacks into the politics of the nation were also made during this period. The New Deal won blacks over from Republicanism for a period of decades; at least some of the great urban political machines—in Chicago and New York, most notably—undertook the task of mustering the black voter to their uses, incidentally providing blacks with political offices and patronage. As a result, black "submachines" appeared. Although these organizations used the mass of black voters for their own ends and as dependencies of the white organizations, at least some blacks were given an education in the art and craft of white politics.

Moreover, the NAACP began to win court decisions, which, lacking as they did administrative teeth, nonetheless began to eliminate formal barriers to black participation in United States society. The national government, under the pressure of its own ideology, made some concessions to the black presence.

Two events marked the beginning of a new era in black history. The United States Supreme Court decided in *Brown* v. *Board of Education* in 1954 that school segregation must come to an end; and in 1955 Mrs. Rosa Parks refused to move to the back of the bus in Montgomery, Alabama. These events ushered in an era of the direct clash of three viewpoints, a clash that had been foreshadowed during the Civil War but largely suppressed thereafter. One viewpoint held that the status quo should be maintained; if change were to occur then it should be channeled along familiar lines. Schools might be desegregated but not integrated. Black migration should be from a rural ghetto to an urban ghetto. The second viewpoint held that desegregation should be assimilative; the black should be regarded, treated, and absorbed as a white man of darker skin tone. White society should open its institutions to blacks; blacks should "prepare" themselves by absorbing white skills and values. The third viewpoint held that blacks were culturally and attitudinally different, but difference should not be a basis for discrimination and deprivation.

These conflicting attitudes continued through the 1960s, a decade punctuated by riots and individual violence. Politicians, and leaders of black and white groups, searched for workable formulas, proposals for solving the problems ranged from civil rights acts to nonviolent resistance, revolution, and a "restructuring" of American society. Black power took on many meanings: black votes cast in bloc for white candidates, black votes cast for black candidates, black economic institutions, community control, and, for some, machine guns and molotov cocktails.

Martin Luther King and the Southern Christian Leadership Conference (SCLC) dominated the early 1960s and appeared to achieve marked gains. White youths participated in voter registration campaigns and the integration of public facilities. The Civil Rights Act of 1964 and the Voting Rights Act of 1965, the "War on Poverty," and heightened public awareness seemed to mark the coming of a new openness in the nation. In contrast to these promising developments, however, the Mississippi Freedom Democratic party failed to win anything but nominal recognition at the 1964 Democratic National Convention. King's efforts to apply his nonviolent techniques in the North met crippling resistance; he accomplished little. Young blacks came to feel that they were being asked to make sacrifices to no avail. In 1966, Stokely Carmichael became chairman of the Student Nonviolent Coordinating Committee. Although not completely modifying the set tactical pattern, he gave it a new context with the cry for "black power" and an emphasis on black self-help rather than total dependence on a black-activist-white-liberal coalition. The great urban riots underscored the fear that whites had of minority "excesses" and the potential threat that minorities posed to the "system."

Three basic lessons came out of the struggle of the 1960s. The first was that blacks could and would make demands upon the political system in their own behalf and through their own groups. The content and style of the demands might vary, including face-to-face bargaining over patronage and the threat of massive disruption, but the demands themselves became a permanent feature of the political terrain. Second, white-dominated institutions would make concessions to these demands. Again, the concessions might vary from the nomination of a black candidate for political office to the hiring of "token Negroes" or the appointment of a study commission, but the crucial point was that the demand-response interaction was established. Third, blacks had "invented" a new style of politics that was to be adopted by students, American Indians, women, homosexuals, and to an extent by Chicanos and other groups hoping to assert their political presence.

The new black politics was not without its forebears in the slave era, in labor unions, in the peace movement, and in the community organization movement, but it appeared as a new amalgam. The basic characteristics of the "new" style were:

Multi-front assaults on dominant institutions. The courts, the legislatures, administrative agencies, boycotts, strikes, and the ballot box were all equally valid and simultaneous approaches.

Eschewing prior judgments about the propriety of tactics and strategies. Despite criticism about the "appropriate" way in which to gain concessions from the political system, blacks found that propriety rules were generally calculated to support the status quo.

A willingness to challenge the validity of institutions and processes by testing the stated function against the actual results of these institutions and processes. A claim, by a dominant institution, to openness and progress was regarded as insufficient unless the claim was matched by results.

The frank and open espousal of power as a rhetorical symbol and a tangible goal.

Aspects of the new style will be examined in greater detail in Chapter 16, but it must be stressed that with variations and permutations, the contribution made by black Americans was basic to the development and formulation of what is here called "minority group politics."

Status

Measured against the indexes of deprivation, the gains made by blacks in America were substantial by the beginning of the 1970s. The median income of black families increased from approximately $3,000 in 1960 to $6,500 in 1970. College enrollment of blacks in 1971 was nearly double that of seven years before. Public health care appeared to have improved and political and social recognition was far greater than twenty, or even ten, years before. There were, however, unquestionable signs of lag. Unemployment continued to be consistently twice as high for blacks as for whites, and sporadic efforts to open labor unions to black membership produced few results. Ghettoization continued, and, more important, from a political stand-point, blacks continued to experience subjective deprivation.

Although blacks won high political office—twelve were in the House of Representatives in 1971, one was a United States senator, and several were mayors of cities—the status of the black American continued to be relatively low on the white American's list of priorities. A decade and a half of intense political pressure had put the blacks on the agenda, but their demands were subject to fluctuating interest: inflation, recession, the War in Indochina, the environment—all could demand the attention of the American public and policy-makers, often at the cost of black aspirations.

There was occasional white impatience with black demands, and not only from those who could be easily labelled "bigots." As in the past, black interests only approximately and occasionally coincided with white interests, at least as whites perceived their interests.

There was, moreover, no unanimity within the black population itself. Divided by income, education, age, and geography, not all blacks agreed on strategies and tactics. Organizations acting as spokesmen for black interests covered a wide spectrum, including the venerable NAACP, the SCLC, the Black Panthers, and a full panoply of local organizations. Although each adopted a more militant rhetoric than was popular in 1960, beneath the rhetoric there were substantially differing concepts of the validity of violence and the desirability of assimilation, integration, pluralism, or separatism.

From the perspective of 350 years of black history in the United States, several broad generalizations can be made about what seems to have shaped the present status of the black in the nation.

First, a good part of black politics has been a *reaction* to white politics. Slave revolts, riots, black political organizations, and even black separatism were efforts to respond to the political decisions, or nondecisions, and themes of the dominant society. Only in the last decade or so has this changed, and the change marks a significant break with the past.

Second, for better or worse, black Americans have been dependent on the "good" white man for ultimate decision-making power. Those whites who for one reason or another enlisted in the black cause, whether abolitionist, philanthropist, white member of the NAACP, justice of the Supreme Court, or Robert F. Kennedy, have provided the primary instruments for black access to the institutions and means of power. Thus blacks have been forced to operate in a world in which they depend on the political power and friendship of those who lay outside their cultural category.

Third, however, blacks have come to occupy a strategic position in American society. Twenty-three million blacks represent a potential bloc of enormous power, especially if capable of acting as a bloc. Blacks, by virtue of their isolation in the major cities of the nation, stand to inherit a key position in society. Granted that the cities face physical, social, and economic problems of staggering proportions, the United States cannot abandon them. Thus blacks, perhaps coincidentally, stand to benefit from transfers of funds and attention to the cities. Moreover, the possibility becomes ever greater that blacks will have at their control established political jurisdictions through which they can exercise political power.

Bibliography

Aptheker, Herbert. *American Negro Slave Revolts*. New York: Columbia University Press, 1943. The most complete history of the black politics of revolt during the slave era.

Barbour, Floyd B. *The Black Power Revolt*. Boston: Expanding Horizons, 1968.

Brisbane, Robert H. *The Black Vanguard: Origins of the Negro Social Revolution, 1900-1960*. Valley Forge: Judson Press, 1970. An excellent history and interpretation of a critical period in the evolution of black consciousness.

Carmichael, Stokely, and Charles V. Hamilton. *Black Power: The Politics of Liberation in America*. New York: Vintage, 1967.

Cruse, Harold. *The Crisis of the Negro Intellectual*. New York: Morrow, 1967.

Glenn, Norval D., and Charles W. Bonjean, eds. *Blacks in the United States*. San Francisco: Chandler, 1969. An outstanding collection of readings covering every aspect of the black experience in the United States, including white reactions toward black political movements.

Gosnell, Harold F. *Negro Politicians: The Rise of Negro Politics in Chicago*. Chicago: University of Chicago Press, 1935. A classic study of the processes by which black politics was incorporated into white political institutions and styles.

Holden, Matthew, Jr. "On Misunderstanding of Important Phenomena." *Urban Affairs Quarterly*, 4 (September 1968): 111-129. A thoughtful and penetrating review of writings on black politics to that time.

Holloway, Harry. *The Politics of the Southern Negro: From Exclusion to Big City Organization*. New York: Random House, 1969.

Jordan, Winthrop D. *White Over Black: The Development of American Attitudes Toward the Negro, 1550-1812*. Chapel Hill: University of North Carolina Press, 1968. Essential to understanding the evolution of racial attitudes in the United States.

Litwack, Leon F. *North of Slavery*. Chicago: University of Chicago Press, 1961. A basic and vivid history of the experience of the blacks during the slave era in those states not having slaves.

Logan, Rayford W. *The Negro in American Life and Thought: The Nadir, 1877-1901*. New York: Dial Press, 1954. The standard work for this period of black history.

Marx, Gary T. *Protest and Prejudice: A Study of Belief in the Black Community*. New York: Harper & Row, 1967.

Pinkney, Alphonso. *Black Americans*. Englewood Cliffs, N.J.: Prentice-Hall, 1969. A short, lively, and scholarly examination of black history, politics, social life, and present status in American life.

Wilson, James Q. *Negro Politics*. Glencoe Ill.: Free Press, 1960. Although somewhat outdated by the passage of time and events, still a very useful study of the problems of black leadership in dealing with white political structures.

Six
The American Indian

America has been haunted by a double image of the American Indian: the lofty rhetorician of the Leatherstocking Tales and the wielder of a bloody scalping knife. No doubt white ambivalence is due to the circumstances of fighting the red man. Unlike the black American, who was brought to this country in servility and who for the most ruthlessly practical purposes was designated as inferior, the Indian was conquered; yet he resisted conquest. For the U.S. Army cavalryman, there was little romance in the Indian wars, but eighteenth and nineteenth century Europe and America still believed that enemies on the battlefield were, if they fought well and hard, objects of admiration, even as they were being destroyed.

The key to understanding the relationship of whites to Indians in the United States is to realize that it was part of the longest colonialization movement in world history, beginning with the Spanish colonialists in the early sixteenth century and not yet concluded today. Of all the peoples of America, the Indians can most accurately claim the dubious distinction of being "colonial peoples."

If colonialization is defined as the appropriation of the soil and the destruction of the national integrity of a technologically weaker people by a stronger through force of arms, the Indian perfectly fits the definition. For despite continued bitterness over the "broken treaty" diplomacy of white relations with the Indians, the dominant characteristic of the relationship was military. Foreign affairs were conducted via rifle and artillery piece. From 1607 to the Wounded Knee Massacre (1890), there were only brief periods during which no white man was fighting an Indian. The consequences were stupefying. The Indian population decreased from an estimated 2,000,000 at the beginning of contact to 200,000 in 1900, an attrition unmatched by the Black Plague, the Thirty-Years War, or any modern war.

Aside from the demographic destruction, there was also the forcible removal of traditional societies from their homes and religious roots and the partially successful engraftment of a new religion, property system, concept of diplomacy and warfare, and language. The enforced status of "Indian" forged a unitary collectivity on cultures as diverse as the Pueblos, the Blackfeet, and the Iroquois. That these diverse cultures could be regarded as one culture was the white man's idea; and because he possessed the power to do so, he was successful in making the concept a reality.

Historical Sketch

At the time of the white man's arrival, what is now the United States was composed of peoples having approximately five loosely related life-styles. Within each of these were a number of separately identifiable cultures, perhaps as many as fourteen altogether. The Pacific Coast was largely populated by Indians who lived a sedentary life, depending heavily on either agriculture or fishing for their economic base. The Southwest contained the Pueblos and the Hopis—people with a complex, urban way of life, although already suffering from incursions by nomadic peoples from the north, particularly the Navajos.

The vast plains area was inhabited by nomads. Largely dependent on the buffalo for sustenance, clothing, and religion, their tribal congregation and dispersal cycles coincided with those of the buffalo. In the broad area of the East, both north and south tended to be populated by quasi-agricultural, quasi-hunting peoples. The politically sophisticated Iroquois confederacy in the north was the prototype for similar confederacies elsewhere, such as the Powhatan confederacy of Virginia and the later Creek confederacy of the Southeast.

This simplified classification of a highly diverse population should not obscure the significant differences of tongue, religion, customs, economics, and politics. For America in 1600 was not populated by "Indians," but by a number of distinctive, separate cultures of long tradition and stability.

Within the context of diversity, however, there were some unifying characteristics. Some of these were to have major implications for Indian-white relations and help to explain the enormous destructiveness wrought by three centuries of warfare.

First, the Indians had a close and basically nonexploitative relationship with the natural environment. They used the world around them, without changing its condition. For many tribes the environment was peopled not only with the present generation, but with past generations and those yet to come. Each Indian, and his tribe, was a trustee of the land on which he hunted or farmed, not an owner. Consequently, most Indians were culturally and psychologically dependent on the world around them. Dislocation, whether forced or voluntary, was wrenching and disorienting. Although the close relationship of the Indian tribe to its terrain gave the Indian soldier a tactical advantage in wars with the whites, it inflicted a strategic disadvantage upon him. He had little room to maneuver without surrendering something of fundamental importance to him, his ancestors, and his descendants.

Ultimately, the Indians were forced to engage in defensive warfare. When driven from a familiar environment they could not regroup to fight from a new position of strength, but felt impelled to regain what had been lost.

Second, although Indians showed a degree of technological development and innovative capacity, their prior relationship to their environment had not been a primarily technological one. Few tribes had invented sophisticated agricultural tools or weapons. Before coming into contact with whites, they did not need such developments to insure survival. Once the need came, Indians showed ingenuity in adopting the modern weapons and skills they acquired from whites (just as whites adopted tactics and skills from Indians.).

Third, although warfare was a ritually, economically, and individually significant activity, the Indians generally pursued a policy of limited warfare. To effect a coup by touching a live and armed opponent mattered more to the Plains tribes than to kill him. The capture of slaves, horses, food, or other goods was more important than a "military" victory in the European sense. Few wars were won or lost; they served as a means to create tribal, family, and individual histories. The white, however, fought the Indians with direct, concrete purposes in mind. Increasingly, the warfare became unlimited, resulting in total destruction of the opponent, whether Indian or white. Because few of the Indian tribes had the basic organization necessary for protracted conflicts, organizations had to be built from scratch, with no tradition or model as a guide. Consequently, few of their coalitions had any staying power. Whites had an organizational advantage in their relations with the Indians, one that improved exponentially as a professionalized military cadre developed.

Fourth, the Indians lived in an approximate equilibrium with their world that was as delicate as it was balanced. The white invasion disrupted that equilibrium beyond all restoration. And, the price for the Indian was extraordinarily high. With few exceptions, the great Indian leaders were "reactionaries," men fighting desperately to return to a prior state of affairs. They rarely attempted to absorb, adapt to, or take advantage of the changes that were occurring, although whether whites would have allowed it is also a matter of question. The Indians, once so powerful in relation to their worlds, suddenly were rendered powerless, because the changes set in motion were beyond their capacity to control.

These characteristics plus those of the whites—their technological superiority, their ever-increasing source of manpower, and their emphasis on economic advantage and exploitation—insured the Indian's doom. Even though neither side showed much statesmanship or wisdom, our sympathies are with the Indians, for it was their land that was being taken.

One of the consequences of the relationship between Indians and whites, a relationship based on warfare, was that Indians were isolated and thus denied the chance to learn from whites. The isolation was exacerbated by two conflicting property systems: one stressed collective and continuing ownership; the other stressed individual and temporary ownership. The Indians, to maintain a semblance of their traditional lives, found it necessary to live on reserves; whites, motivated by the convenience of putting the Indians to one side, not only acceded but adopted the reservation as policy.

The reservation policy enabled Indian culture to survive in some fashion, but it meant that the great mass of Indians were more thoroughly ghettoized than the blacks ever were. Furthermore, the Indians were also thoroughly "objectified," reduced from the status of humans to that of objects. Their major contacts with the white world were to be via anthropologists, merchants, government officials, and missionaries, who wanted to study, exploit, or manipulate the Indian. Indians became something for whites to do something to or something for; they were resident outsiders, available for observation, modification, or preservation, but clearly different and properly delineated by the steadily decreasing boundaries of the reservations.

The period of major warfare concluded in the 1870s. By that time, most Indians had been installed in government-supported reservations under the corrupt care of the Bureau of Indian Affairs and the indifferent interest of the military. The reservation system, however, had already proven to be a running sore: it encouraged sporadic revolts on the part of starving people and claustrophobic warriors; it cost the government enormous sums of money, large quantities of which found their way into the pockets of others than those for whom it was intended; it was ideologically questionable, for the concept of reservations ignored those of private property, free enterprise, and capital acquisition; it kept whites from acquiring the large acreage that they wanted; and, for many who had observed the Indians first-hand, it was inhumane, degrading, and un-Christian.

The problems associated with the reservations led to the first major attempt to implement a "termination" policy, that is, an effort to extricate the federal government from any responsibility for the Indians and their future welfare. The Dawes Act of 1887 (The General Allotment Act) was a compromise between those desiring to help the Indian, those coveting the land still held in reservation, and those who simply wanted to get rid of the "Indian Problem" once and for all. The goal was to make the Indian a landowner; the effect was to dispossess him of vast tracts of land. Rather than producing a class of landowners, the Dawes Act actually impoverished large numbers of people who then became beggars or wards of the various states.

The census of 1900, which showed that Indians were well on the way to becoming extinct, stirred a white reform movement that culminated in a massive survey during the 1920s and the Reorganization Act of 1934. The latter enabled tribes to achieve corporate status through charters, thereby enabling them to continue their existence in a collective form and to gain a measure of representation and self-determination. Principal control remained in the hands of the Bureau of Indian Affairs, however, and, though more enlightened, the 1934 act was the older reservation policy with modern trappings.

In 1946, the Indian Claims Commission was established, charged with returning the lands lost under the Dawes Act. In 1953, under a Republican Administration, a strong resurgence toward termination began. Congress requested the Bureau of Indian Affairs to begin to work itself out of a job, and the Bureau introduced a succession of bills to terminate thirteen groupings of Indians. Although government officials consulted with Indian tribes, the policy met with resistance from Indian leadership and their supporters. The reasons for the resistance were similar to those which explained the failure of the Dawes Act program. Some Indians were thrown into white society without the skills or means to survive; a sizable proportion of Indian land was again appropriated and most of it sold to whites; and those tribes that were terminated were subject to state and local taxation without an economic base from which to pay the taxes.

By 1958, the new termination wave began to recede. And, in 1961, the Kennedy Administration brought it to a standstill. In the 1960s, an indigenous economic development was encouraged and federal control over education was reduced. Under the Nixon Administration, lost land or cash equivalents were restored and self-determination increased.

Major themes emerge in this brief history. First, Indians have been relatively powerless in their contacts with whites. During the decades of warfare, they were forced to react to white initiatives and, despite brilliant tactical victories, were strategically overwhelmed. More fundamentally, however, Indians were concerned with preservation in the face of powerful innovation. Ultimately, Indians could not preserve their life-styles against the effect of the railroad, the telegraph, the Gatling gun, and the permanent fort. They became almost totally dependent on white institutional willingness to continue past traditions. That this willingness was at best whimsical and at worst hostile was evidenced time and again by broken treaties, termination policies, the transfer of Indian youths to white-dominated schools, and subtle and not-so-subtle encouragement to give up reservation life and the old rituals and traditions. The Indian could cling to the past and seek continuity, but he could do so only with enormous conscious effort, at the price of economic deprivation, and in the face of contrary governmental actions. As proof that they were not totally powerless, many Indians preserved their cultures, however modified, through succeeding generations. But to the white world, the Indian persistently remained an object to romanticize, to preserve, to eliminate, or to use for commercial advantage.

The very ambivalence of governmental policy, its fluctuations between preservation and isolation and between termination and accommodation, accurately reflects the more fundamental ambivalence of the American white population. And, the Indians have been helpless in the face of these fluctuations. On occasion, they have resorted massively and dramatically to the politics of revolt—exodus and war; or to smaller acts of revolt—individual flight, suicide, alcoholism, the use of peyote, and, increasingly, pressure-group politics.

Second, the Indians have been inextricably involved in the political process, either as objects of diplomacy and warfare or as a domestic, colonized people. Unlike some minorities who might possess a theoretical option to choose political action as a means of achieving their goals, Indians have had no such option. Concurrent with their involvement in politics, Indians have been denied legally established political rights longer than any other single major grouping—not achieving even partial citizenship until after World War I, and not achieving the right to vote in all state elections until 1946. Along with a lack of civil status has been an almost complete dependence, at least on the reservations, on government for support, ranging from food and medical help to agricultural practices and education. In order to seek almost any collective goal, they must go through the agencies of government.

Third, this long-standing dependence on the political process and the good will of government has been a mixed blessing. On the positive side, the federal government has maintained the reservations, prevented the extermination of the Indian (which might well have happened), and provided a minimum of welfare benefits. On the negative side, it has been consistently niggardly in its appropriations for basic needs and has been consistently inconsistent in its long-term posture toward Indians. Security, whether physical or psychological, has not been one of the benefits derived from governmental supervision. Thus, on the one hand, some potential for identity was maintained; on the other, a dreadful cost has been exacted for maintaining that potential.

Fourth, Indians have been dependent on whites to act as intermediaries in the political process, whether these whites have been officials of the Bureau of Indian Affairs, committed anthropologists, or reformers in and out of government. This dependence, like that of blacks, has not been entirely unfortunate for Indians; but, like blacks, they have been subjectively deprived, underscoring the powerlessness of a deprived minority to gain results for itself.

Fifth, Indians have been politically and organizationally divided historically. The few grand coalitions that came into being, most notably Pontiac's "conspiracy," Tecumseh's league, and Sitting Bull's alliance, had limited cohesive power. Although white counterresponses contributed to their collapse, divisions within a coalition were equally significant. Indian political organization was generally unable to extend beyond the "tribe," and when it did, it had little staying power. Thus, despite white insistence on regarding the "Indian" as a single phenomenon, Indians themselves failed to build a pan-tribal identity. In the face of the enormous institutions of government, their dividedness was only an added political liability.

Status

Measured by most objective indexes, the status of the American Indians at the end of the 1960s, was the most deprived of any minority grouping in the United States. In 1968, the average life-span of white Americans was 70.2 years; of Indians, 42 years. Unemployment was ten times the national average, that is, it ranged from 40 to 60 percent, depending on general economic conditions. It was estimated that 50 percent of the housing available to the Navajo was unfit for human habitation and that as much as 90 percent of all Navajo housing was below minimum standards for health and safety.

Indians living on reservations had one of the highest infant mortality rates in the world; and the reservations were one of the few remaining areas of the United States in which tuberculosis was still a common disease.

In 1966, out of a total population of about 700,000, only 1,900 Indians were enrolled in college, or 1 in 300, compared with a ratio nearly ten times more favorable for the population at large. In that same year, 120 Indians graduated from college. The rate of illiteracy was estimated to be 50 percent.

These figures improved steadily through time. The life-span of the American Indian, for example, increased in the years 1968 to 1970 by two to four years, depending on the estimate.

More fundamental to the quality of Indian life were certain other characteristics, however. The Indians were still primarily agricultural and pastoral in a nation undergoing the "postindustrial revolution." Their farms were generally small at a time when agricultural methods and economics had long since been mechanized and giant agricultural corporations dominated the economics of farming. In addition, their farming and herding generally took place on unproductive land, of which large acreage was required to support minimal activities. In short, they were operating with inappropriate means in a world of corporations and corporate economic power.

The Indians seemed to suffer from serious identification problems. Torn between past traditions and present demands, many were driven to self-destructive behavior and escapism, such as alcoholism and suicide. Whether these problems are a result of "deculturation" or the grating frustration of perennial poverty and illness is impossible to ascertain, although presumably one reinforces the other. Taught to have a close identity with family, clan, and tribe, an Indian grows up to find that the white world prefers that he lose that identity. Material rewards can come only if he makes at least a physical break from his traditional identification groups.

Although finally in possession of the nominal rights of citizenship, the Indians still faced serious problems. Few candidates offered themselves for public office as spokesmen for or representatives of Indian interests; voter turnout among Indians was low; and the population was widely dispersed geographically, inhibiting interaction and organization on the basis of political activism. Although some groupings of Indians, especially the Navajo, were in a position to exercise a voting influence in state politics, no real effects had emerged by the early 1970s.

Although the picture was bleak, it was not hopeless. Health showed improvement. Through the efforts of the Nixon Administration, basic benefits were granted to various Indian tribes, including the restitution of land to the Taos

Indians and concrete and symbolic steps toward greater freedom from supervision by the Bureau of Indian Affairs.

In the 1960s there was also an emergence of major groups representing Indian claims and aspirations, as well as a strengthening of older groups. Some Indians rallied to the "Red Power" movement; others chose a more moderate approach through such older groups as the National Congress of American Indians, the Association on American Indian Affairs, Arrow, Incorporated, and the Indian Rights Association. Even the "established" groups began to adopt a more militant rhetoric. All began to gain greater national prominence and to receive attention from such political figures as Barry Goldwater, Robert Kennedy, and Richard Nixon.

Three problems continued to plague the Indians as a minority grouping, however. The first was a lack of resources—financial, human, and organizational. Like any severely deprived minority, the Indians faced the difficult problem of finding the resources and energies to make their potential influence felt. Geographic dispersal, lack of education and organizational skills, and a sense of powerlessness were all serious handicaps.

Second, the Indian "community" itself was by no means unified. Although it is difficult to assess either the magnitude or intensity of various viewpoints, it seemed that four major positions existed among the Indian population:

The traditionalists. Those Indians who wanted to preserve the reservation way of life and native customs set their priorities in terms of isolation from the white world and maintaining old rituals, trades, and skills. Basically, their goal was to preserve the status quo by resisting economic development, agricultural and pastoral innovation, and incursions of nontraditional political positions or practices. The price of traditionalism may be continued deprivation.

The progressives. Those who wanted to modify the reservation way of life to bring it into line with existing economic realities turned to economic development, better farming methods, tourism as a source of income, and increased federal assistance in order to progress from poverty status to one of lesser economic deprivation. They hoped to preserve the reservation system as an envelope for identification groups by making it economically viable. The difficulty with this position was the unanswered question: Is it possible to change some basic practices without modifying the entire cultural pattern?

The terminationists. There were those who felt that the reservation system was intrinsically a dead end. They wanted Indians to be fully assimilated into American society and the "cultural mark" to be eliminated forever and completely. Based on their assessment of the reservation as an economic and social trap, the terminationists had as their primary goal the preparation of Indians to leave the reservation as quickly as possible through educational and skill-oriented training programs.

The militants. Rapidly emerging were those who felt that white society was itself in serious trouble, afflicted by social, political, and economic ills. The Indian thus should have the power to make his own way, should recognize the intrinsic superiority of the Indian culture in contrast with the materialism and competitiveness of white society, and should reject that society in favor of "Red Power." In some respects, the militants combined the goals and attitudes of both the traditionalists and the progressives, but rather than depend upon the whims of white society or work through the traditional tribal councils, they sought new group vehicles to mobilize Indian will and resources. Further, their emphasis was different, far more separatist than either the status quo position of the traditionalists or the adaptation to white customs implicit in the progressive position. The reservation would be preserved, but it would become an entirely new unit of self-identification and power.

In large measure, the divisions themselves are related to differences in age, experience, education, and tribal status. Young Indians, for example, who learned the rhetoric and goals of the black-power movement, tended to adapt it to their own situation, whereas the older generation (like the older blacks) were inclined to view militance as unreasonable and self-defeating.

Third, the Indians continued to be dependent on whites, whatever their goals or strategies. Even the militants required the cooperation of whites to achieve their ends, either by supplying resources or through governmental action, which would provide the desired independence.

Despite the failure of white Americans (or perhaps because of that failure) to take the Indian movement seriously, red militance mounted. In 1969, a small band of Indians seized Alcatraz Island after it had been abandoned by the federal government. Although totally dependent on outside logistical support, the Indians held the island for eighteen months. They argued that the island was land owed the Indians; more important, however, the seizure symbolized a new mood prevalent among Indians, since representatives of several tribes were present and support came from all across the nation.

Direct action was also launched at other federal areas, especially military posts. In 1971 in New York City (which contains about 10,000 Indians), a statue of George Washington was defaced, in symbolic protest against the history of oppression of Indians. In 1972, when Raymond Yellow Thunder was killed in Nebraska under mysterious circumstances, Sioux from Nebraska and South Dakota organized a protest and investigation that carried undertones of the threat of violence.

Certain lessons can be learned from the Indian experience as a minority grouping. The first, and most obvious, of these is that a minority would be imprudent to depend on the good faith and good judgment of the dominant political system. That system has not been indifferent to the Indian all of the time, nor have all officials lacked compassion; even so, the Indian's forced dependency on white support and help has brought him few benefits beyond marginal survival. The lesson may seem too harsh; it may assume that the dominant system is incapable of learning from its own errors. But a young Indian reading a history of his people could understandably draw the inference so clearly laid out before him. It would also seem that minority status carries with it certain serious liabilities beyond those of objective deprivation. As noted in the chapter on blacks, there are major problems in trying to build organizations, strategies, and tactics. Indians have tried diplomacy, warfare, accommodation, and subservience; today they are experimenting with the new strategies and tactics of the politics of revolt. Thus far, none of their efforts have produced major gains, although experimentation with the politics of revolt is too recent and too disparate to evaluate fairly.

Moreover, Indians as a minority have disadvantages that blacks do not have. They are much fewer in number: 700,000 Indians versus 23,000,000 blacks. They live in rural areas instead of strategic urban centers. Population concentration and numbers are important resources for a minority, often the only resources.

Bibliography

Collier, John. *The Indians of the Americas.* New York: Norton, 1947. One of the very best works on the American Indians, written by the most famous and compassionate director of the Bureau of Indian Affairs.

Daniels, Walter M. *American Indians.* New York: Wilson, 1957.

DeLoria, Vine. *Custer Died for Your Sins: An Indian Manifesto.* New York: Macmillan, 1969.

————. *We Talk, You Listen, New Tribes, New Turf.* New York: Macmillan, 1970. Both of DeLoria's books are sharp, clear statements of the anguish of the contemporary Indian and his resolution to do something to produce radical change in his circumstances.

Josephy, Alvin M., Jr. *The Patriot Chiefs: A Chronicle of American Indian Leadership.* New York: Viking Press, 1961. A valuable study of leadership among the Indians during crucial periods of history.

Kluckhorn, Clyde, and Dorethea Leighton. *The Navaho.* Cambridge, Mass.: Harvard University Press, 1946.

Kramer, Judith. *The American Minority Community.* New York: Crowell, 1970. Contains a very good chapter on the Indians, with special insights into the effects of the "peyote cult."

Steiner, Stan. *The New Indians.* New York: Harper & Row, 1968. A valuable look at the new political activism of American Indians.

Tebbel, John, and Keith Jennison. *The American Indian Wars.* New York: Bonanza, 1960. A handy, brief guide to the major landmarks in this grim phase of white-Indian relations.

Seven
The Mexican-American

Perhaps for the vast majority of Americans, the most invisible of the new minorities is that consisting of Mexican-Americans. This is, in part, attributable to the fact that most of the Mexican-American population is concentrated in five southwestern states. Population distribution, alone, does not explain the lack of general public awareness of Mexican-Americans, since the American Indian population is largely regional as well. Only recently has the Mexican-American movement emerged as an "issue."

Black Americans have evoked strong passions for much of their history. A major war was fought with slavery the nominal cause. Although often treated as objects of ridicule, they have also been stereotyped as being threatening or dangerous, potent and untamed. The same has been true of American Indians, although they have been stereotyped in a different way. Even as they were fought, defeated, and consigned to reservations, a romantic legend was created and still persists.

Latins, especially Mexicans, have on the other hand rarely been regarded with the same ambivalence. They have been stereotyped as being lazy, constantly taking siestas, speaking with a foreign accent, and being interested in banditry, bullfights, and guitars. They were comfortably regarded as small children. An analysis of American movies would reveal that blacks have virtually never been depicted as villains and that, in recent years at least, Indians have been cast as perhaps savage but nonetheless sympathetic characters. Rarely, if ever, has a Mexican-American been portrayed as anyone but a bandit (usually incompetent), who is ultimately done in by a heroic Anglo-American[1] cowboy.

An equally important contributing factor to the low visibility of the Mexican-American has been the slowness with which a political consciousness directed at

---

[1]In this chapter the term Anglo-American is used instead of white American to distinguish those of British or European descent from those of Spanish descent.

overcoming subjective deprivation has emerged. The Chicano movement did not appear until the second half of the 1960s. Compared with the controversial spokesmen that shaped the women's movement, the black liberation movement, and the Indians' struggle for independence and survival, the Mexican-Americans have, until recently, had few to speak for them, either from their own ranks or from a small number of sympathizers. To explain almost a century and one-half of silence, it is tempting to assume that Mexican-Americans have suffered less than other minorities, or that their history has been less filled with discrimination and deprivation than that of blacks, Indians, or other groupings. The facts do not bear out the assumption, however.

It is also tempting to draw analogies. Like blacks, Mexican-Americans were originally predominantly rural and have rapidly become urban. Like blacks, Mexican-Americans have been exploited for cheap agricultural labor and have paid the price of exploitation by short life-spans, malnutrition, poverty, and disease. Like both blacks and Indians, Mexican-Americans are physically distinguishable from Anglo-Americans and are culturally marked by their distinctive speech patterns. Like Indians, they live in particular regions and have become a minority by virtue of conquest rather than by either forced or voluntary immigration.

These similarities to other minority groupings only partly disguise an important underlying reality. Mexican-Americans have a rich and unique tradition, with its own political driving force and its own specific potential. The basic ingredients of that tradition are found in their history, in their distinctive culture, which has survived both in spite of and because of discrimination, and in a pattern of objective and subjective deprivation that has imposed bitter hardship on a large and growing population.

Historical Sketch

Anglo-Americans celebrate the founding of what was to become the United States by marking the anniversaries of Jamestown (1607) and Plymouth (1620), but by those dates the southwestern segment of the new nation had already been explored and colonized by Spaniards. The process of settlement was slow, however, because of the vast spaces, an often inhospitable environment, and hostile Indians.

By the time the Mexican nation won independence from Spain in 1821, a clearly defined set of societies had been established in what is now Texas, New Mexico, and California, with Arizona and Colorado being much more sparsely inhabited by Mexicans. In 1821, Texas had an estimated population of 4,000 Mexicans, most of them farming or raising livestock. In New Mexico and California, large-scale ranching was the common economic base. In Arizona, persistent warfare with the Indians held settlement to a minimum until well into the nineteenth century. In fact, each of the areas has a distinctive history, inasmuch as the settlers were forced to cope with different environmental problems.

Although the patterns of settlement and economics were different, the Mexican settlers had certain common characteristics. One was a strong tie to their Spanish heritage and culture. Even though Spain's imperial power had rapidly declined (the Mexicans having contributed to the decline by seeking independence), many still thought of themselves as being of Spanish origin and were committed to preserving the traditions of language, literature, religion, and life-style. This commitment was stronger among the upper classes, but it was shared by the lower classes as an aspiration if not an achievement.

Also contributing to the Mexican heritage was the legacy of the Indians who originally inhabited the land that the Spanish had conquered. The arts, crafts, and foodstuffs of both, together with a more than occasional mingling of blood, produced a people that was neither Spanish nor Indian but definably Mexican. Like Anglo-Americans, Mexicans had a sense of heritage from a mother country, but the passage of time produced changes in language, physiognomy, diet, and even religious practices. Mexico was more than a political unit; it was also a "New World" way of life.

A third common characteristic was the close interrelationship of family, religion, language, and culture, with family being the most crucial element. The ties of blood and marital relationships were the cement of the Mexican social system. Family commitments shaped political and economic issues. Given the importance of *machismo* (masculine virility), the social structure of the family was patriarchal. It is very possible that the ultimate triumph of the Anglo-Americans, which reduced the Mexican-American to a state of subservience, was an especially painful subjective deprivation in a country in which the male was regarded as a potent and dominant figure.

Even before Mexican independence from Spain, there had been contact between the Spanish and the Anglo-Americans along the western frontiers of the United States, and these contacts were not always friendly. Until 1821, however, only a few Anglos had moved as far west as Texas. The birth of the Mexican nation included a boundary settlement with the United States; at the same time, the Mexican government granted permission to Stephen Austin to found colonies in Texas.

From 1821 on, Anglo-Americans poured into Texas and tension heightened. In 1826, they unsuccessfully attempted to seize control of the Mexican province. After years of sporadic conflict, the successful Anglo rebellion of 1836 tore Texas away from Mexico, and nine years later it was annexed to the United States. In the war that followed (1846–1848), the United States acquired most of what is now the American Southwest, together with a large population of former Mexican citizens.

National military victory did not end the conflict among Indians, Americans, and Mexican-Americans. As recently as 1943, in the so-called *pachuco* riots, Anglos and Mexican-Americans clashed; and even today there are still physical confrontations. One result of the protracted battle has been a hardening of attitudes on both sides. Although living in geographic proximity, the members of both Anglo-American groupings and Mexican-American groupings found their basic "we-they" categories sharpened by physical struggle.

During the decades following annexation by the United States, a steady migration of Anglos into what had formerly been Mexican areas took place. Southerners seeking to extend (or escape from) the cotton economy moved west; Anglos from all parts of the nation were drawn by the magnets of gold, railroads, and land. The Mexican-Americans were rapidly displaced from lands that had been theirs to use for generations.

Three major factors contributed to the displacement. First, the Mexicans had quite naturally settled on the most desirable lands in terms of arability, grazing potential, and proximity to water. The Anglo-Americans were determined not to be denied these rich areas simply because of prior occupancy. And their determination was strengthened by the consideration that the prior occupants had been defeated in warfare, spoke a "foreign" language, and practiced a different religion, as well as generally having much darker skin (and it must be remembered that many of the Anglo settlers came from the South).

Second, the Anglo-Americans brought a different economic structure to much of the Southwest. The giant ranch surrounded by barbed wire replaced the open grazing rights of the Mexicans. In effect, "enclosure" occurred in the Southwest as it had in England centuries before with the result that Mexican-owned livestock was prevented from grazing on the best pastures and from drinking from the best sources of water. That many Mexican-Americans were also sheep herders, to the disgust of many Anglos, only exacerbated matters, leading to bloody range wars, the most famous of which was the Graham-Tewksbury War in Arizona in the early 1880s.

Third, the instruments of government had changed hands. The courts were no longer Mexican but American. When a Mexican-American felt his land rights had been illegally or unjustly violated, he had to appear before an Anglo judge and argue against the interests of another Anglo. He invariably lost his case. And the territorial or state legislatures were just as unsatisfactory for legal redress. Language barriers, political intimidation, and legal enactment eventually disfranchised most Mexican-Americans who had hoped to participate in the political process.

In brief, the newly Americanized Mexican had been conquered at war, deprived of his traditional property rights, reduced rapidly to the status of a numerical minority by Anglo migration, and denied the processes of law. There were exceptions, but, in general, in the nineteenth century Mexican-Americans were squeezed out of their holdings, consigned to menial and subordinate economic roles, and regarded as aliens in a land that had been colonized by their ancestors.

The pattern underwent change, however, at the turn of the century. Until that time, the overwhelming majority of Mexican-Americans were native-born. Although migrant workers had been coming across the border, only a few settled permanently. With the outbreak of Mexican revolutionary violence in 1909-1910, immigration to the United States became a major factor in population changes. Since that time, hundreds of thousands of Mexicans have crossed the border, having obtained visas to work and make their homes in the United States. A number have crossed illegally as well. In the late twenties and from 1955 to 1965 great waves of Mexican immigrants arrived.

Chronic labor shortages in the United States, especially during the two world wars, provided an incentive to migrate. Although initially most Mexican-Americans had come as agricultural workers, they began to seek opportunities in the cities of the Southwest. After World War II, Mexican-Americans became increasingly urbanized. In 1950, 66 percent of the Mexican-American population lived in cities; ten years later, 79 percent did.

Immigration was encouraged by the policies of the United States government. The giant farming interests, needing inexpensive and menial labor, lobbied hard for the *bracero* program and managed to keep it functioning until 1964. Under that program, farmers were allowed to import workers for a season and then return them to Mexico. There is no question that many of the workers fled to avoid returning to Mexico, staying on as permanent residents. The program also demonstrated to impoverished Mexicans that there might be better job opportunities in the United States than at home, thus encouraging them to migrate.

Underlying the migration was the familiar bitter problem. Many came expecting to find jobs that did not exist, or to discover that the available jobs were dead ends. They faced discrimination, not only in employment and pay, but in schools, social contacts, housing, and the operations of government agencies. The burden of discrimination was made heavier by their inability to speak English fluently. Often, if private or public help did exist, the immigrant could not find it. In response, a number of immigrant-help organizations came into being, such as *La Alianza Hispano Americana* and *La Sociedad Mutualista Mexicana*. The Roman Catholic Church made a heavy commitment to aid the distressed as well.

Among the advantages accruing to the long history of Mexican-Americans in the Southwest was that many basic cultural institutions survived because they had never been torn loose from their original moorings. Churches, religious practices, neighborhoods, and communities maintained continuity through time and provided a stabilizing context for the newly arrived.

This stability in turn enhanced the development of an organizational life that served not only to help new arrivals, but also to communicate the needs of Mexican-Americans to the outside world. The churches and church-based organizations were very important, but in the years following World War II, a number of more politically oriented organizations came into being, such as the Community Service Organization and the American G.I. Forum. Both sought greater electoral leverage for Mexican-Americans through voter drives and by encouraging Mexican-American candidates to offer themselves for public office. During the late 1950s and early 1960s, Mexican-American organizations increasingly sought involvement in the dominant political process. The Mexican-American Political Association, formed in 1958 and primarily California-based, and the Political Association of Spanish-Speaking Organizations, created in 1962 and Texas-based, were both frankly politically oriented. Both contributed to the demise of the poll tax and to the increase in Mexican-American voter registration. They gained representation in community action and model cities programs as these programs came into being.

All the organizations had problems, however. They had little contact with urban young people and often even less with agricultural laborers. They appealed primarily to the middle-class of a grouping in which a large proportion of the population suffered severe economic deprivation. Finally, although Mexican-American in composition and avowed purpose, they adopted the tactics and values of Anglo society rather than having an essentially Mexican-American identity or approach.

The rising tide of black militance provided a model for many disaffected Mexican-Americans. A major result was the Chicano movement, which began in 1966. The potency of the movement lies in its strong appeal to Mexican-American solidarity and to the young, especially those in colleges and universities, and in its masculine symbols of "brown power." Branches of the Chicano movement were most commonly found in California in the early 1970s, but they also appeared in Colorado, New Mexico, Arizona, and Texas.

New Mexico has also been the scene of protracted, although virtually bloodless, guerrilla warfare. Under the leadership of Reies Lopez Tijerina, Mexican-Americans were seeking the restoration of lands originally held by Mexican-Americans in the northern part of the state. Tijerina emerged as a folk hero for Mexican-Americans in search of an authentic cultural mode of expression. Tijerina's rebellion, moreover, carried profound political overtones: its objective was land reform, so long a symbol of revolution in Mexico; it also came close to advocating separation from Anglo society.

The most compelling struggle was that of Cesar Chavez and the United Farm Workers Organizing Committee in their effort to win union recognition for the grape pickers of the Delano area of California. On its surface, the conflict was closer to a classic labor-management confrontation than a struggle between a minority and a dominant group. The points of negotiation were the familiar issues of labor organizing drives in the 1920s and 1930s. As important as the bread and butter issues were, the overriding and compelling force of the effort was Chavez himself. He emerged as a passionately charismatic leader, an expression of generations of oppression, a spokesman for the Mexican-American's desire to reclaim his manhood, and a religious leader with the mystic qualities of a Ghandhi. For many of his followers, the real issues were less the economic ones than those of whether

Mexican-Americans could defeat their exploiters. It was to this that Robert Kennedy responded in his 1968 primary campaign in California, his sympathetic reaction winning an outpouring of support from Mexican-American voters.

When Chavez finally won his battle in 1969, the victory was all the more impressive because it was so hard-won, required so much sacrifice, and was, originally at least, so expected to fail. The lesson driven home was that Mexican-Americans could organize and, with organization and leadership, could win against long odds.

One of the effects of the heightened self-awareness was the growth of a large number of organizations embodying the Chicano ideology. In 1968, the Brown Berets appeared, claiming twenty-six chapters located primarily in California and Texas, but in other states as well. Their enunciated aim was to seek "a restoration of the dignity of the people." At about the same time, the Mexican-American Youth Organization (MAYO) appeared in Texas and in 1969 formed an alliance with the Denver-based Crusade for Justice led by Corky Gonzalez. MAYO emphasized the establishment of Chicano capitalism and worked with the indirect assistance of a major foundation until blocked by Congressman Henry Gonzalez of Texas, who argued that MAYO was a disruptive influence. Despite the setback, MAYO continued its organizing efforts and spread rapidly to college campuses throughout the Southwest.

The story of MAYO embodies the evolution of Mexican-American consciousness taking place in the late 1960s and early 1970s. The older, more firmly established segments of the population preferred to "work within the system," seeking a gradual growth of Mexican-American voting power, the election of moderate spokesmen to state and national legislatures, and the gradual assimilation in economic terms, at least, of the population. The younger generation was clearly more impatient and angry and with increasing frequency turned to the politics of revolt to express their grievances. Although the strategies and tactics of the various new organizations differed, almost all adopted militant rhetoric; many spoke in the language of popular Marxism, and although claiming nonviolence as a credo, carefully pointed out that they were willing to resort to arms for "self-defense."

The pattern of development for Mexican-Americans was one, then, of a long era of suffering in silence, during which they were deprived and disfranchised. The explosion, when it finally happened, was perhaps all the more potent because of the decades of quiescence that had gone before. The precise directions of the Chicano movement remained uncertain. It was more than clear, however, that the Mexican-American insisted on being heard and that he spoke with a voice that was specifically his own.

Status

According to the 1970 census, the Mexican-American population was slightly over 5,000,000, with 80 percent living in California, Texas, New Mexico, Arizona, and

Colorado. The median family income of the Mexican-American in 1960 was estimated to be $4,164 compared with $6,448 for Anglo-Americans and $3,644 for blacks in the Southwest. Tentative estimates showed that the absolute family income for Mexican-Americans had improved by 1970, but that the gap between Anglo- and Mexican-American incomes narrowed only slightly. Fifty-two percent of the Mexican-Americans in rural areas had incomes that fell below the official poverty line; 31 percent of the urban families had incomes below that line.

Unemployment among Mexican-Americans, although not as high as that among blacks or Indians, is nonetheless twice or three times as high as that of the total population of the United States. Health statistics are equally grim. Malnutrition, infectious respiratory diseases, and infant mortality have remained endemic within the Mexican-American population, partly as a consequence of the lack of public health services in the *barrios* (Mexican-American ghettos).

On the positive side, concrete gains have been made, largely through improved "outreach" in programs sponsored by the federal government as a part of its War on Poverty of the 1960s. Local government agencies hire an increasing number of Mexican-Americans and Mexican-speaking service personnel to reach those who would otherwise be excluded from assistance because of language barriers.

Mexican-Americans have made substantial gains in terms of political clout. Although far from the goals set by voter-registration drives, the number of registered and active Mexican-American voters has increased steadily since the 1950s. A 1967 survey of the five southwestern state legislatures showed that of the 603 members, 48 were Mexican-American: the New Mexico legislature having the greatest number–33; and Texas having 10 (Grebler, Moore, and Guzman 1971, p. 560). New Mexico was also represented in the United States Congress by a senator of Mexican-American extraction.

The federal government, moreover, has given increasing recognition to the needs of the Mexican-Americans. In 1964, the bracero program was finally terminated, and thus one of the most ugly symbols of exploitation vanished. Federal funds began to be available for research into the problems and aspirations of the Mexican-American population, and limited funds were appropriated for language educational programs. The language issue has been a bitter one in the Chicano movement, since abundant evidence has emerged to show that Mexican-American school children are discriminated against for their use of Mexican and are punished for their failure to master English. The refusal to accept the cultural tongue has been seen as a direct effort to destroy Mexican-American cultural heritages. The creation of bilingual school programs continues to be a major aim of Chicano organizations.

Most of the larger southwestern universities now acknowledge the presence of a Mexican-American student constituency on their campuses either through special study programs or the addition of individual courses to traditional curricula. And, the scramble to hire Mexican-American faculty has become as lively as the hiring of blacks, in no small measure as a consequence of pressures from the U.S. Department of Health, Education, and Welfare. The pattern, however, is a confused one, like that of other minorities. Some of the "progress" is concrete: improvements in the health, economic conditions, and housing of Mexican-Americans have reduced the objective deprivation of the grouping. Some of the progress, however, falls far short of the demands generated by the sense of powerlessness among the Mexican-Americans, especially when compared with rising aspirations. The Chicano movement has only begun to realize its hope of *La Raza* (a sense of peoplehood), the same hope expressed in Tijerina's cry: "Our god is our language, our blood."

And, there is far from universal agreement within the Mexican-American grouping regarding the validity or the ultimate benefits of a "peoplehood" approach. The most severe splits are generational. Those inclined to be moderate can look to a growing body of those who have attained middle-class status and a degree of acceptance within the Anglo society. Patience, hard work and frugal habits still seem to pay off. Although many of the forms of Mexican-American culture could vanish with prosperity, the moderates hope to retain their religion and language as a part of the private life of the individual and the family.

A large number of young and some older Mexican-Americans are suspicious of this gradualist philosophy. Not a few are the sons and daughters of those who have attained middle-class status and are willing to challenge the emptiness of affluence without identity, as they see it.

The split is exacerbated by the suspicion among the young that the Church is a (perhaps unwitting) tool of Anglo domination and oppression, or at best a drag on organizing and consciousness-raising efforts. Even though a strong movement within the Church towards social commitments has placed it often in the forefront of battles for responsive programs, many activists see the Church as an institutionalized force for status quo thinking. Older people are apt to feel that the Church and the family are totally intertwined, the basic institutions that symbolize heritage and tradition and the primary sources of comfort and security for the individual and the people. The attack on the Church is, inevitably, an attack on the family in their view. As a result, the split between generations and between positions on the Church divides not only the population as a whole but families.

Most observers agree that of all the major minority groupings, Mexican-Americans have long suffered the most from a lack of organization and leadership. Mexican-Americans are consequently left without the political traditions or skills to engage in a protracted struggle with dominant groups in a modern, postindustrial, and urban society. Factionalism, "Uncle Tomism," and the quest for personal instrumental goals among those group leaders who have arisen in the past only contribute to a sense of despair and ineffectiveness among the larger population. Even in the 1970s, although the Chicano movement advocates unity, in its practical workings it helps create divisions within the total population.

Yet the Mexican-American does occupy a strategic position in American society. A large portion of the population of the southwestern United States could, potentially, subscribe to *La Raza*. There is a common cultural heritage, one that has been less undermined than is often the case for minority groupings. Political experience is rapidly being accumulated. The problem is whether the aspiration for peoplehood can be translated into the imperatives of politics.

Bibliography

Cabrera, Y. Arturo. *Emerging Faces: The Mexican-Americans.* Dubuque, Iowa: Brown, 1971. Especially useful as an expression of basic grievances and needs.

Dinnerstein, Leonard, and Frederic C. Jaher, eds. *The Aliens: A History of Ethnic Minorities in America.* New York: Appleton-Century-Croft, 1970. Contains a vivid essay by Marjorie Fellows on the Mexican-American laborer.

Grebler, Leo, Joan W. Moore, and Ralph C. Guzman. *The Mexican-American People: The Nation's Second Largest Minority.* New York: Free Press, 1971.

Hansen, Niles M. *Rural Poverty and The Urban Crisis.* Bloomington: Indiana University Press, 1970. Contains an especially useful chapter setting the Mexican-American in the national context.

Heller, Celia S. *Mexican-American Youth: Forgotten Youth at the Cross-Roads.* New York: Random House, 1966.

Madsden, William. *The Mexican-Americans of South Texas.* New York: Holt, Rinehart, and Winston, 1964.

McWilliams, Carey. *Brothers Under the Skin.* Boston: Little, Brown, 1964. One chapter is devoted to the Mexican-Americans and is a concise statement of their history, problems, and treatment by Anglo society.

Moore, Joan W. *Mexican-Americans.* Englewood Cliffs, N.J.: Prentice-Hall, 1970. A brief and up-to-date summary of current research.

Steiner, Stan. *La Raza: The Mexican Americans.* New York: Harper & Row, 1970.

Eight
Students

To regard students as a minority grouping raises interesting intellectual and practical problems. On the one hand, students–here used to refer to students at institutions of higher learning–would, by most standards, be designated a privileged elite. In the absence of universal higher education, uniform distribution of intellectual talents, and an equal distribution of family resources, all Americans cannot enjoy the immediate and long-term benefits of a college or university education.

Student life often has its hardships, including real poverty, long hours, holding multiple low-paying jobs, insecurity and anxiety, and conformity to a variety of rules and standards, the logic of which is often obscure. College graduates, however, can look forward to higher salaries, higher status, cleaner and more interesting work, and, in general, broader opportunity structures than their less educated counterparts. Furthermore, a college student's deprivation is limited in tenure–four years, six years, perhaps eight years–and he is released from his "bondage" to reap the deferred benefits he has earned. As a minority member–if he is one–the student enjoys an advantage that no other deprived minority member possesses, the knowledge that he is to be amply rewarded by society for his transient status as a minority member.

On the other hand, the very status of "student" itself defies ready description. The student role can be viewed from a variety of perspectives. And each of these has implications for understanding the position of the student as a member of a minority.

First, the student can be seen as a voluntary member of a complex organization. As such, he is a direct participant in the life of the organization. Perhaps more than any other view, this is the "traditional" one. Students are assumed to go to college and graduate school because they choose to do so and because they have the intellectual talents and financial resources required for admission. They are thus intellectual apprentices, expected to learn from the journeymen and masters, "doing while they learn" through laboratory experiments, papers, and discussion. Nothing keeps them in school except their own willingness to put up with the requirements, since they can refuse student status by not enrolling in the first place or by dropping out later. Within the context of the organization, they have a great variety of opportunities to pursue, depending on personal predilections, capacity, and the size of the school. Those who hold this opinion of the student role argue that college life represents a broadened opportunity structure for the individual in intellectual, economic, and social terms. Taking advantage of the opportunity offered is purely voluntary.

There are costs—in terms of money and energy—and requirements for organizational conformity, variously called "intellectual discipline," "achievement," "realistic progress," "good grades," and a "passing average." There are also identification expectations: "school spirit," "commitment," and "motivation." These requirements and expectations are expressions of organizational expectations. In return for the university's or college's stamp of approval (the degree), the student will conform to the standards that older, more experienced members of the organization (faculty and administrators) hold as basic expectations. Coupled with these primary organizational expectations are related standards governing behavior that might threaten the organization's viability and outside sources of support and resources. Thus, the student must behave in a way that will not discredit the institution. He must surrender certain "normal" privileges, such as car ownership, freedom to consume alcohol, or freedom in sexual behavior, and he must comply with certain generalized standards of decorum, some of which stress his status. In exchange for these compliances, he enjoys both formal and informal licenses that are sanctioned by the organization. It will protect him if he gets into trouble with civil authorities, grant a form of sanctuary on the campus, and wryly tolerate outbursts of "youthful exuberance."

From the organizational standpoint, the college or university is a group—or a series of interlocking groups—of a primarily instrumental character. The hierarchy, status differentiations, rules, and requirements are logically related to the preservation of the institution and the fulfillment of its instrumental function. The student is a member of this group of groups (institution) by choice, subject to membership screening, which is performed by established members of the institution. He is obliged to accept the basic bargain of all instrumental groups: the attainment of one's own goals assumes behavior that is supportive of the group's existence and expectations. Greater privileges and rewards are granted with longer membership and in proportion to group participation that is supportive (good grades, participation in extracurricular activities, model behavior). A number of identification groups develop within the context of the instrumental functions, such as fraternities and sororities, friendship groups, and informal seminars. Because they help to bind the student to the institution, the institution itself endorses and supports these identification groups.

Second, the student can be seen as a client or customer of the institution. As such, he is less a member of the organization than a purchaser of whatever it offers that will benefit him. This relationship of student to institution is complex, because it is assumed that the customer is entitled to shop until he finds the product he desires, but the institution itself is expected to provide products with the potential customers in mind. It is conceivable, even probable, that the customer knows better what he wants than the producer, but as a nonmember of the establishment he has no right to dictate the management's decisions. Presumably, "market forces" will take care of any imbalance between customer expectation or demand and management's failure to satisfy that demand. The student, then, is inevitably an "outsider." Although he may be catered to, cajoled, threatened, or tantalized in an effort to attract and hold his custom, his participation in the organization is limited.

As two separate forces working on each other, the institution and the student-as-customer may attempt to modify each other, but they must accept some degree of difference and independence of action. The student must be willing to tolerate managerial idiosyncrasies in rules and requirements. If he feels that the basic product is what he wants, these idiosyncrasies are merely part of the price he pays. The institution itself must accept that the student will demand more attractive products and will seek to pay the lowest possible price to obtain them.

Third, the student can be seen as the function of the university. The institution's existence can be explained only by the presence of the students. Its validity as a social institution is not based on whether the student is a member or a customer, but on whether the institution provides a habitable environment in which the student as a human being undergoes beneficial development. In this respect, the institution is not in a superordinate or a bargaining relationship with the student, but in a subordinate relationship.

Although by trial and error the institution may have evolved what it considers more effective means of meeting the student's needs than other means available, organization norms and standards, that is, "group needs," are secondary unless they directly contribute to an individual student's needs. If they are barriers to student development, they should be removed, even at the risk of destroying the organization itself. It is, after all, illogical and inappropriate for an organization to perpetuate itself by means that stifle its function. Stressing procedures and forms that are supportive of the organization but may reduce its functional effectiveness is not in accord with the definition of the relationship of student to institution. Faculty tenure—if it keeps in the classrooms "ineffective" teachers—course requirements, parietal rules, codes of conduct, and refusal by administrations to commit institutions to the opposition to public policies that are counter to student interests are all suffocating anachronisms stressing organizational survival at the expense of student development.

The institution should be engaged in a steady quest to further its function as an environment for the students, and this should be its primary criterion of "goodness." Although most of the standard activities of a university would continue as presently constituted – teaching, research, administering, and governing - they would be re-evaluated from time to time.

Fourth, the student can be seen as a captive of the institution and of the society that it reflects. In the United States, dominated by a middle-class culture, if students can meet all the requirements (intellectual and economic), they *must* go to college. They are taught to accept this imperative by their parents and their elementary and high school teachers. They are informed of it by a social system that denies them managerial, educational, professional, and many governmental positions if they fail to go to college.

Except for those unable to go to college because of insufficient education or financial capability, the young are faced with a highly limited opportunity structure. Go to college and, once there, conform to its standards or be dismissed from it, and if dismissed, realize what the social, economic, and physical risks are. Enduring the captivity has its material rewards, but the rewards are pseudo-rewards, perpetuating the system that put the student there in the first place. They prepare him for a life situation in which he will continue to be a captive of the corporations and bureaucracies that shape the institution's function to their own benefit.

Institutions of higher learning, then, are extensions and reinforcers of the current social system. Their primary function is to program the young to the norms of the system (which include the value of higher education as presently constituted). As a result, insistence on many of the values embraced and defended by these institutions and their supporters is at best hypocritical, at worst cynical. Academic freedom excludes social issues for fear of angering the sources of financial support; rational debate is restricted to reasoning from unchallenged premises about the correctness of the social order; tolerance of dissent refers to dissent encapsulated by predetermined standards of behavior; and intellectual discipline means the absorption and acceptance of socially accepted norms. The basic values contained in the concepts are desirable, but society and its institutions, including colleges and universities, have robbed them of all but a manipulative and deceptive value.

The bargain is a simple one. If a student conforms and gets "good grades," which is to say he learns what he is told to learn, then he is eventually rewarded with a degree that society promises to validate with a high salary and comfortable employment and social status. If he gets "bad grades," he is "in trouble"; a sufficient number of bad grades causes his dismissal from the institution. The ultimate hypocrisy is that he is told *he* has "failed," as though the error was his, the lack was in himself. Although the forms of freedom of opportunity are reserved, largely by constant reference to them, the substance is nonexistent. A student comes to an institution hoping to be educated in the broader sense of the word; he is, instead, educated to realize that the price of success is to submit, to support the system by participation on its terms, and to keep his mouth shut unless told to open it.

In short, the student is a "nigger" in an admittedly fairly benevolent system. Like a black, if he stays in his place, white society will be kind to him. A "good" student is deferential, obedient, mildly amusing, and willing to accept his place in the system. A "bad student" is assertive, challenging, independent, and hostile or rebellious, if he objects to the droning lectures that have been delivered verbatim for twenty years and to stifling rules that control and limit him. And a bad student is soon shown the error of his ways. But if he fails to toe the line after that, he is punished by expulsion.

These four perspectives from which the role of the student can be viewed are not necessarily exhaustive. However, they demonstrate two crucial points. First, individuals who participate in the activities of an institution and who are in agreement regarding its importance can interpret differently the status of a certain category of people within that institution. Second, the various interpretations indicate that whether or not students can be defined objectively as a "minority" is irrelevant. If a number of students at a given time and place adopt postures approximating the third or fourth perspective listed here, they are *subjectively* defining themselves as a minority and will adopt the patterns of action of a minority group.

Even though students are students for only a brief period of time, occupying a status that they will no longer have in less than a decade, faculty and administrators must deal with the perceptions and actions of the students that are currently enrolled. The argument that students are transient and that their successors may have a different set of priorities will not dissuade them from being concerned with the present state of affairs.

Historical Sketch

Student activism is not a new phenomenon in the United States. At least since the beginning of this century, campuses have been the scenes of agitation for and against war, peace, imperialism, organized labor, and civil liberties. On occasion, the activism has been accompanied by violence. In general, however, the early activism was directed not at the college or university itself but at society and its governing institutions. The campus was a convenient place from which to launch organizations; it provided an arena for making speeches, recruiting members, and raising money. There were, however, sporadic revolts against the colleges or universities themselves, usually in the form of resistance to rules that restricted student "rights and privileges," as they have come to be known. These outbreaks were largely spontaneous, were guided by little or no "ideology" or coherent logic, and received little national attention.

Although the decade of the 1950s was generally considered to be a period of quiescence and even conformity for American students, there was some activism, especially in the peace movement. Students campaigned against the spread of nuclear arms, and they organized to resist the encroachments of McCarthyism. Nonetheless, the efforts were directed at society, and the college or university served as a sanctuary and a site of the ferment of ideas.

The catalyst for the "student movement" was the civil rights movement. In the early 1960s, large numbers of committed students travelled from all over the country to the South to protest racial inequality. They picketed establishments in their own communities as well. Confrontations with the police became commonplace, and overnight or longer imprisonment a badge of honor. Three other developments took place. One was the growth of student organizations that had protest as their central political tactic. Students for a Democratic Society (SDS), the Southern Student Organizing Committee, and the Student Nonviolent Coordinating Committee (SNCC) were, among others, vehicles for communication and political education on a pan-campus basis. In addition, older and more conventional organizations such as the National Student Association became progressively more activist.

Second, cadres of students became expert in the political style that had been developed by black Americans. Many students considered the needs and the social role of blacks to be similar to their own. By virtue of their age, their nonvoting residence in the college community, and their ghettoization on the campus, students were in many respects marginal citizens or noncitizens—objects to be acted upon by others and powerless, like blacks. The politics of revolt was a logical style, in no small measure because students, like blacks, possessed no direct political power but were expected to depend on intermediaries for any influence over the institutions that controlled their lives.

Third, students were "sensitized" by the civil rights movement. In their search for racist institutions, they found certain incongruities on their own campuses. Housing offices maintained segregated off-campus housing lists. There were pathetically few blacks in the student body and even fewer on the faculty. The black presence on campus was confined to custodial personnel who were generally paid wages that kept them below the poverty line. The ills of society, about which scholars wrote, talked, lectured, and criticized endlessly, were as present on campus as off: depersonalization, bureaucratization, militarism, denial of civil rights, corporatism, and materialism. Students were taught the techniques of social analysis, and they learned from the black movement the political techniques by which to apply their analyses.

Although the first great eruption occurred on the Berkeley campus of the University of California in 1964 with the Free Speech Movement, its precursor was a sit-in concerning freedom of speech and a university ban on certain types of outside speakers at Ohio State University in 1963. The Berkeley revolt, however, received national publicity and established a pattern for student-administration conflict. The basic elements are an administration ruling that appears to violate a student "right," student mobilization of protest, including the expansion of the original grievance to include others, efforts at negotiation, resistance to compromises, and often a "show-down" that might include the use of force on both sides. The Berkeley revolt in fact was the prototype for the vast majority of subsequent campus revolts. The scenario at Berkeley to be repeated time and again consisted of:

> Conflict over the relation of the student to the institution. How much power was the institution to exercise over student lives and affairs and how much power were students to have in governing themselves and the institution?

> Introduction of other issues as proof of the intransigence and callousness of the institution's governing authorities, which served to involve larger and larger numbers of students and faculty.

> Street tactics applied against the institution itself instead of the outside society.

> Organized and protracted conflict, pressing authorities to resort to counter-responses in an effort to restore stability and helping to radicalize even more students.

> Return of stability, as much a result of mutual exhaustion as the resolution of the issues.

The intensity of the war in Vietnam added an ingredient that was missing prior to 1965. Students were vulnerable in a way that they had not been before, for their draft deferments depended on their academic standing. They became "captives of the system," and the institution, by dismissing a student for failing to meet its academic standards, became an inadvertent handmaiden to the selective service system. Gradually, radical analyses of society became fashionable. Perhaps for the first time in the history of American higher education, students began to look closely at their colleges and universities: to ask who governed them and what characterized the people who were governors; to question the functions that the institutions served and how they served them; and to examine the sources of financial support. The answers, for many students, proved the radical hypothesis. Governing boards consisted of men of wealth, corporation executives, and political figures—people who had no special credentials for understanding or making educational policy. Colleges and universities seemed better designed to produce future business and government executives, tomorrow's capitalists and their lackeys, than men and women with a sense of social obligation and commitment. And much of their financial support came from the Defense Department, private industry, and political maneuvering that served "special interests."

Some students began to accept the idea that students were "niggers"; a relaxation of the rules and the "tokenism" of putting "student leaders" on university committees were merely means by which administrations deceived the more naive students into believing that they were making progress. To continue the same system of rule would be supportive of the pattern of suppression of a sick society, albeit in a shrewdly disguised form. The cry for "black power" was echoed by the cry for "student power."

Weaving through the numberless struggles to determine whether students would sit on committees, be members of governing boards, or have a voice in hiring and promoting and in the general policy-making processes of an institution were issues of war and race relations. In some instances, disputes over race relations led to a wider conflict over the structure of the institution (as they did at San Francisco State College in 1968–69); in others, militarism and the relation of the institution to the community precipitated the confrontation (as they did at Columbia in 1968). Usually, however, these clashes were only the dramatic incidents, overshadowing in the mass media the student attempts at numerous other universities and colleges to strengthen student governing bodies, to gain student rights of consultation and participation, and to force the institutions to divest themselves of what activist students considered out-moded practices and traditions.

For most of the decade, violence was generally unilateral. Student leadership usually fell into the hands of those who advocated nonviolence. Many perhaps half expected to be "busted," either literally or figuratively, by the police, but they did not expect to counter with violence in turn. From 1968 on, however, violence was often reciprocal. The use of fire bombs, high explosives, rocks, and bricks against campus buildings and the presence of the police on campus became common. So did personal encounters between "straight" students and protestors. Nonetheless, most students, perhaps recognizing their helplessness in the face of organized violence, preferred to continue nonviolent, albeit increasingly disruptive, tactics.

The national elections of 1968 emphasized the ambivalence of the student's position. Students, correctly or not, could reassure themselves that they had influenced President Johnson's decision not to run for re-election and had had notable influence in some local elections. Some, however, were physically beaten in the streets of Chicago during the Democratic National Convention, and although very few of the total number of the nation's students were present, all could see what was happening on television. Nixon was elected, and in 1970 he launched a military invasion of Cambodia, which precipitated a demonstration at Kent State University in Ohio in which four students were killed by the National Guard. This in turn set off a chain of revolts at other schools throughout the nation. Although the war was the nominal issue, demands affecting the structure of the schools themselves were usually a part of the protests.

By 1972 the campuses were "cooler." In many instances, it seemed that the reduction of military strength in Southeast Asia had reduced the effectiveness of the war as a catalytic issue. Administration and faculty flexibility in allowing some students to participate in policy-making helped to funnel "moderate" student energies into administrative tasks. Many radical students had become so committed to guerrilla tactics that they went underground, ceasing to organize on campus and to speak in public. The older organizations, moreover, were in disarray. The Southern Student Organizing Committee had terminated its existence; SNCC had become an all-black organization and then dissolved; SDS had become divided over ideological and tactical issues, and its Weatherman faction became an underground terrorist organization. The National Student Association and various peace organizations continued to command national followings, but they had neither the local cadres that the other organizations had had nor the same tactical and rhetorical grasp of local campus issues.

Although the "student revolt" continued as a reality, including sporadic bombings of campus buildings (at St. Louis University in 1971, for example), the approach and attitude of most students changed in the early 1970s. Student power was still an issue, but student tactics moved away from a politics of revolt.

Status

The term "student," like "black" or "Indian," refers to a grouping rather than a group, and a wide variety of divergent characteristics can be found among students. One study summarized the social characteristics of protestors: they attend prestigious and major colleges and universities; they rank high academically; they come from families whose incomes and social status are high and whose political orientation is liberal. Many protestors do not conform to this general description. But the implication is that students who attend less "good" schools, who rank lower academically, and who have more modest and conservative family backgrounds tend *not* to be protestors. Further, students in pre-medicine, business and commerce, agriculture, pre-law, medicine, law, and engineering are far less apt to participate in the politics of revolt than students in the liberal arts and sciences. In short, a large number of students do not participate in protest movements against their colleges or universities or against other social institutions.

The reasons for the differences are not simple. Students themselves hold various positions on the four perspectives regarding student status given at the beginning of this chapter. Many, if not most, of the 7,000,000 students in this country may feel that they are voluntary members of an instrumental group; they accept the requirements of the institution in exchange for a degree that will broaden their personal opportunity structures.

Most colleges and universities tend to emphasize (and perhaps help to create) a plurality of student interests in many ways:

By organizing themselves into separate schools and departments.

By separating their undergraduate courses of study into upper and lower divisions.

By dividing upper-division curricula into separate disciplines.

By intellectually segregating graduates and undergraduates.

By physically segregating various disciplines and activities.

By providing for and accommodating a broad range of identification groups.

By stressing close identification with a major field of study, an advisor, a school, or a professor.

By selecting both students and faculty from diverse age, geographic, and social groupings.

Such a structure does not necessarily prevent the formation of a concept of universal "studentness," but it inhibits it. Even when the concept is formed, the structure discourages easy interaction, especially in a large institution. Inevitably, therefore, diversity and division occur within the grouping generally labelled "students."

A student is a transient and a member of a transient minority in two senses. The first and most obvious sense is that he is a student for only a limited time. Although he is on campus for four years, his first year is largely absorbed in becoming oriented; his last in decisions about his future. He is also a transient in the sense that when he leaves the campus to go to a job, to take a vacation, to socialize with nonstudents, or to politic or whatever, his "studentness" is reduced. He does not, like a black, an Indian, or a woman, carry his status with him, except insofar as his youth, dress, and mannerisms mark him. In short, the student can "pass" as a member of the dominant society at some times and in some places.

Youth is, of course, a mark, and for people from certain social backgrounds, youth almost automatically means "student" as well. The possibility of an imposed identity always exists, but it tends to be most salient on a campus, and less so the further one is from a university community.

One of the traditional standards shaping the relationship between student and institution has been limited in recent years. The doctrine of *in loco parentis,* which grants a college or university the same legal relationship to a student as a parent has to a minor child, has been weakened by either voluntary institutional restraint or court-imposed limits on an institution's freedom to ignore due process in disciplinary actions, censorship, and arbitrary judgments. Universities and colleges are relaxing parietal rules governing overnight privileges and dormitory behavior. They have also granted students more direct control over the adjudication of student offenses and violations of rules.

The effect of allowing students greater freedom, which often includes participation in the affairs of the institution, is to relieve some of the pressure placed on a sexually and intellectually mature adult living in what has been called "imprisonment in kidhood." An individual student is less likely to encounter situations in which his "studentness," to the extent that it implies inferiority or powerlessness, is stressed.

There are severe limits on a student's capacity to regard himself as a member of a minority and to organize on that basis. "Studentness" as a characteristic simply may not be sufficiently salient to override academic institutional definitions of disciplines and status; it may not be able to prevail over such distinctions as skin color or sex. It may not be able to affect identification with career preferences and informal and formal (such as fraternities or athletic teams) groups. Decreasing administrative rigidity reduces the salience of "studentness" further.

There are forces that work to make "studentness" salient. The faculty is still the evaluator and the student is still being evaluated, although efforts to lessen the distinction between them through curriculum and individual course evaluations are popular. However, student evaluation of faculty performance does not necessarily have an effect, whereas faculty evaluation of student performance always has. The first is an act of powerlessness, the second an exercise in real power. As academic requirements become more rigorous and as the competition for positions in graduate schools and for employment heightens, the evaluator-evaluated relationship stresses the characteristic of studentness: the more time that a student spends studying, the more he assumes the role of a student.

In place of *in loco parentis,* partly at the prodding of the students, colleges and universities have moved toward creating a "total environment" within the campus. Athletic facilities, recreational facilities, living quarters, meeting rooms, on-campus coffee houses, drinking rooms, and entertainment are provided, and the student spends less time away from campus. He is, in many ways, voluntarily ghettoizing himself. The opportunities to interact exclusively with other students are increased as is the shared awareness of student status.

Faculties and administrators will probably act to increase the salience of student status. There are inherent limits in the amount of power that faculty members and administrators are willing to surrender to students. As long as students continue to think of their relationship to the institution as a power relationship, there will be conflict. And, with each conflict student awareness is reemphasized.

Finally, external events act as catalysts. Antiacademic legislation, "class legislation" designed to control student revolts, or, as the events of the 1960s showed, war or the efforts of other minorities may all precipitate revolt and a search for identity.

In no small measure, of course, the continuity of a student's perception of himself as a member of a minority depends on the degree of continuity within a transient minority. "Generational turnover" is rapid in the student population, and it is not clear at this time that the student "subculture" is transmitted from one college generation to the next, in a form coherent enough to provide a basis for minority group politics.

In terms of resources, students do seem to suffer the same deprivations as the other, more permanent minorities. Many possess no voting power in state and national elections; they possess no economic power other than that which any group of consumers can exert on a local economy; and their numbers, although impressive, are divided into scattered, isolated clusters. Further, few of their organizations seem to have real staying power, except those endorsed by the institutions themselves, such as student councils.

Yet, within the context of their particular arena, students possess enormous potential power, if they can achieve self-awareness and organization. As they have shown, they *can* shut a university down, especially if they are willing to risk a "bust." The drama inherent in the closing of a major institution of education, even for a brief time, enables them to command the attention of the society, especially by means of television. Further, to the extent that there is a conflict between generations, it is at the colleges and the universities that the young live in circumstances that are suited to expressing grievances against the older generation. The nature of the academic experience is such that the student learns new techniques of analysis, responds to the newest social ideas, and acquires the ability and the opportunity to make use of tactical innovations if he chooses to do so.

In part, then, the university is not only an arena for the working out of strictly academic issues, but a place in which other issues become the subjects of political action. The student, therefore, occupies an important strategic place in the society.

Bibliography

Avorn, Jerry L. *Up Against the Ivy Wall.* New York: Atheneum, 1969. One of the best student statements by a student on the conflict between students and institutions of higher learning.

Barzun, Jacques. *The American University: How It Runs, Where It Is Going.* New York: Harper & Row, 1968. Although addressed to larger issues of the governance of the American university, Barzun's analysis is nonetheless one of the more influential statements against protest.

Bell, Daniel, and Irving Kristol. *Confrontation: The Student Rebellion and the Universities.* New York: Basic Books, 1969.

Farber, Jerry. *The Student as Nigger.* New York: Pocket Books, 1969. Perhaps the nearest thing to a manifesto of the student left.

Foster, Julian, and Durward Long, eds. *Protest: Student Activism in America.* New York: Morrow, 1970. One of the most useful collections of readings on the student movement, including a variety of analyses of the causes, issues, and nature of student rebellions.

Jacobs, Paul, and Saul Landau. *The New Radicals: A Report with Documents.* New York: Vintage, 1968.

Kennan, George F. *Democracy and the Student Left.* Boston: Little, Brown, 1968. The famous "debate" between student protestors and the author, which manages to produce an excellent profile of a variety of positions on student activism.

Schwartz, Edward, ed. *Student Power: Philosophy, Program, Tactics.* Washington, D.C.: National Student Association, 1968.

Wallerstein, Immanuel, and Paul Starr, eds. *The University Crisis Reader: The Liberal University Under Attack.* New York: Vintage, 1971.

_____. *The University Crisis Reader: Confrontation and Counterattack.* New York: Vintage, 1971. These two volumes are the best single collection of articles, manifestos, and research on the student movement.

Nine
Women

Of all the minority groupings in American society women evoke the most amusement and the least apparent anxiety. The battle of the sexes, after all, is a historical fixture–a source of numberless jokes, farces, and ironical comments. Whether to regard women as members of a minority, at least in the numerical sense, is debatable, since they comprise more than 50 percent of the nation's population. There are some women, as well as some men, who are quick to point out that women in this country live in greater comfort than ever before in history; they are perhaps better off than the women of any other nation in the world. They live longer than the men they marry. Except within certain minority cultural groupings, they are not encouraged to bear more than two children. Modern labor-saving devices provide them with more time than they have ever had to pursue their own interests. Although a "typical" woman may for the most part be restricted to her home until her children are old enough to go to school, her life after marriage is far freer than her spouse's, inasmuch as men are obligated, by tradition, to support their wives.

Some would also argue that the anger that women direct toward men is based on a misapprehension of the roles and activities of both men and women. Although it may be true that some men regard women as "sexual objects," this may be due less to deliberate lasciviousness, or to an effort to humiliate women, than it is to the natural order. The basic relationship between men and women *is* biological; it is the way in which nature worked out the process of attraction between the sexes. Now that women have been freed from the Victorian mores that dictated that no decent woman should openly enjoy sex, there is no reason why women should not regard men as sexual objects in turn. Sexuality is, after all, part of every human's person and personality. And to argue that women suffer the drudgery of life and men have the glamour, excitement, and glory is to forget that most of men's economic activities are painful drudgery, fully as confining, stifling, and deadening as housework. Women, it could be said, are suffering from a grass-is-greener problem.

It could also be said that men and women are by nature mutually dependent on each other for the survival of the species, and for psychological comfort, mutual self-esteem, and the pleasure of human companionship. Complete separation of man and woman is unattainable, for even "artificial insemination" requires sperm cells from a male source. Although the male-female relationship has probably not been worked out to the satisfaction of women, that relationship has undergone changes in the last century, and today it is difficult to say who suffers the heavier burdens.

With that line of argument in mind, many men and some women dismiss the women's liberation movement as a fad, a harebrained scheme concocted by female homosexuals, disappointed divorcees, frustrated spinsters, and bored housewives looking for entertainment. That a healthy, prosperous, pampered, long-lived, educated American woman could see herself as "deprived" or in a situation analogous to that of a black, a Mexican-American, an Indian, or even a student, is on its face laughable. The predicament of the black or Mexican-American woman is, of course, another matter; but the roots of the problem here lie not in discrimination because of sex but because of other cultural marks.

The foregoing arguments may well have merit. The crucial point, however, has been stressed and restressed. The relevant political data are not whether objective standards of deprivation exist, but whether subjective ones do. Moreover, women as a grouping *can* be considered to be deprived if their economic and social-status opportunity structures are compared with those of men.

The complexity of understanding women as a minority grouping lies in the complexity of biological roles. Societies have always made distinctions between men and women: in dress, in work activities, in training, in "rites of passage," and in kinship relations. Some of the distinctions seem to be quite "logical," that is, women bear and nurse children, whereas men do not. The male, therefore, has a degree of physical mobility that the female for periods of time does not. In a primitive society, men do the hunting and the fighting, whereas women have a more sedentary role, since women who are pregnant or nursing would be severely handicapped in these activities. Two obvious questions arise. First, because of their biological differences, are there intrinsic psychological differences between men and women–differences significant enough to warrant continued cultural, economic, political, and social differentiation? Second, are the biological differences fundamentally related to the functioning of a modern, industrialized, and complex society?

To answer either question on a scientifically objective basis is impossible. To answer the first one, we would have to assume that all cultural factors could be eliminated; that is, that the effect of treating males and females differently from the moment of birth could be omitted from consideration. It would be necessary to establish a laboratory situation in which human beings, both male and female, could live from birth in an environment that is completely free of cultural pressures from societies that make distinctions between male and female roles.

The second question is also difficult to answer. Women have in the past and still do fight in wars—in Russia and Israel, for example. They perform the functions of chiefs of state (e.g., Queen Elizabeth I, Queen Victoria, Golda Meir, and Indira Gandhi). They operate complicated machinery, do research, speculate in the stock market, write poetry, and get elected to political office. The development of modern contraceptive methods has enabled women to be sexually active without the possibility of pregnancy. Motherhood has become a matter of choice, competing with other options.

Science, then, has in part eliminated some of the effects of the "natural" differences between the sexes. What science has not changed directly, a technological society has developed indirectly: relative equality in formal education and an acceptance of women as legal citizens of the society. It could be argued that even that traditionally masculine preserve, the conduct of war, is no longer logically the domain of men. There was a time, perhaps, when the superior musculature (a function of childhood training) of males was an important prerequisite. To wield a shield and a spear, to control a war-horse or a chariot team, to hoist cannon balls into the muzzle of an artillery piece, or to engage in fighting with bayonets demanded the stature and strength of a man. But, both men and women can pull a trigger, push a button, or control the movements of complex machinery. Yet, it is unimaginable to most Americans that women could serve in the infantry.

The reduction of certain barriers owing to technological advances has not eliminated all the sources of women's grievances. Women maintain that they are paid less for the same work done by a man, hired last and fired first, assumed to be unqualified for certain jobs, limited in postgraduate educational opportunities, and socially ghettoized in myriad ways. They also maintain that men have the power to preserve the status quo, which they do by objectifying women (and thus humiliating them), by stereotyping them, and by insuring that women remain powerless except in those roles that a male-dominated society has assigned to them.

Historical Sketch

In 1848, female leaders of the Abolitionist movement met at Seneca Falls, New York. The prime movers were Elizabeth Cady Stanton, Ann Green Phillips, and Lucretia Mott. The Seneca Falls "Declaration of Sentiment" was hammered out and became the first public statement against the status of women in the United States. Because all of those at Seneca Falls were Abolitionists, it seems likely that the struggle for black freedom clarified their understanding of the status of women in society. Further, increasing educational opportunities for women contributed to their awareness and their ability to interact and communicate with each other on the basis of that self-awareness.

Following the Seneca Falls convention, a series of meetings were held. The movement, under the leadership of such feminists as Susan B. Anthony, grew more militant in its rhetoric and its demands. Significant gains were made in the four decades that followed, with limited suffrage granted to women in sixteen states. There were "radical" aspects to the early stages of the movement. Women stressed their exploitation and enslavement; they made an issue of the depersonalization of women in society and in the family. Elizabeth Oakes Smith, for example, said in 1852: "We aim at nothing less than an entire subversion of the present order of society...." In the second half of the century, however, women activists began to soften their rhetoric and to modify their strategic aims. They moved from a primarily sexist interpretation of the movement, which demanded a major revision of the male-female relationship, to a limited political interpretation. The central issue became that of granting suffrage to women as an extension of political rights and ideals, while social and economic deprivation were progressively deemphasized. From 1890 until the ratification of the Nineteenth Amendment, the women's movement concentrated almost entirely on the single issue of suffrage.

The shift from numerous issues to a single issue is partly explainable by the difficulty of appraising a culture and its life-style. Without being able to offer concrete alternatives, the militant woman had to persuade her married sister that home and family were instruments of oppression. Then, as is probably true now, most people assumed that a woman's proper place was in the home fulfilling her biological role. Few professions were open to women; those jobs which a rapidly industrializing society made available to them were rarely an attractive alternative to domesticity. The right to vote, however, was an objective that would not necessarily set a woman against her prescribed social role.

Activist women faced the same problem that faces every deprived minority: the necessity of winning the support of dominant groups and institutions in order to achieve change. Women were dependent on male votes in order to obtain the right to vote themselves. They got this cooperation from the progressive reformers, who were willing to align themselves with the women's movement on the faith that women would vote differently from men. The reformers hoped that women voters would have a morally uplifting, cleansing, and softening influence on the affairs of government, thereby helping to control the rampant graft and corruption that permeated American civic affairs. The need to win male support propelled the movement into a single-issue focus. With the single issue emphasis came a rapid diminution in the radicalism of the movement.

After 1920, the women's movement declined drastically. The prosperity of the 1920s and the Depression of the 1930s contributed to this decline. Other, more pressing issues diverted attention away from that of the role of the woman in society. And, the fate of single-issue politics befell the movement; that is, once the goal is achieved, the basic cohesive force is lost.

Both Woodrow Wilson's "New Freedom" and Franklin Roosevelt's "New Deal" took the issues that the women's movement had raised into account. In 1920, the Women's Bureau was created in the Department of Labor; and the League of

Women Voters became a permanent pressure group in an increasing number of states and localities.

Liberal spokesmen for the New Deal made sporadic attempts to articulate women's interests. With Eleanor Roosevelt as an ally, Frances Perkins, the first female cabinet member, was concerned about the status of the American woman. Owing to the heavy economic bias of American affairs, however, efforts were concentrated on wages and working conditions; women were simply another category of exploited workers and no attempt was made to search out the fundamental cultural biases. New Dealers assumed that the extension of social security benefits, minimum wage laws, governmentally imposed limits on working conditions, and encouraging women to get a "useful" education would ultimately remedy whatever hardships women suffered.

World War II put women in jobs, thereby changing their roles in society. They moved quickly to fill positions vacated by men who were going into the armed services or created by the enormous expansion of the defense industry. They also served in the military. Women performed jobs previously thought to be suited only to men. Although at the end of the war many working women willingly or grudgingly surrendered their positions to the returning men, some stayed on, especially those whose husbands resumed their educations with the support of the G.I. bill of rights and the incomes of their working wives.

Women's increased restiveness in the 1950s and early 1960s may have been caused by the experience of the war years. It may have stemmed from postwar saturation of material things and the increasing social mobility of the American middle-class family; or it may have come with the expansion of education, with the ghettoization of the female reinforced by rapid suburbanization, and with the steady increase in the number of working women who encountered male prejudice face-to-face on the job. Whatever its causes, it was accompanied by intellectual ferment. In 1949, Simone de Beauvoir, in the *Second Sex,* articulated a view of women reminiscent of the radical days of the 1840s and 1850s. More than a decade later, Betty Friedan, writing a forceful and popular work entitled *The Feminine Mystique,* explicitly laid out the dimensions of women's deprivation and the effects of a male-dominated society.

In 1961, President Kennedy issued Executive Order 10980, which established the President's Commission on the Status of Women. Two years later, the commission released its report. As Margaret Mead observed in an epilogue to the report, the document was based on three major assumptions: first, "anything peculiarly feminine is a handicap"; second, women achieve complete fulfillment only through marriage and child-bearing, but "that no fundamental sacrifice should be made of them, nor should sacrifice be made to them"; and, third, one should be able to work for money to achieve full humanity in American society. The report stressed the right of all Americans to make basic choices, and by stressing that right suggested that women were deprived of as full an opportunity structure as men enjoyed.

The report was, in its official way, a militant document, articulating in formal language the experiences of women throughout the country. It pointed out that women had never really exercised their right to vote in an organized fashion and that, in fact, women were in many respects second-class citizens.

The growing militancy of the civil rights movement—its gradual conversion from a struggle to remove barriers to one that sought an affirmative place for the black in American society—provided a valuable training ground for many young women. They joined students' groups, observing and participating in tactical exercises, but also frequently encountered discrimination even there. The Black Panthers averred "Power to the brothers and love to the sisters." One militant black leader said that the only position for a woman in his organization was on her back. Women activists were often expected by their male counterparts to do the cooking, cleaning, and secretarial work but to stay out of the way when "man's business" was being done. Women discovered that even men who were profoundly concerned about freedom and liberation were talking only about liberation and freedom for men.

In 1968, the advocates of women's liberation received nationwide publicity in their protest against the Miss America contest. Although many commentators found such a protest laughable, the women were dead serious and continued to protest against sexist institutions in American life. The publishers of women's magazines experienced picket lines and sit-ins, as did at least one publisher of a men's magazine. In 1970, a Women's Strike for Equality included marches and demonstrations in a large number of cities.

In 1968–1970 many new women's organizations came into existence. Some, such as the National Organization for Women (NOW), were strongly oriented toward economics, aiming to enforce antidiscrimination laws in colleges and in businesses. Others, such as the Redstockings, the Women's International Terrorist Conspiracy from Hell (WITCH), and the Feminists, took more radical positions, in some cases adopting Marxist-Maoist rhetoric and analysis, training their members in self-defense, and searching for precise resistance techniques. Local organizations proliferated. Their primary purpose was "consciousness raising," that is, making women aware of their subordinate status and imbuing them with a sense of sisterhood.

Concrete gains were made. Women were appointed to commissions, were given national publicity, and won a victory for an equality amendment to the U.S. Constitution, a proposal that had been brought before the Senate Judiciary Committee every year for twenty years. Abortion laws, a major issue of the movement, were repealed and relaxed in a number of states.

Status

Despite progress either incidental to or as a result of the movement, women continued to be discriminated against by employers. By 1970 most women still received only 60 percent of the salary paid to a man for doing the same work. In addition, women were typically occupying the more menial and less powerful positions of the economic structure. Even college-educated and professional women often found that their employment opportunities were far more limited than those of men; and women cross-pressured by marriage and work often surrendered the latter or accepted temporary, dead-end jobs that paid less than their qualifications warranted.

The two major political parties had long given recognition to women, by assigning them to committees, through campaign techniques aimed at reaching women voters, and by including in their campaigns issues that were assumed to be of concern to women, such as education, child welfare, recreation, and health. Nonetheless, few party organizations attempted to articulate their positions on the role of women in society or to give attention to militant women's organizations.

Fewer women voted than men, and they rarely occupied important public offices. In 1965, only two women were in the United States Senate and only eleven were in the House of Representatives. Five years later these numbers had not significantly changed. No woman was ever a justice of the Supreme Court; only two had ever held Cabinet posts. In state and local governments, the number of women in high-ranking posts was larger, but typically they were appointed or elected to posts in "women's areas," such as education, health, welfare, and libraries.

The women's liberation movement, a category comprising a wide variety of organizations and an even wider variety of tactics, has gradually formulated a systematic view of the woman in American society. The elements of that view have been couched in a number of vocabularies, often in the radicalese of the New Left, occasionally in traditional class-struggle terms, and now and then in modern pluralistic language, but the basic ingredients are always about the same.

First, although American women are numerically a majority, their basic condition is that of a deprived minority.

Second, the essential characteristic of that condition is what has been called a limited opportunity structure. The restraints imposed on women's opportunity structures are the result of certain assumptions about the female role: that is, a woman's primary function is to have children; she must choose between career and family; she should not compete with men for employment; certain jobs are appropriate for women but others are not; and this arrangement is immutable, "natural," and necessary.

Third, the female status is that of a dependent. Economically and socially a woman is dependent on her husband; in cultural terms she is dependent on and defined by her sexual role. If sufficiently attractive as a sex object, she can expect men to reward her with attention and economic benefits; to be attractive should therefore be the focus of her energies.

Fourth, the pattern of female life is created and reinforced by a set of self-perpetuating cultural institutions, including child-raising practices, informal and formal education, advertising, social norms, and role prescriptions. Women are trained to accept the role that society assigns them because men assume it to be "natural." From early infanthood they are taught what it is to be "feminine" and womanly, which they in turn teach their daughters. After they have mastered the lesson, women must act out the role prescribed for them: flaunt themselves sexually, but remain chaste; bear children, but only after marriage; concentrate on domestic chores, but always look alluring; compete with other women for masculine attention and favors, but not so aggressively as to embarrass a male; and inspire their husbands to assume their rightful place in the masculine-dominated society, but never be demanding. Thus, they are expected to act in a way that reduces their capacity for self-development, that undermines their self-esteem, and that supports a power system in which they themselves are powerless.

Fifth, there is but one institution in which woman theoretically holds sway – that is the family. This is ostensibly her special preserve, the cultural institution created to protect her biological functions of breeding and nurturing, over which she has full control. To the intellectually liberated woman, however, the theory is a myth; it is based on the same kind of logic that convinces the servant that his master could not exist without him. The cold reality is that the man's economic dominance enables him to control the family. Conceded that his wife may be allowed to decide where they go on vacation, he determines if they can afford to go – or if they go. She may participate in choosing a new home or a new car, but again he makes the fundamental economic decision, the legal and binding decision.

The semblance of female dominance within the family hides the actuality of male predominance. A woman is supposed to make a "good home" for her mate in order that he may be free to achieve success in his career. The important aspect of family life is his job – his success, his salary – the masculine world dominates the female preserve and the criterion by which she is judged to be a success or a failure is the well-being of her husband. If his occupation demands it, the home and family will be moved across the country; her task is to make the move go well, to accept it without even thinking of questioning its validity, and to conceal, even from herself, any unhappiness about moving at all.

She is the primary child-raiser for the first six years of each child's life, but this task is also structured by the demands of her role. She must transmit the same values that are operative in her life: "You'd better be good or Daddy will punish you," or, "Keep quiet, Daddy's tired because he's been working so hard." She does the drudgework: the feeding, bathing, cleaning-up-after, and diaper-changing. Once the children reach the age when they begin to reason and can serve as companions, they are turned over to the schools.

The woman can and often does have her way in the family setting, but she does so by resorting to domestic guerrilla tactics. She must use her powers of seduction, play on her husband's emotional commitment to her, and use her capacity to threaten revolt and disruption to win her way. These are the weapons of the relatively powerless.

Women comfort themselves by pointing out that "all men are babies," that "they ought to know what trying to run a household is really like," or asking "what would they do without us?" but these are actually unconscious confessions of weakness and self-hatred. They say, by implication, that the wife's life is dominated by the husband, who is less knowledgeable, less emotionally mature, and less rational than herself.

It can be (and often is) argued that women themselves accept and even yearn for this role. The cultural milieu that fosters the belief that women want domesticity as it is currently structured is an effective force in maintaining her dependence. Every woman, whatever her talents, education, intelligence, or predispositions, is assumed to be abnormal if she does not want to be a wife and mother. As a result, society, including other women, generates pressures to force each woman into her predetermined role. And, because she has been subjected to these pressures since childhood, each woman, restless and haunted by a sense of a wasted life, is apt to blame herself, to feel guilty about her own inadequacy as a woman rather than question the system itself.

The family, then, is viewed by the proponents of female equality not as a sexual or social institution, but as a power system in which culturally determined sexual and social roles are part of the raw materials of the system, and woman is seen as dependent, preprogrammed, and powerless in relation to her mate and to society.

Although a large part of the women's liberation movement, unlike the suffrage movement, has concerned itself with equality of employment, it is hardly a single-issue campaign. In concrete terms, the aims of the movement are:

Equal pay for equal work.

Hiring and promotion based on talent, skills, and merit.

Free day-care centers for children so that women may work without having to surrender the choice of motherhood.

Re-examination of marriage as an institution, and of the superior-subordinate roles that the culture establishes in the context of marriage.

Revision of child-raising practices so that women are not programmed to preset social roles.

Revision of educational practices to the same end.

Political organization to achieve the program.

Underlying the concrete program is the intention to effect a major cultural innovation: the elimination of prescribing roles on the basis of sex.

Women as a grouping are, like other groupings, divided by age, marital status, income level, social status, and life experiences. By the beginning of the 1970s, the movement had been given somewhat more than sporadic attention by the media, but it was not clear how far it had been successful in organizing any sizable segment of the female population of the country into a self-aware minority group. Colleges and universities were beginning to acknowledge the demand for analysis of the status of women by including special courses in their curricula but, as nearly as could be ascertained, women's liberation had barely tapped the potential strength represented by the number of women in the population.

Bibliography

Amundsen, Kirsten. *The Silenced Majority: Women and American Democracy.* Englewood Cliffs, N.J.: Prentice-Hall, 1971. One of the most useful works to come out of the women's liberation movement, in that it combines an analysis of the status of women with careful political research and theory.

Bird, Caroline. *Born Female: The High Cost of Keeping Women Down.* New York: David McKay, 1968. Focuses primarily on the economic status of working women.

Flexnor, Eleanor. *Century of Struggle: The Woman's Rights Movement in the United States.* Cambridge, Mass.: Harvard University Press, 1959.

Friedan, Betty. *The Feminine Mystique.* New York: Norton, 1963.

Gruberg, Martin. *Women in American Politics.* Oshkosh, Wis.: Academia Press, 1968. A valuable survey of women's roles and accomplishments in American politics.

Kraditor, Aileen. *Up From the Pedestal.* Chicago: Quadrangle Books, 1968.

Mead, Margaret, and Frances Bagley Kaplan. *American Women: The Report of the President's Commission on the Status of Women.* New York: Scribner, 1965.

Millet, Kate. *Sexual Politics.* Garden City, N.Y.: Doubleday, 1970. One of the more influential statements on the status of women in America.

Morgan, Robin, ed. *Sisterhood is Powerful.* New York: Vintage, 1970. An excellent collection of readings, covering a wide array of problems associated with women's status and reactions to that status.

Tanner, Leslie B., ed. *Voices from Women's Liberation.* New York: New American Library, 1970. Another excellent collection of readings, particularly valuable for its documentation of the women's movement in the nineteenth century.

Ten
Why Politics ?

As the preceding five chapters have indicated, deprived minorities in America must resort to politics to redress grievances. Minority groups consisting of blacks, Mexican-Americans, or Indians turn to political action partly because it is through the political process that they can obtain the things they need from government; women and students resort to politics not so much to obtain specific benefits from government but to obtain power.

Both approaches are old and well-established American traditions. From the beginning of the republic to the present, interest groups have sought material and other benefits from government. Even in the heyday of laissez-faire capitalism—the 1860s, 1870s, and 1880s—railroads and other corporations received direct subsidies from government in the form of land grants and tariff protection. Today, defense-related industries make the same demands. The frank appeal to power is somewhat different, although it is also "traditional." As A. A. Berle observed, "Current American thinking has regarded power as a dirty subject, and desire for its possession a naughty emotion" (p. 18), and this was probably also true a century ago. American politicians and businessmen have usually disguised the quest for power in the rhetoric of the public welfare, in the promulgation of issues and ideas, and in statements to the effect that the "best men" should rule. Nonetheless, they have sought and continue to seek power.

What is true of other interests is equally true of minority groups. Minorities today are generally deprived less through the deliberate policies of government than through the workings of the economic, social, and political systems as presently constituted. Few laws now on the statute books of federal, state, and local governments overtly deny the rights and privileges of citizenship to minority groupings, and the enforcement of such laws that do exist is progressively being relaxed. Yet, almost unanimously, minorities turn to the political process in an effort to mitigate their deprivations. One reason minorities engage in politics is based in part on the nature of minority deprivation and in part on the nature of the state and the potential role it can play, which includes the passage of statutory law and the coercive and redistributive powers that governments exercise. Another reason is that politics is the exercise of power.

Laws and Regulations

Although today there are relatively few laws that deliberately impose special burdens on minorities, some do exist. For example, state laws and regulations that set minimum residence requirements for eligibility for public welfare benefits severely handicap Mexican-American and black migrant workers, who may be seeking the money needed to support life and family. Such regulations were often designed to discourage migration. Abortion laws, requiring proof of physical or mental disability, oblige women not desiring children to bear the burden of having them. To change such laws, the minorities affected by them must turn to the political process.

Although not deliberately designed to do so, every law places a burden on someone and benefits someone else. Because of their relative powerlessness, minorities are apt to bear the burdens, and they are apt to suffer from them more than dominant groups would. Thus regressive taxes, stringent zoning laws, and proof of eligibility for various government services and benefits, such as loans or contracts, work serious hardships on the deprived. The increasing use of the sales tax by cities means that the poor spend a disproportionately greater part of their total disposable income for necessities than do the more affluent, and the "poor" in the cities are usually blacks, Puerto Ricans, Mexican-Americans, working women, and the elderly. Even though the tax is frequently imposed to raise money for programs that are supposed to benefit the poor, such as welfare and education, the cost is highest to the deprived. Zoning laws aimed at preserving the "integrity and amenities" of attractive residential areas make decent housing too expensive for those of limited means—on occasion deliberately so. Proof of eligibility for government loans may prohibit a member of a minority from establishing a business because such eligibility is based on standards he can never meet. The intention to guarantee that public funds are used honestly and with prudence can mean that public funds do not reach those who need them the most desperately.

In such situations, minorities must either forego the benefits that could be derived from government, thereby accepting the burden, or try to have new programs established and old ones changed. If they do not accept the status quo, they must turn to legislatures, courts, and administrative bodies for change; in other words, they must politick. And, once they take part in the political process, they tend to continue to do so.

Redistributive Powers

Federal, state and local governments are empowered to redistribute money and the other benefits of society. Although the primary means of redistribution in America remains the private sphere of the economy, accomplished through the transfer of money from consumers to corporations, who then pay wages, salaries, pensions, and dividends, this process is often indirect. Moreover, for a member of an economically deprived minority, it is inaccessible since the point at which one breaks into the cycle is employment. If a member of a minority is unemployed or subemployed, he must depend on some other source for money. In some cases, it may be a private source: a charity, a foundation, or, for a woman, her husband. But government has a larger redistributive capacity than any of these other sources, especially as far as blacks, Puerto Ricans, Mexican-Americans, students, and Indians are concerned.

Government intervenes in the private redistributive cycle by taking a portion of the money for its own use and diverting it to those who are either not in the cycle or only marginally so. By its power to tax and spend, government makes direct payments (welfare payments) to individuals who are either not paid or underpaid by the private sphere. It can also directly provide goods and services that might be purchased in the private sphere by the economically less deprived (free school lunches, free textbooks, housing, physical and mental health services, food stamps, food surpluses, day-care centers, and education).

Government is a source of employment as well. Federal, state, and local governments directly employed approximately 12,000,000 persons in the late 1960s of a total work force of about 80,000,000 in the United States. Although many of the jobs are menial, or are patronage positions held in reserve by the political parties to pay off the faithful, there is, nonetheless, a large potential opportunity for individuals to gain government employment. To the extent government is more open than certain sectors of the private economy, a member of a minority can benefit from the redistribution of wealth gained by taxes and paid to him in wages, salaries, and fringe benefits.

Coupled with direct employment is the potential impact of governmental policies regarding the hiring of minority members by those holding government contracts. Manufacturers, research agencies, contractors, printers, suppliers, universities—all who engage in directly selling goods and services to governments—can be required to conform to "fair employment" practices as a proviso of their contracts. Government, as a large consumer of privately produced goods and services, is in a position to use its special powers to demand that the jobs paid for by governmental revenues must be allocated to minority members.

Government also occupies a special position in terms of its revenue potential. The power to tax allows governments to carry out programs with little regard for profit or loss. They can therefore provide high-risk loans and high-risk insurance or low-cost loans and low-cost insurance for a variety of purposes, including business ventures, housing, agriculture, and urban development. Although many such governmental programs are expected to break even, unlike private enterprises they may suffer losses for an indefinite period of time without being affected by the consequences. Such programs allow people who are denied access to private sources of funds because of discrimination or economics to obtain government loans or insurance at lower interest rates or premiums than those of private enterprise.

Finally, some of the governmental programs that are designed to help the general public can benefit deprived minorities. Public transportation systems make it possible for the unemployed of the central cities to reach jobs in the suburbs. Improved urban services for everyone can mean improved services for the deprived. Efforts to control inflation benefit the poor more than anyone. In other words, when government redistributes benefits, goods, and services, conditions under which the deprived live can be improved, either intentionally or incidentally.

Four major principles control the role of government as a redistributive agent. The first is that government is a special kind of economic agent. Unlike private enterprise, it need not conform to the conditions imposed by competition. It can sacrifice economy and efficiency to attain other ends. A business firm, for example, would be reluctant to hire someone whose productivity might be less than optimum; government, however, can tolerate the "loss" in productivity in order to guarantee a reduction in welfare costs, to extend opportunity, and to relieve political and social stresses.

Second, government's power to act as a redistributive agent is limited by the political process. If people in positions of power expect government to perform like a private firm, it cannot act with a free hand. Legislatures can require programs to break even financially or to demonstrate that employees are productive. Every government official is aware of the political pressure connected with spending the taxpayer's money.

Third, certain practical considerations limit government's activities. Local governments are often inhibited by state constitutional and legislative dictates. State and federal governments recognize that the economic consequences of their actions can trigger a political response. Extensive spending programs are inflationary, unless one program (such as defense) is reduced to finance another (such as social welfare). But to modify one program in order to strengthen another may cause those who benefit from the former to suffer. Governments thus are invariably tempted to add on rather than reallocate. The price of adding on is higher taxes, higher costs of government, and increasing taxpayer resentment. Governments may have to face "taxpayers' revolts" and, ultimately, legislative revolt. In the ensuing struggle, the programs that are paying off are apt to be the ones that are preserved intact; the ones that can show no quantifiable benefits are sacrificed. And, the programs that specifically benefit minorities are the most difficult to express in favorable "cost/benefit" terms.

Fourth, as a result of the practical limits, the redistributive powers of government are rarely fully used. The untapped potential, however, invites minority groups to enter the political process to transform the possibility into actuality. Federal, state, and local governments can do more; the problem confronting minority groups is to get them to do more, by expanding existing programs and creating new ones.

Coercive Powers

Aside from the tangible benefits that governments can distribute, they possess the potential for modifying human behavior. Government does possess enormous coercive power: governments may require individuals to behave or to refrain from behaving in a number of ways. For minority groups this power is significant, since the law can be used to forbid discrimination in employment, housing, education, transportation, public facilities, election laws and procedures, and public communications.

Government can use coercive powers either negatively or positively. The removal of barriers that exist by law or custom through the passage of new laws that repeal the old is negative use of coercive power. Positive use includes not only the removal of barriers but the creation of conditions that would have existed had the barriers never been in effect. School desegregation is an example of negative use. A barrier was removed, but there was no guarantee that schools would be integrated. Integration, however, places blacks in predominantly white schools and whites in predominantly black schools, creating a situation that might have existed had skin color not determined where children go to school.

Governments have four methods for achieving either the removal of barriers or the affirmative elimination of the effects of deprivation and discrimination.

First, they may use *suasion*. The government takes a position of "leadership" and calls upon individuals, groups, and institutions in its jurisdiction to follow its preferences. A governor or a mayor who favors school integration, for example, will avoid sending his own children to segregated private schools and will let it be known that his children attend racially integrated schools. Federal government agencies will increase their hiring of minority members and will ask private enterprise to do the same. Suasion is effective to the extent that there are those who agree with the position that government has taken and are convinced that a commitment by government affords them community approval and protection (thus allowing them to do something they might have been wary of doing before). It is also effective among those who are anxious to defer to authoritative leadership. But, among those who disagree with government leadership, suasion can be totally useless.

Of the alternative methods available to government, suasion is the least expensive. Although it requires the assertion of governmental authority, it involves a negligible commitment of power. For minorities, the principal value of suasion is symbolic: an acknowledgment by government officials of their existence, status, and the difficulties that they face. Recognition can be the first step toward action.

Second, *mutual self-interest* may be used to achieve compliance. By offering concrete benefits to individuals and institutions, governments can use self-interest as a means of achieving affirmative or negative compliance. The federal government may deny states or localities grants-in-aid, and private firms contracts. It can show preference by awarding grants, loans, or contracts to jurisdictions or organizations. Although frequently labelled "dictatorship," the use of self-interest as an incentive poses a simple dilemma for the recipient: either continue a policy with which the government disagrees, thereby foregoing the grant, or change that policy in order to obtain the grant. Examples of "forced" compliance are the integration of southern school districts, nondiscriminatory hiring by industry, and membership policies of labor unions.

The advantage of using mutual self-interest is that few institutions are willing to surrender the benefits they want in order to retain discriminatory practices. But, it is a costly method: it breeds resentment. It also requires constant supervision to be sure that grants or contracts are not being given to those who do not comply.

Third, there are *limited sanctions.* Government can dictate that a procedure be followed and can impose a fine for failure to comply. For the sanction to be "limited," the penalty must be limited. Like that of mutual self-interest, the problem is one of enforcement. For a penalty to be levied, there usually must be an administrative hearing, and often a trial and an appeal. The process is time-consuming and costly. Further, the burden of proof frequently lies with the person who has been discriminated against, or with the government if it is acting on behalf of the injured party. Moreover, limited sanctions are usually used for individual cases—correcting individual violations of the law but allowing numberless others to go unpenalized, simply because no action has been brought against the violator.

To a member of a minority, the process is often so drawn-out it becomes meaningless. A point of principle may be won and other discriminators may be warned, but the tangible benefits awarded to the aggrieved individual or group may long since have lost their value.

Finally, government can resort to *maximum sanctions,* that is, jail sentences or ruinous fines and penalties for failure to comply with the law. Understandably enough, such penalties are usually reserved for extreme cases, and government agencies are reluctant to invoke them.

Governments have a variety of means with which to bring about compliance with official policy, but the use of these means is affected by both the willingness to invoke them and the effort required to make them effective. Both elected and appointed officials prefer to employ the least coercive means, resorting to the most coercive only very reluctantly. Few politicians want to be accused of imposing a major burden on any institution or segment of society, especially for the benefit of an unpopular grouping, unless the demand for it is overwhelming. For this reason bitter battles are fought over how a policy is to be "implemented," because the means used to ensure implementation determine how effective the policy will be. The consumption of time, the administrative costs, and the results to be expected determine the means by which government chooses to enforce a policy, rather than the substance of the policy itself.

From the perspective of minorities, however, the failure of governments to use strong measures indicates official reluctance to correct obvious injustices. Governments have the powers: they simply must be made to use them vigorously and consistently. Government can force changes in behavior (if not in attitude); thus minorities always have an incentive to enter the political process to produce the changes.

Governmental Distortions

In the American system there is substantial room for discretion in the application of policies at any level of government. An administrator, theoretically charged with following the law to the letter, is rarely able to do so: first, because the law is rarely explicit enough not to require interpretation; and, second, because it is physically impossible. A traffic policeman is charged with apprehending all violators; in reality, however, he apprehends only a few. Who they are depends on what criteria he uses, what his preferences are, and what the demands on his time may be. Moreover, in a federal system of government, a "federal" program passes through a number of hands and is usually administered by locally hired officials in local governments. Programs, then, tend to lose force, to be modified, or to be distorted in practice as they pass from one set of administrators to another. Low-income housing can become a means for furthering ghettoization, urban renewal can become minority removal, training for employment can become a way in which to funnel members of minorities into noncompetitive occupations, and public welfare can become a patronage system. In 1970, for example, Section 235 of the National Housing Act, which was intended to help impoverished people acquire rehabilitated housing, in some instances was misapplied by local real estate speculators who foisted unrehabilitated housing on those who believed they were receiving the protection of a federally sponsored program.

It can be argued (and it is probably true) that distortions of this kind are inevitable in a complex system of government. There are always some corrupt administrators; there are always some who are too overworked to supervise the details of every program for which they are responsible; there are always some who unintentionally misinterpret the meaning of the law; there are always some who are willing to bend the law to conform to "local conditions," to satisfy a powerful legislator, governor, mayor or pressure group. The cumulative result is some degree of distortion at any given time. The principal means of protection against such distortions is through active pressure groups and legislators who are anxious to see that whatever distortions exist do not harm their interests.

Another form of distortion exists in governmental "priorities." Government programs and activities can be vehicles for minority deprivation. Examples of such programs are: a new highway designed to run through a black residential area rather than a white area; a new recreation area located near a comfortable, wide-lawned middle-class area rather than a crowded slum; a new municipal swimming pool that is more accessible to whites than to racial minorities; a new coliseum financed by a city too strapped to increase welfare benefits. Although members of dominant groups are often unaware that any distortion exists, members of minorities are acutely aware of it. They sense their powerlessness to do anything about it even though it affects the quality of their lives; their objections are met with stolid indifference or, worse, a stubborn insistence on keeping them deprived.

Besides these obvious differentials is the bitter debate over the allocation of governmental resources. Is it better to spend money on bigger and more extensive antiballistic missile defenses or on improving the conditions of poverty? Should society instruct its law enforcement agencies to root out subversives or to enforce the laws governing equal opportunities? Unquestionably, groups stand to benefit whichever road governments take, but the question is which groups and how much?

Minority leaders who observe the political process realize, sooner or later, that such decisions are made and are going to be made. Either the decisions can totally disregard minorities, or the "system" can be made aware of minorities' needs. To make the system aware, the minority itself must undertake the burden of political activism.

Accessibility and Generality

Another impetus toward political action by minority groups is the relative accessibility of governmental institutions. Governmental institutions are not equally accessible to all groups at all times, but compared with other segments of society, any governmental institution might seem more open.

Once the basic rights of citizenship are attained—that is, the right to vote, to petition (i.e., engage in group activity), to pursue grievances through the courts, to nominate and support candidates for elected and appointed office—a degree of *opportunity for access* exists. The realities, or perceived realities, of that opportunity will be explored in the next few chapters, but government is accessible in a way that private spheres of society are not. This is in part because the vote, whatever its strengths and weaknesses, is a political resource that has no precise equivalent in economics or social life.

Government, moreover, has a subjective accessibility. To those excluded from full social or economic participation, the prominence, emphasis, and drama given politics makes government seem more open. It is psychologically easier to turn to political activities on a large scale than to do the same in the economic or social spheres of society.

Closely related to accessibility is the quality of a potential victory won in the governmental and political arena: the quality of generality. A minority seeking equal employment opportunities, for example, could undertake the task of convincing every firm in the country to hire on an equal basis; it could alternatively attempt to persuade Congress to pass a law to achieve the same effect. The latter course might require years of work, but it would have a degree of generality and would be far more efficient than the former course could ever be. Moreover, although the minority would have to be the sole monitor of the results won by its own campaign, it could hope that government would be the primary monitor of a law passed in its name. The consideration is hardly a trivial one. For groups with limited resources, it is necessary to commit those resources to those areas in which the most generalized victories can be won.

The Search for Power

Pervading all these considerations is the most significant of all. Governmental and political institutions are specialized institutions for wielding power in contemporary society. They are designed to act as instruments of power for those who can gain some influence over their performance. Although they do not have a monopoly of power in the society, they exist primarily to bring the massed capacity of the state to bear in whatever directions the political processes select.

For the powerless, those who feel they have little control over the forces that shape their lives, to share the direction and control of these instruments is inherently desirable. Not only can these institutions be used for the direct benefit of a minority, but they can be deflected from being used against it. And with control comes the subjective rewards of power: self-esteem, pride, a sense of accomplishment, and a greater security about the future.

Minority politics, however, are not limited to the specialized institutions of power we call government. Students apply their power analyses to universities, institutions previously inviolate to the cold speculation of power politics. Women examine the family and the male-female relationship in terms of a power relationship, a view formerly held only by Adlerian psychoanalysts.

Bibliography

Anderson, James E. *Politics and the Economy*. Boston: Little, Brown, 1966. An extremely useful survey of the role of government in shaping economic decisions and the impact of economic institutions on governmental policy-making.

Banfield, Edward C. *The Unheavenly City.* Boston: Little, Brown, 1970. A thoughtful–and controversial–examination of the distortions that have occurred in efforts to relieve the conditions of poverty discrimination.

Berle, A. A. *Power.* New York: Harcourt, Brace and World, 1969.

Clark, Kenneth B., and Jeannette Hopkins. *A Relevant War Against Poverty.* New York: Harper & Row, 1969. A careful analysis of the successes and failures of the "War on Poverty" programs.

Kershaw, Joseph A. *Government Against Poverty.* Chicago: Markham, 1970.

Lockard, Duane. *Toward Equal Opportunity.* New York: Macmillan, 1968. An excellent study of the problems of eliminating discrimination in a federal system.

Morgan, Ruth P. *The President and Civil Rights.* New York: St. Martin's, 1970.

Wilcox, Clair. *Toward Social Welfare.* Homewood, Ill.: Irwin, 1969. One of the most useful examinations of government as an actual and potential agent for the redistribution of social benefits in American society.

Part Two
MINORITY POLITICS

Eleven
The Political System:
A Dominant View

A source of contention between minority groups and dominant groups engaging in politics is the nature of the American political system. When minority groups and dominant groups are in disagreement, it often is about what the political system is and what it should be: what strengthens it, what overburdens it, what it can or cannot produce, what it should do and how. When most Americans turn to politicking, they generally accept the political system for what it is, the basic issues being who will control it and what use will they make of it. The new minorities, however, feel differently: to a great extent, they attribute their powerlessness to the nature of the system and therefore challenge its structure and processes. One result is that both minorities and dominant groups have been forced to try to understand and analyze what that system is.

Describing politics is describing a summation of human actions; and human actions are a product of individual understandings applied to other human beings and either imposed, modified, or abandoned in the process of application. The political system is in large part what each "political person" thinks it is at any given point in time.

In the context of minority group politics there are two central—and divergent—views. One can be called the dominant view, presumably held by a large number of people who are not members of minorities. The other can be called a minority view, which is quite different from the dominant view. It must be noted, however, that only *one* dominant view is being presented here. In reality, there are probably dozens of dominant views of the political system that vary from each other in detail if not in basic thesis. Most Americans have not really attempted to put together a coherent and systematic view of their political system. Even though they may understand various parts of it and may be aware of certain processes, few except the specialists attempt to make a complete picture of what they read, hear about, see on television, and experience.

Any description of what can be called the dominant view of the political system, then, must be very general and therefore possibly unsatisfactory to many. The effort is necessary, however, because it helps to bring into focus what is under attack and what the conflicts are. The most direct method of describing the political system is to regard it first as a set of processes and then to look at what the processes produce in generalized terms. In part, however, even this simple method is arbitrary and invalid, because the process often *is* the most important product from a dominant point of view.

The Political Process

The American political process is often described as a method of resolving conflicts, a means by which clashing interests are brought into a common arena and settled under terms that channel and limit both the scope and the intensity of the conflict. The most prominent aspects of this system are the electoral process, the informal and formal norms or "rules of the game" (which impose predictable patterns on the participants' behavior), the temporary quality of most political decisions, and the role of compromise and bargaining.

The Dominance of Electoral Politics

In the dominant view, party politics—or, more precisely, electoral politics—is the predominating feature of the American system. It is the means by which most persons in power are formally chosen and by which power is transmitted from one set of politicians to another and from one generation to another. It is an ingenious solution to the eternal social problem of choosing a leader of a society, and, of course, it is the formal standard that sets democratic regimes apart from dictatorships, aristocracies, and monarchies.

Electoral politics is an activity in which a large number of citizens can readily and inexpensively participate. Legislators must calculate their maneuvers and the votes they cast in their chambers on the basis of the impact of their actions on the electorate and on their chances for re-election. Although many administrators are isolated from the direct influence of the electoral process, their chief executive is usually chosen by popular vote, and they must be sensitive to the political risks that he and the legislators who are responsible for the appropriation of public funds might incur. Even judges are reluctant to move directly against the public opinion that is revealed in election returns. And judges, for that matter, are themselves either popularly elected or chosen by those who are popularly elected.

Correctly or not, the rewards of an election are considered valuable. Those winning an election can hope to put their programs into effect; those who have supported a winner can expect to be rewarded directly or indirectly for their help. To win office, to defeat one or more opponents, to be a public figure, to hold some power, to command the attention of the media, to have (perhaps) patronage to distribute, to be able to share in making public policy—all are rich and desirable attainments. As a result, elections have drama. They are contests between persons who are seeking to satisfy ambition and to please large numbers of people. An election can hold the attention of large segments of the public and by doing so can persuade them to participate by casting a vote. Aside from its more serious aspects, an election can be entertaining. American elections are contests in which winning itself is one of the major purposes of the game.

Two additional factors contribute to the importance of elections. One is that the contests between the two major political parties have significantly structured American political thinking. Although the number of self-styled "independents" has steadily increased in the last decade or so, apparently most politically conscious Americans still identify with either the Republican or the Democratic party. Such identification is, moreover, deeply rooted psychologically, acquired at an early age, and maintained for a lifetime. Thus, not only are the election contests themselves intrinsically important, but the two great political parties are important. Either party continues to be an almost absolutely necessary route to political success. Those who aspire to political power gain the money, organization, support, and votes to attain that power by means of the political parties. As such, the parties are intermediaries in electoral contests. They are the general rubrics under which diverse ambitions, interests, and values are accumulated and more or less success-fully compromised, bargained, coordinated, and converted into votes for either party's candidate.

The political parties help to make the electoral process work; some would argue they alone allow it to work. They are the means by which voters can organize a complicated political universe into a manageable form. They are the means by which voters can participate in effective political action. And they are the means by which the resources for obtaining power and holding it produce leadership for the nation, states, and local governments, making that leadership responsible for its actions.

Second, elections are important because of their periodicity and frequency. Somewhere in the country, a campaign, an election, or active preparation for a campaign or election is always going on. Both periodicity and frequency require the perpetual existence of political organizations, generate a huge appetite within the parties for candidates, and require a steady appeal to voters and to contributors for support. The sheer number of elected officials is impressive: 522,295 or approximately 1 out of every 400 persons in the country, excluding the various party officials who, in some states, are elected in party primaries but do not hold any other elective post. An enormous number of Americans are directly involved in electoral politics, running for office, supplying advice, money, and work, and challenging incumbents.

Frequency can lead to voter apathy, to sheer fatigue and boredom with the constant repetition of demands for money and support. At the most, 60 percent of the registered voters turn out for an election, indicating that either the appeals of the parties and their candidates fall short of attracting the voter or the voting public is less than enchanted by the whole business. Nonetheless, the opportunity for extensive participation exists, and even those not actively participating may do so passively, by reading or listening to the constant bombardment of propaganda and objective information provided by the media.

Certain structural features of the political system contribute to the importance of electoral politics. An elected official controls government revenue. Legislators, through appropriations, and elected executives, through budgets and vetoes, determine how revenue will be raised and how it will be spent. Although some appointed administrators, such as city managers, possess some authority, the purse-strings are generally held by elected officials, who jealously guard the tradition. Elected officials also make the laws and set the administrative machinery into motion to enforce them.

The significance of the dominance of electoral politics is fourfold. First, if political power does rest with those elected to office, then that power is widely dispersed among a large number of individuals, even though the amount of power varies (e.g., the influence of the president of the United States cannot be compared to that of an elected member of a school board in a small rural community). Each elected official has his own base of voter support, and so long as he retains that support, he can defy other, more powerful officials. Moreover, a legal responsibility is associated with each individualized base of support. An individual elected to office is supposed to carry out certain duties of that office, and the office itself, its duties, the electoral base, the elected individual, and the exercise of power constitute one complex package, separate from all other similar packages.

Second, the base of voters is itself dispersed. Voters may be strongly influenced by well-organized machines; they may be subject to manipulation, intimidation, or outright purchase. But at the polls a voter makes a secret decision. That decision—whether rational or irrational—is surprisingly independent of direct control, which is evidenced by the enormous persuasive effort that goes into campaigns. Candidates for public office are never so sure of winning that they can forego attempts to reach the voters by some means. In this respect, the power of an elected official is dependent on his constituents. It is measured by his last set of election results, his prospects for re-election, the risks of competition, and those risks inherent in alienating a significant segment of his base of support. The power of a legislative committee chairman, for example, is often a function of his seniority, which in turn is a product of the voters' willingness to elect and re-elect him to office.

Third, participation in the political process is generalized. An enormous variety of individuals—roughly eighty million—are participants through the act of voting alone, and this does not include those who are too young to vote but who nonetheless campaign for their candidates. A large number of people engage in political activity in addition to voting. They do campaign work, hold party offices, make contributions of money, and try to persuade family, friends, and acquaintances to vote for the candidates they support. Political power, then, is hardly focused or unified, but is dispersed and shared through widespread participation.

Finally, the electoral process is aggregative. The political party is a mechanism for accumulating voters as individuals, blocs, jurisdictions, and neighborhoods to form a winning coalition. "Coalition" is the operative word. To master the crucial majority or plurality, diversity must be turned into at least temporary unity. The political parties and their candidates are impelled to move toward a modal distribution of the voters' attitudes and perceptions. Although any given grouping can be ignored by both parties, one or the other is always tempted to expand its base and to accommodate new attitudes and interests in an attempt to assure itself of victory. To fail to do so is to surrender the opportunity to the other party. In the short run, both parties may by tacit agreement exclude a potential bloc of voters, as they did the blacks during the post-Reconstruction era, but the essential goal of either party is to win. And so, sooner or later, either party or both will attempt to bring that bloc into the fold; the Democrats have tried to bring the blacks into the fold ever since the New Deal. By means of the process of aggregation, each interest brought into a party can make some claim on it and its candidates once an election is won and thus share not only in the process of winning but also in the tangible rewards of victory.

The dominance of electoral politics is vital to the political system not only because it provides the primary route to power individually or collectively, but because it is the motivating factor in generalized, frequent, and dispersed participation. Power and its sources (votes) are not concentrated but generalized and individualized. A single voter may seem like a small pebble on a large beach, but as a part of a bloc or a party, the voter is the goal and root of political power and thus *is* political power.

To say as much is not to ignore the other power-wielding agencies: vast bureaucracies, interest groups, or even (especially in local governments) the influence of certain well-placed individuals. But, it can be argued that their power is substantially derivative. The influence of an interest group on a legislator stems from the group's ability to supply him with votes, or money, or information and cues, or moral support on issues at a time that will amplify his electoral chances. A legislator who comes from a safe district can and will safely ignore the pressures of an interest group that has no influence in his district, unless he can be bribed into doing things that will not harm him with the home folks anyway. Despite all the power of bureaucrats and bureaucratic organizations, elected officials can cripple or destroy that power at will, if they sense that they have the support of those who have elected them to office. Bureaucracies rely on elected policy-makers for money, discretionary power, and the shape and content of the programs to be administered.

Even well-placed individuals can usually exercise power only in direct proportion to their organizational backing, which in turn is directly or indirectly related to the capacity to influence voters.

If governmental institutions are the specialized agencies for the exercise of power, the electoral process is the specialized process by which individuals and groups can most directly attain access and control over those institutions.

The Rules of the Game

The struggle for power by whatever means is not an unlimited conflict. There are norms that govern the behavior of the participants and thereby limit the scope, intensity, and rigor of the conflict. In the parlance of political science, these norms are called the "rules of the game."

There often is disagreement on the rules. Some politicians at some point in their careers seem willing to violate them, but usually these violations are costly and lead to their political demise. The constitutional guarantees of freedom of the press and of speech make it possible for violations of the rules to be publicized, sometimes influencing the voters to exercise the ultimate sanction of electoral defeat.

Despite continued violations, certain rules are generally accepted and followed, however reluctantly. The most important are:

First, adherence to the basic legal forms of the political system; that is, the formal processes are obeyed. In the United States, elections are not suspended because of crisis but are held on schedule—even in time of war, such as the Civil War and World War II. Court orders are usually obeyed. Requirements for filing for public office, accounting for the use of funds, and accepting policy directives are obeyed in the letter if not the spirit. Unlike certain nations, the United States generally obeys its constitutional and statutory mandates, although where there is room for disagreement, there are arguments over interpretation. This obedience has important implications. It insures predictability, stability, and a degree of orderliness. There is a minimum point of reference: what the law says must be done or cannot be done. And because the rules are relatively fixed, those in power cannot simply suspend them to maintain their power. If an election is scheduled to be held, the regime in power cannot refuse to hold it for fear of losing.

Although it is customary political practice to attempt to manipulate the legal forms to the advantage of one interest or another, their existence is a limitation on the exercise of power. Even changes in the rules must be accomplished by procedures set down by the rules, so that possession of the instruments of government does not guarantee a perpetuation of that possession, especially in conjunction with the electoral system.

Second, the voluntary acquiescence in a change of hands in government. The losing regime turns over the reins of power to the regime-elect. Again, this is not universal practice. An incumbent regime could resort to violence in order to maintain its power, jailing its opposition, barricading itself in its offices, and defying its opponents to oust it with brute force. But, except for occasional individuals in isolated instances, such behavior is not an American practice. Among other things, this rule of conceding the loss of an election indicates that the ability to amass votes is more important than the capacity to accumulate physical force. In the United States, the functional equivalent of armed supporters is committed voters.

Third, eschewing the political destruction of one's opponents. In general —although there are exceptions—it is not considered fair play to eliminate the opposition. They may be forced into a condition of permanent incapacity to win control of the government, but it is assumed that they will be allowed to exist. The constitutional forms—freedom of speech, assembly, and petition—are further insurance of the opposition's continued existence, but a self-serving logic supports the rule, too. To attempt to root out all of the opposition would insure that they would do the same if they attained power. The electoral system helps to maintain this state of uncertainty and restraint. The knowledge that today's victors may be tomorrow's losers is a strong incentive for the victors to be compassionate toward their foes. As a result, committee assignments in the legislature will include members of the opposition; the electoral laws will not be modified to place the opposition in an overwhelmingly disadvantageous position; some positions in the administration may even be allotted to the losing party; and the police force will not be used to prosecute opposing leaders or to hound them into exile. There is, in effect, a tacit bargain of mutual preservation that also provides mutual benefits. There is always a reason to muster energies for a new effort, or the opposition may gain power.

Fourth, the expectation that a political professional keeps his promises. The expectation is not limited to those to whom a promise has been made, but extends to other observers and to the politician himself. The logic is simple. In a system in which power is dispersed and each individual or bloc must depend on others to aggregate enough power to be effective, a promise is the only assurance that each participant in a coalition can be relied upon. A promise is to a politician what money is to a businessman: the currency of exchange. Promises are broken, of course, but usually a politician will specifically ask to be relieved of his obligation and will make another in return, if the price of his keeping the first one is political survival. Those who consistently renege on their promises can expect to be quickly isolated and abandoned.

It should be noted, however, that there is a difference between promises made to other politicians and promises made to the public. Those made to other politicians are binding, the necessary currency passed between officeholders, or between officeholder and interest group or party leader; those made to the public constitute an effort to rally a mass of individuals, and although a politician will often attempt to honor his promise, he does not feel compelled to do so.

The rule of promises given and promises kept also produces predictability and stability in political relations. Each participant knows what is due him and what he is obliged to deliver; he knows the shape of his immediate future. Legislators, chief executives, party leaders, and interest group leaders can thus grasp the network of relationships and can estimate the future performance of any given individual and the part of the system within which he works.

Finally, there is an emphasis on orderliness. A candidate for public office must campaign within certain limits. Overt bribery, systematic violence and intimidation, deliberate lying and slander, and disruptiveness are considered to be illegitimate even though they are occasionally used. Within these limits, there is room to maneuver within the shadowy reaches of political behavior, including ambiguous falsification, covert or indirect deals, and boisterous spirits, but even these maneuvers are to be avoided if there is any chance that they may become known to the mass of voters. The rules call for a "middle class" brand of politics, which emphasizes issues and appeals to reason, assumes that the voter makes rational, literate choices after evaluating competing arguments, and assumes that contending parties and interests use persuasion rather than threats, force, or deception.

It is conceded that "rationality" may include, perhaps should include, an appeal to the materialistic, selfish interests of the voter, and it is legitimate for one party to attempt to out-promise another. But these commitments are within the context of the rules, to be honored or not as conditions dictate. The essence of the rule of orderliness is that informal behavior will conform to the formal norms; laws are to be obeyed, restraint is to be exercised, and potential power, especially the power of brute force, is to be held in restraint.

The rules of the game, then, postulate a political system in which the acquisition and exchange of power are basically orderly, law-abiding, and although competitive, competitive within limits. The pursuit of power, however intense that pursuit, must be within the limits of legitimacy and accepted norms. If otherwise, the acquisition or retention of power may be denied, by public exposure, public distaste, or legal prosecution. Furthermore, an individual or group whose quest is unbridled may be branded as "unavailable" to hold power—too deviant, too unreliable, too unpredictable to be allowed access to the instruments of power—and thus may be refused support, money, votes, and political office or recognition.

The effect of the rules of the game is to shape American politics to fit a normal pattern of human behavior. At the extremes there may be violence at the polls, bribery and corruption, and deliberate flouting of public opinion and values. Presumably, however, the central tendency is one of orderliness, promises made and promises kept, obedience to the legal forms, tolerance of the opposition, and a peaceful change of power when changes occur. Presumably, also, this central tendency reflects the basic attitudes of those constituting the dominant culture of the society, and to win their support, the politician must conform to their norms.

The Nonfinality of Decisions

Reinforcing the rules of the game is the recognition by those in politics that they cannot always be winners and will not always be losers. The absence of ultimate wins or losses characterizes the political system as a whole. Although certain institutions of power, like courts or legislatures, make binding decisions, they are temporally limited, binding only until changed by a shift in political fortunes or values. Within a few years, seemingly "final" decisions may be revised, which happened in the late 1930s when the Supreme Court changed from economic conservatism to liberalism. Further, decisions may be changed even more swiftly. A legislative enactment may be vetoed; a veto may be overridden by the legislature; a law may be declared unconstitutional by a court; the composition of the court may be changed by executive appointments. Constitutions themselves may be changed; bureaucrats may undermine the most seemingly binding policy decision. At no given time can anyone say with complete surety, "We have won *that* battle."

One effect of the nonfinality of decisions is that those who are defeated in a political struggle always have recourse. General policies may seem to be finally determined, but they can always be modified, expanded, or contracted by a variety of means. One legislative session will appropriate a certain sum for a given program, the next, however, may take up the issue again with possibly different results. Since the defeated never need abandon the field, those who win once cannot safely abandon it either. Political issues tend to be continuing, carrying over from one year to the next, one generation of politicians to another, and one institution to another.

There are a number of advantages in the nonfinality of political decisions. In the first place, no single institution or interest can claim absolute power; the ability to establish immutable commitments does not exist. Second, an evaluative process is implicit in such a system. If issues must be fought over and over again, they will be examined over and over again, and the consequences and effects of past action will become part of the renewed struggle. As a result, periodic evaluations in response to changing circumstances are forced upon decision-makers. Although the process may seem inefficient to a systems engineer in that it requires the reargument of stale questions and sometimes produces no fundamental changes, it is nonetheless a method of reassessment by which adaptation to political and social change is achieved.

The nonfinality of decisions guarantees a dispersal of power opportunities. Since no single institution possesses a monopoly of power, those seeking to influence the process can turn to a variety of institutions and mold their tactics and resources to whichever target seems most promising.

Bargaining and Compromise

Obviously, a system that disperses power among a variety of institutions, groups, and individuals, which limits the finality of decisions, and places restraints on the extent of conflict must have generated some means by which decisions are made. The possibilities for reaching a deadlock and for violating the rules of the game are so great that there must be a means of resolving conflicts.

The means that has evolved is the process of bargaining and compromise, which requires a willingness on the part of disputants to make concessions to each other in order to get on with matters. It could be said that the opponents of an issue prefer to get half-a-loaf than to deadlock to the point that no one gets even a crumb. Moreover, since the decision arrived at through bargaining and compromise is not final, each side can hope that sometime in the future greater gains will be made, that further concessions can be forced and that there will be better opportunities to force those concessions.

To work, the process of bargaining and compromise requires several conditions. First, the proponents of an issue must be willing to surrender something. Their objectives cannot be absolute. Otherwise, there is no basis on which negotiations can take place.

Second, each side must have something of value to give the other. The number and kinds of valued objects in politics are almost limitless: promises of present or future support of other issues; the relaxation of opposition to the issue in question; special considerations for an important constituency; jobs, favors, or contracts; and the delivery of a voting bloc, to name a few. Depending on the proponent and the circumstances, each side has some valued objects but not others; some are available to bargain with and others are not. But, there must be a mutually useful exchange.

Third, the proponents must be willing to negotiate, whether face-to-face or through intermediaries. Thus, ideological, political, or personal differences must be secondary to the basic desire to find a mutually convenient position on a given issue at a given time at a reasonable price.

Bargaining and compromise is, then, another means by which conflict is channelled and controlled. More than that, however, it is a way in which diverse interests can accommodate one another. A politician seeking office will bargain with or act as a bargaining intermediary among blocs of voters and their leaders whose support he needs for election. Once in office, he will bargain with fellow officeholders, with pressure groups, with bureaucrats, and with party leaders to avoid being caught in an irreconcilable conflict and to create the base of support required for re-election.

Although the process of bargaining and compromise rarely produces a completely satisfactory solution for any of the participants, it is a device by which conflicting and competing interests can be committed to support of certain of one another's proposals, thus, despite the dispersal of power, enabling decisions to be made and results to be attained. The process has the additional effect of strengthening weak positions; a politician who might be totally defeated in open combat can, through bargaining and compromise, achieve at least part of his goals by trading on the time and effort it would take to defeat him.

Process Products

Although there are other elements of the American political process that could be included in a dominant view of the system, electoral politics, the rules of the game, the nonfinality of decisions, and bargaining and compromise are the most significant. They suggest a system based on logic and order, which prevents breakdowns in human relations by avoiding absolutist positions, and which provides for change, adjustment, and generalized sharing of power, or, at the least, widespread participation in the use of power. The system can also be characterized by its products—the results it achieves in a general or a specific sense. Describing its products can be as difficult as describing the system as a process. As already noted, there are really two sets of products that come out of the American system. One set consists of "substantive products," the actual programs of government and political activity; the other consists of "process products," conditions or circumstances that are the result of the processes. Process products tend to characterize every policy area and affect every program, which makes them worth examining first.

Incrementalism

Incrementalism is a consistent product of the political system. Major changes in policy and the evolution of policy commitments take place gradually. The great changes—such as emancipation, the welfare state, and the creation of a permanent defense establishment—although virtually forced by prevailing circumstances, were produced only by an intricate series of bargains and compromises. Incrementalism as a product of the system does not prevent change; it merely insures that change occurs slowly, each step being assimilated before the next is attempted. A system that stresses electoral politics, the dispersal of power, and bargaining would, of course, tend to conform to this pattern. The pressures of moving toward a modal distribution of public awareness and attitudes force even those who consider themselves to be leaders to operate on a one-step-at-a-time basis. Thus there are no abrupt shifts; even changing to a regime dedicated to innovation or retrenchment produces only incremental changes in public policies.

Multiple Access and Multiple Veto

Policy changes are incremental and few decisions are final because there are multiple points of access to the political system and multiple points of veto; in other words, points at which action can be initiated and points at which it can be stopped. The system of checks and balances built into the federal government is one factor. Congress may block the president, the president may block Congress, the Supreme Court may block both. There are other systems, too: the relationship between the upper and lower houses of Congress and between the committees (and subcommittees) within each; the relationship of the administrative agencies to the president, to Congress, and to each other. The pattern is repeated in state governments and in many of the 20,000 local governments that carry on more than one function of government. Often a state or local government can block federal action, and the federal government can force action upon states and localities.

Thus literally thousands of centers of power are available to those who want to initiate or stop action. It is easier to stop action than it is to initiate it, however. To initiate action, it is necessary to wend through a series of institutions. To block action requires setting up a stopping point at only one institution. Those who are fighting defensively, trying to prevent change, have an important advantage over those seeking to innovate.

However, the mere existence of multiple points of access and veto does provide the system with a degree of openness. Aggrieved citizens have a variety of alternatives—legislative, executive, administrative, and judicial, in local, state, and federal governments—open to them. They may not win, but they have a chance to fight for their goals and to seek a battleground that is favorable to them.

Multiple Allegiances

The multiple points of access and veto represent a wide variety of institutions, groups, and interests. They indicate, too, that many individuals have numerous separate allegiances: to their families, their local governments, their state governments, their national government, their jobs, their professions, their churches, and their friends. Only on occasion are all these allegiances really compatible, especially on political issues. Although individuals tend to seek out mutually compatible instrumental and identification groups, they are not always successful, having relatively limited opportunity structures in the quest. A person anxious to see his children's education improved is not always as anxious to see his local taxes increased; a university administrator eager to receive more government funds for his institution may be troubled by governmental emphasis on defense-related work; a person loyal to a political party may find its programs inadequate in terms of an environmental protection group to which he belongs. The dilemma is, of course, simply a matter of cross-pressures. Because of multiple allegiances the ties of group interests are weakened. Unable to avoid being cross-pressured, an individual is not apt to be single-mindedly devoted to any one interest.

Cross-pressuring is, on balance, accepted as a healthy characteristic of American politics. Like the rules of the game, it prevents politics from becoming too heated and from nurturing ideologues fanatically devoted to only one cause and willing to pursue it at any cost. Multiple allegiances also make compromise and bargaining possible. Since conflict is dampened and absolutist positions are avoided, each individual and group constantly makes new evaluations of the political situation and environment.

Stability and Flexibility

One of the most signal aspects of the political system in the United States is its stability. Although historians note various political "revolutions," such as the Jacksonian era, the Civil War, and the New Deal, the basic forms of American government, federal, state, and local, have changed little since 1789, and the processes by which these forms operate have changed even less. Whereas other nations experience periodic upheavals, consisting of violence, the rewriting of constitutions, and the rapid shift of power from one set of interests to another, incrementalism dominates the American pattern of handling change.

A stable political order has, of course, profound social, economic, and psychological rewards and benefits. Social classes, although perhaps made anxious by change, are not forced into cohesive groups to press for change or to fight it. Political stability helps to explain why Americans have never been as class conscious as most Europeans. For the economy, stability guarantees predictability and thus aids the entrepreneur in making capital investments, in making commitments to research and development, and in developing markets and financial sources to expand his enterprises. American corporations have been relatively free to grow without the threat of a sudden disruption of the civil order and the basic patterns of producer and consumer relations.

Psychologically, stability reduces individual and mass anxieties. The aura of confidence characteristic of Americans, underlying a large part of their social and economic order, is probably an individual psychological phenomenon; an American knows that the word "revolution" is more rhetoric than reality, that the American way of making revolutions is by slow change, by piecemeal combat in elections and legislatures, and by the gradual shifting of public opinion from one position to another. He knows comfortingly that, historically, redistribution of the wealth and benefits of society has rarely included the expropriation of the possessions of one interest to benefit another. An American, quite literally, does not expect to awake to find that a new regime has taken over the government overnight, or that a battalion of soldiers is fighting the navy in the streets, or that the local television station has been seized by a junta. Although his taxes increase, governmental restrictions cover more aspects of daily life, and policies change, these changes take place after long discussion and they rarely remain settled issues. Arguments of the New Deal were also arguments of Nixon's "New Revolution": pump-priming, deficit spending, the welfare system, aid to local government, and war and peace.

Stability is not only a condition but a necessity. In a complex social and economic system, in which economic interdependence has become the pattern, the consequences of discontinuities and disruptions are felt nationally. Through mass media, geographically remote disruption becomes immediate to vast audiences, creating psychological disturbance. Riots in California create anxiety in Virginia, which in turn gives rise to a more generalized fear and uncertainty. Although there is no logical connection between the president's health and the fluctuations of the stock market, a president's illness invariably leads to a decline in prices. Government as a source of information, funds, regulation, and symbolic performance, emphasizes the need for stability in political affairs.

There are other, subsidiary reasons for making stability a primary goal. Bureaucratization, by definition, is the search for routine methods to accomplish tasks. Not only government agencies, but corporations, unions, and educational institutions are bureaucracies. The flow of human beings, whether workers, consumers, students, or residents, requires accommodation and therefore predictability. The potential massed impact of people behaving in certain ways cries out for analysis, understanding, and reduction to predictable terms. For businessmen to cope with suppliers and markets, for government to handle planning and development goals, for universities to prepare for changes in enrollment, and for individuals to integrate and accommodate environmental change, stability must exist. The political system is not alone in providing for stability, but through its processes and products it is vital in guaranteeing that disruptions will not take place or, if they do, that an institution with power will handle them.

Emphasizing the stability of the system and its stabilizing influence, however, should not obscure the flexibility that exists. For one thing, the system is not perfectly articulated; there is "slack" in it. A change in one part does not produce immediate change in another; resistance to change in one part does not mean that all other parts will be equally resistant to change. More basic, perhaps, the processes of the system accommodate change. The electoral process provides for changes in leadership. The rules of the game allow agitators for change to press their causes. The process of bargaining and compromise presupposes change: it is a dialectical process by which divergent interests find solutions to problems.

Often, inconsistent goals and policies may exist hand in hand. Government encourages the elimination of environmental damage at the same time that it encourages the construction of more and more miles of pavement on which to drive air-polluting vehicles; a legislator fights for budget reductions at the same time that he attempts to increase expenditures for his district; one agency is charged with pursuing the means for disarmament while another is granted funds to build weapons of destruction. The examples suggest that inconsistencies are due less to the "irrationality" of politicians than to the capacity of the system to tolerate simultaneously competing and divergent interests.

Substantive Products

Aside from the process products, there are impressive substantive products that can be attributed to the American political system. For one, Americans live in a state of unparalleled prosperity. Although there are pockets of poverty, they become progressively smaller with each decade. The political system cannot claim full credit for what a naturally rich area produced or for what a vigorous economic system made use of, but it can be credited with the creation of a social environment in which the development of national resources and an economic system could dovetail.

Substantial steps have been taken to guarantee a reasonably equitable distribution of the nation's wealth through the regulatory and redistributive powers of government. Social security, medicare, public hospitals, public schools, public health programs, housing support (for both private and public development), employment programs, and support of physical mobility—all broaden the individual and collective opportunity structures of the nation's populace.

What has emerged is a highly literate society, whose members enjoy good health, long lives, and a fair degree of physical security. Although much is made of "crime in the streets," Americans have fought five wars in seven decades, and their own country has remained inviolate.

Large numbers of immigrants have been integrated into society—not without stress, certainly—but the Irish, Italians, Germans, Slavs, Jews, and Scandinavians have increasingly found social, economic, and political advancement more easily attainable. Discrimination exists, even toward the old minorities, but at a diminishing rate.

Obviously, the society is not without flaws, but the temptation to concentrate on its failures should not obliterate its achievements. Whether by luck, chance, divine guidance, or human intent, the American political system can be argued to have served its people well. To note the problems yet unsolved is, first, to acknowledge that they have been recognized and, second, to admit that humans have not yet achieved an earthly paradise. Present inadequacy is no proof of future failure in a system capable of preserving itself while maintaining sufficient flexibility to solve newly recognized problems.

The view of American politics presented in this chapter can be called "liberal pluralism." It assumes that power is widely dispersed and available for general participation. It holds that power must be assembled from diverse interests—dozens, or hundreds, or thousands of small power points—and that this can be done only through bargaining and compromise and in obedience to the rules of the game. Further, it stresses stability but with enough flexibility to accommodate change through incremental steps.

Embedded in this view are obviously important values: avoidance of violence, adherence to order and rational means, and the use of prescribed channels to bring about gradual change. If openness consists of recognizing the diversity and heterogeneity of interests and of those in power, then, according to this view, the American political system is an open system. Those impatiently seeking immediate and rapid change fail to realize that the price of such change is the concentration of power, together with the loss of the generalized participation of so many people and institutions. The system is capable of changing to meet the needs and desires of all Americans, assuming that they are willing to accept that the system in its turn makes demands upon them.

These demands will be discussed in another context later, but in brief they include: learning the system (that is, gaining the information needed to work within it); organizing; willingness to obey the rules of the game; willingness to bargain and compromise; recognizing that change occurs incrementally in order to protect the needs of others; and willingness to build political power by allying with others and by negotiating with a large number of highly dispersed powerholders. Competition is desirable, but it must be limited; change is good, but it must not affect the stability of the system.

Assuming that this is a reasonably fair picture of liberal pluralism, how many Americans actually subscribe to it? It is an almost impossible question to answer. High school and college textbooks, the columns of editorialists and correspondents, and scholarly analyses and criticisms attempt to provide the answer, but none tell us with any precision what exactly is in the minds of the public. Probably most Americans who think about their political system consider the dominant view to be what the system ought to be, even though it may fall short in some respects. Further, if one argues that belief must at least loosely fit reality in order for the reality to exist, then most Americans believe that their system does function according to this view, and, in fact, so it does.

Bibliography

Brogan, D. W. *Politics in America*. Garden City, N.Y.: Doubleday, 1960. One of the most useful examinations of American politics by an outside observer, in this case an Englishman.

Campbell, Angus, Phillip E. Converse, Warren E. Miller, and Donald E. Stokes. *The American Voter*. New York: Wiley, 1960. A classic study of the behavior of the voting public.

Dahl, Robert A. *Pluralist Democracy in the United States: Conflict and Consensus*. Chicago: Rand McNally, 1967. This study, by one of America's most respected defenders of the pluralist perspective, is invaluable for understanding the liberal pluralist position.

Free, Lloyd A., and Hadley Cantril. *The Political Beliefs of Americans*. New York: Simon & Schuster, 1968.

Key, V. O., Jr. *Public Opinion and American Democracy*. New York: Knopf, 1964. A thoughtful examination of the nature of representation and the relationship of public attitudes to governmental institutions and performance.

Rose, Arnold. *The Power Structure*. New York: Oxford University Press, 1967. Despite its title, this book is a deliberate effort to refute those who believe that America is run by an elite.

Sayre, Wallace S., and Herbert Kaufman. *Governing New York City.* New York: Russell Sage Foundation, 1960. Although a study of only one city, this work most clearly lays out the basic method of analysis and findings of pluralist political science.

Sorauf, Frank J. *Party Politics in America.* Boston: Little, Brown, 1968.

Truman, David B. *The Governmental Process.* New York: Knopf, 1960. The most widely used and the most sophisticated explanation of pluralism.

Twelve

The Political System: A Minority View

Just as there are many dominant views of the American political system, so there are many minority views. Generally, these minority perspectives have several themes in common. One theme is that the pluralist viewpoint is culturally biased: it is a view of the system that, if true, is true for only a part of American society. Second, the dominant view is rife with what may be called "myths," hoped-for conditions that do not exist and never have existed. And, third, the pluralist view stresses empty forms or processes while ignoring the results of those processes. It should be noted that these criticisms are not only made by members of minorities; in fact, they are often generated by those who are firmly established in the dominant institutions, such as Floyd Hunter, C. Wright Mills, John Kenneth Galbraith, and Paul Goodman. Moreover, some minority group leaders are more sympathetic to the pluralist interpretation of American politics than others. Again, it must be stressed that the view presented here is only *one* view, but it is useful to examine it because it helps to show that an important subjective difference exists concerning the nature of politics and what is to be done to achieve effective action through the political process.

The Cultural Bias of Power

It will be recalled that one pluralist interpretation of the distribution of power holds that power is dispersed among many individuals and centers, whether voters, officeholders, or institutions. From a minority point of view, it can be argued that such an interpretation is at best unrealistic, at worst a deliberate fraud.

The Power Curve

If it can be assumed that power is actually held by those who seem to hold it—that is, by elected officials, appointed officials, party officials, interest group leaders, and other individuals—it is possible to illustrate graphically the major concentration of power in United States society. Some of the positions of power are private or quasi-private, such as corporate executive positions, union leadership positions, and interest group leadership positions. Some are public, that is, public office or party positions. Obviously, there are wide variations in the amount of power that accrues to these various positions. A leader of a small union local is hardly as powerful as the president of the United Auto Workers. A mayor of a small town is hardly comparable to the president of the United States. But the greatest amount of power, whether in private or public positions, is held by only a few.

Individual voters, minor civil servants, small businessmen, and local lawyers are at the lower points of the power curve. They possess power, but it does not equal that held by the giants at the highest point of the curve. Similar graphs could be used to illustrate the distribution of power among the various classifications included in the power curve; that is, federal, state, and local governments, corporations, unions, and so forth. The distribution of power within a family could be graphed in the same way. In each case, the curve illustrates that the higher positions, and therefore the greatest amount of power, are held by a small number of people; the number of people increases as the amount of power they have decreases.

Who are these powerholders? In addition to the approximately 522,000 elected officeholders in the nation at large, there are 12,000,000 civil servants (whose positions rank from high to low within federal, state, and local governments) and an estimated 10,000 party officials (two county chairmen—one for each of the major parties—for each of the 3,000 counties in the country, plus cochairmen, city party officials, and minor party officials). Although the numbers are difficult to assess accurately, perhaps we should allow for about 3,000,000 pressure-group leaders,

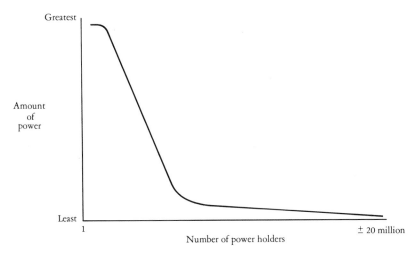

The power curve: the number having positions of power increases as the amount of power they have decreases.

including those who head corporations, labor unions, and other national, state, and local associations. The total is approximately 16,000,000. Even if we add another 25 percent, which is a generous allowance for any oversights, we get no more than 20,000,000. In other words, out of a total population of 204,000,000 only 10 percent can be called powerholders.

It could be argued that these 20,000,000 hold power largely by the consent of others. If so, what are the criteria for obtaining that consent? Those who hold positions of power generally have certain characteristics in common. They are white, male, over 35 years of age, middle-class, and fairly well educated. The greater the amount of power they hold, the more pronounced these characteristics are. Those women, blacks, Indians, Mexican-Americans, or young people who have positions of power are at the lower points of the power curve. It is difficult for anyone to move toward the top, but especially for minority members. This is true for those who hold public positions as well as those who hold private and quasi-private positions.

If a position on the curve does require the consent of others (and not all require the consent of the electorate or anything approximating the electorate), there appears to be a consensus on the qualifications for admission to the charmed upper reaches of that curve. This consensus may be the product of a number of circumstances. Those who occupy the higher positions on the curve *are* in positions of power, which includes the power to recruit and advance other people.

Those who are in possession of power share many of the same values, predispositions, and attitudes. Certainly, they may strongly disagree on any number of matters. They compete with each other for certain benefits and prerogatives (including advancement on the power curve), but since most of them share the same cultural background and have roughly equivalent educational and income status, their agreements will inevitably be more fundamental than their disagreements. It is they who have written the rules of the game; it is they who share common attitudes about the political system and its purposes; and it is they who are in a position to enforce the rules and to impose their values.

Their commonality is what produces the "politics of irrelevance." The members of the dominant groups well situated on the power curve can discuss the merits of a new space program while children go hungry; they can debate the validity of more war-related research grants to institutions of higher learning while students protest against the war in Indochina; and they can worry about unrest in the high schools while dozens of people die of narcotics addiction each week. Outer space, defense, and high school unrest are subjects that are relevant to those situated at the higher points of the power curve simply because they are drawn from a limited portion of the population and because they know little and care even less about matters of concern to the rest of the population. In fact, they find it hard to imagine why others cannot be as fascinated with their interests as they themselves are, and they engage in enormous efforts to generate an equal interest within the whole population.

The Power Structure

To assume that power is shared, even unequally, by 20 million individuals, however, is further than many critics of pluralism are willing to go. Many argue that the "power structure" or "power elite" does not consist of 20 million people, but of a great many less than that.

Although the expression "power structure" is as often abused as it is used accurately, frequently being employed to refer to everyone except the user and his immediate supporters, in its more rigorous sense it applies to those who really wield power in contrast with those who are in positions of apparent power. According to those who hold that the American political system is nothing more than a power structure, those officials who have apparent power really do not have it and are totally dependent on others for support, financing, and instructions. They are pawns—the front men of those who are actually in power. Occasionally, the actual members of the power structure may be visible to the public eye, but their preference is for anonymity, quiet control, and the reality of power rather than the vulgar public trappings associated with elected or high appointed office.

Membership in the power elite is determined by a position in the nexus of economic power. Although not all corporate executives or board members are necessarily members of the power structure, the individuals who are members are most often top-ranking corporate executives. Wealth alone is insufficient. Artists, performers, and individual entrepreneurs could have the money without having the corporate organization, the availability of legal talent, lobbyists, public-relations personnel, technical, "inside" information, command over jobs and services, and control over the flow of goods and products that membership in the power structure commands and requires. Members of the power elite sit on the boards of universities and multiple corporations, constitute the governing bodies of newspapers, radio stations, and television stations, are the financiers of politicians and pressure groups, and are the men to whom presidents, governors, and mayors give attentive deference.

In addition to being drawn from the same social class and possessing the same values, the members of the power structure, in many cases, know each other. Their primary purpose is to expand their interlocking corporate empires, not only nationally but internationally. They view most social and welfare legislation with equanimity and even magnanimity, because in most cases the limited programs passed by the politicians under their control dampen discontent and draw attention away from the more important questions of tax legislation, corporate regulation, international trade, and the defense industry.

The crucial point, however, is that political power, as well as social and economic power, is concentrated in their hands. They determine not only how issues are to be resolved but which issues will even be raised. Their power is not total, although it is greater than that ever vested in any single group. The primary function of the law enforcement agencies, from the Federal Bureau of Investigation to the local sheriff, is to protect the property and interests of the elite from incursions by the people; the major missions of the Defense and State departments are to defend their overseas investments and purchase their goods through military contracts; and the major function of the political process is to act as a cover for their activities.

The principal problem facing the power structure is keeping the political process in hand. As long as voters agree that elections are important, as long as rebellious groups can be convinced to play by the rules of the game, and as long as there is a general faith that politics is substance rather than shadow, there is no problem. Popular urges can be channelled into efforts that have little or no effect on the power structure itself. On occasion, however, there are threats; the people break out of the mold developed for them and select leaders who pass legislation or advocate positions that endanger the interests of the power structure. In general, however, the power elite has managed to absorb these rebellions. The labor movement, for example, was contained and eventually controlled by bringing it into corporate management, by seeing to it that the movement adopted a corporate form, and finally by guaranteeing that labor concentrated on materialistic goals rather than basic political issues.

The power structure can stave off most piecemeal threats simply because it possesses the money, power, jobs, and opportunities to buy off all but the most dedicated opponents. Those it cannot buy off, it can isolate through its public-relations apparatus working through the mass media to control public opinion. In the last analysis, opponents can be imprisoned or killed by law enforcement agencies that the elite control.

The Cultural Elite

A more fundamental view of the American political system is that, whether American politics is dominated by a power curve or by a power structure, it operates with the tacit consent of the greater proportion of middle-class American society. America is a racist and sexist society—a society that rejoices in youth and envies youth's advantages but refuses to entrust the young with power, responsibility, or the opportunity to develop beyond a preset pattern. Whether Americans have been habituated to discrimination by their leaders, have inherited it with their Puritan Anglo-Saxon traditions, or have evolved it as a product of rampant materialism, it can be argued that the cultural bias exists. The cultural categories leading to discrimination are so deeply rooted in the national and individual psyche that they are the conscious or unconscious basis of every religious, social, economic, or political institution. In this respect, it can be argued that the power bias is no more than a reflection of the attitudes of the majority of the populace. Although many—perhaps most—Americans agree that blacks, Indians, students, women, Mexican-Americans, and Puerto Ricans should have greater economic security and benefits, they hold the reservation that these people are not really "fit" to make decisions on their own behalf. They should instead look to leaders drawn from the "better" classes who know best how to organize and work within the system. The minorities should rely on the system itself to rectify wrongs. There is, in other words, a cultural distinction based on those fit to govern and those who are not. The latter must depend on the paternalism, charity, and compassion of the former, because a minority's efforts would be doomed to defeat from its own incompetence.

This analysis of the distribution of American power argues that Americans have extended the same attitude into foreign affairs. The extension is demonstrated by the irresistible American urge to make the world safe for democracy (American-style) and to tell the Japanese, Koreans, Indochinese, Latin Americans, and Africans how to organize their governments and how to model themselves upon the American pattern. The forebear of the new imperialism is the missionary spirit that carried military and economic imperialism into Asia, Africa, and every other continent of the globe.

Members of the dominant institutions resist any transfer of power to minorities not only because it would mean a loss of power for themselves, but also because they feel that the minorities could not exercise power wisely or well. The minority member is told to imitate the dominant pattern, to be patient, and to look to a future time when he may be given a small share of political and economic power, after, of course, he has succeeded in becoming an exact replica of the members of the dominant society. The black who is an "oreo" (black on the outside but white inside), the student who obeys the rules and memorizes what his professors tell him, the woman who accepts without question the "female role," the "good" Indian, the Mexican-American who learns to speak English in a midwestern accent—all will be rewarded for learning to be "responsible," that is, to surrender themselves to the dominant culture. The others, in failing to imitate the dominant pattern, are not yet ready. The struggle, then, is really between cultures, in which the dominant culture possesses the specialized instruments of power—government—and uses them by means of education, law enforcement, welfare programs, employment opportunities, and housing and urban renewal programs, among others, to impose its values on minorities and to attempt to mold the minorities to the dominant pattern.

Politics and the distribution of power are important because through them the dominant influence is most directly brought to bear on the minorities; but, in many respects, the precise distribution of power within the dominant part of society is irrelevant. That distribution, whatever it is, more or less suits the dominants. The real issue is whether it is to be used against minorities or redesigned so that minorities may exercise power within their own spheres of existence.

The Class Interpretation

Often, a class analysis is used to describe the power-bias in American society. In this interpretation, all minorities plus the numerous impoverished whites are a proletariat, a working class and underclass that continues to be exploited for the enrichment of the bourgeoisie. Because political and social systems are no more than artifacts of the economic system, the present power curve is bound to represent a middle-class bias. Although blacks and poor whites, Mexican-Americans and Indians, and other minorities may distrust and fear each other, this results from the age-old bourgeois tactic of dividing the working class to prevent its unification and the development of a true class consciousness.

Working people, including lower-paid white-collar workers, are manipulated and propagandized to believe that if they subscribe to the present system, they will, like a Horatio Alger hero, be rewarded for their efforts. Their fears and insecurity are played upon in an effort to convince them that the threat to their existence comes from other oppressed peoples rather than from those who really exploit them. They thus focus their resentment on blacks and Puerto Ricans who are seeking employment instead of on those in corporate offices and banks who are the real source of their economic bondage to low-paying jobs, mortgages, installment payments, and high taxes. The false gods of nationalism and patriotism are evoked to convince the people that they should support imperialistic ventures abroad and to persuade the young that they should die compliantly in far-off jungles.

The principal differences between a class analysis and a power-structure analysis is that in the latter the exploiters are found to be far less numerous than they are in the former. Further, the power structure is more politically motivated than the ruling classes of a class interpretation.

The power curve, the power structure, the cultural elite, and the class interpretation are by no means mutually exclusive and are often combined in various admixtures. They possess a common set of theses. First, the liberal pluralist view of the distribution of power is both inaccurate and deceptive. There are no real multiple points of access, nor is there any generalized participation, at least not where power is really exercised. Only a tiny proportion of the American population can exercise any real control over what shapes their lives. Second, of this tiny proportion, the beleaguered minorities are at the lowest echelon. Depending on the analysis used, the minorities are either at the lowest point of the power curve, automatically excluded from the power structure, the targets of the cultural bias, or the most exploited by the ruling classes. Third, because they are powerless, minorities can be and are ignored by the dominant institutions, except when they can be "objectified," that is, used as objects or instruments of a dominant interest—for example, as scabs in times of labor unrest or as symbols of "lawlessness" so that society as a whole can be under greater control. The political system is so biased that those who are presently powerless will tend to remain so, especially if they depend upon the good intentions of those who are powerholders within the system.

The Myths of Pluralism

Aside from the unverified faith of the pluralist in the dispersal of power, it can be argued that a number of other myths cling to the dominant view of the political system. From a minority perspective, the myths are important because they prevent Americans from perceiving and correcting the flaws in their system. More important, when minority members subscribe to the myths, they, too, are prevented from taking effective action on their own behalf.

The Myth of Democratic Elections

Because electoral politics dominate the pluralist model of the political system, elections must be a means for the dispersal of power. From a dissenting position, they serve no such function. The electoral process is an oligopoly of the two great political parties, with an occasional third party thrown in to confuse matters. With fairly limited, elitist machinery the parties select the candidates between whom the public must choose. Almost invariably these candidates are spokesmen for well-established interests occupying the highest positions on the power curve. Although the winner is required to have gained the consent of at least a plurality of the voters in an election, the voters themselves confront a structured choice, which offers them very little choice. Conceded that primaries and nominating conventions introduce some degree of competition for candidacies, the candidates who offer themselves are usually of limited representativeness. And, those entitled to vote in primaries are registered party voters; those at the conventions are the party faithfuls, petty officeholders, favor-seekers, and financial contributors.

The electoral system appears to be open but in reality is controlled, limited, and structured, with the opportunities going to non-controversial, long-faithful conformists to the status quo. The refusal in 1964 of the Democratic National Convention to seat all but a token representation of the delegation of the Mississippi Freedom Democratic party, the battle in the streets of Chicago in 1968 while the convention choice was controlled indoors, and the stranglehold of the Nixon-Thurmond alliance over the Republican National Convention in the same year are only the more overt examples of a process firmly embedded in national, state, and local politics.

The myth distorts reality even further, however. Although it is common to stress the importance of each individual's vote in pluralist mythology, only the most arrant optimist can be convinced that his specific vote matters. National, state, and large city elections require the aggregation of votes for them to have any significance; a vote must be a part of a larger bloc directed toward some specific purpose. Otherwise, individual votes are the mere random distribution of personal idiosyncrasies and as such can be regarded lightly by the politicians. It is a function of the parties to prevent such randomness; but to admit the need for the parties is to admit that power is not dispersed among the voters but shared between the party organizations.

Within the context of the party organizations, the important power wielders are either the party machines, which deliver a mass of supine voters to whatever candidate is most attractive to the bosses, or the great pressure groups–the unions, corporations, and farm organizations–which provide the voting blocs, the money, and the organization to fuel the party apparatus.

Under examination, the voter as a center of power begins to fade, as some pluralists would admit. More to the point, the idea that there is a correlation between the desires of the people and the performance of their leaders also begins to vanish when it is recognized that individual preferences are structured on a two-choice basis: this nominee or that one, this party or that one. If there are no basic differences between the parties or their nominees on any given issue, no choice exists at all. If both parties choose to ignore the aspirations of a minority, as they did those of blacks after Reconstruction, the minority is effectively disfranchised, whether it possesses the vote or not.

The Myth of Nonviolence

One of the most important–and attractive–features of the pluralist view is that the political system is orderly and pacific. For reasons of shared values and mutual self-interest, the participants play by the rules of the game, voluntarily surrendering power when defeated, winning power by appeals to reason or reasoned self-interest, and eschewing the use of force. Competition is fierce, but it is fettered.

From a minority standpoint, however, this view is a myth. At the intersection of dominant and minority values, the political battlefield is literally strewn with corpses. For all but about seven decades of the 350 years of contact between whites and Indians, the relationship has been that of warfare. The Bourbon Restoration in the South was accomplished by violence and threats of violence against Negroes, and the pattern created then was continued in the widespread use of lynching well into the twentieth century. The civil rights movement had its landmarks in the bodies of black and white workers, the clubs and dogs of the police, and the bombing and burning of churches and schools. Kent State University, Jackson State University, Southern University, and elsewhere give evidence of the consequences of student revolt. And these are only the most famous, overt instances of violence. Jailings, beatings, threats, harassment, insults, and humiliations are the chronic currency of minority-dominant relations. It can be argued in response that, first, many of these instances were unsanctioned, and, second, that they occur only when the system is placed under unusually severe stress. The first rebuttal, aside from being empirically incorrect, can be interpreted to mean that members of the dominant culture obey the rules of the game only in relations with each other; the second, that the rules of the game will be ignored if there is any threat to dominant power.

As researchers have shown, the American political system is far more violent than it pretends. Aside from the individual, private acts of violence, Americans have been at war, often with several peoples simultaneously, from colonialization to the end of the Philippine Insurrection. And, in the six decades since, they have fought in four major wars. A system could conceivably be warlike in its foregn affairs but pacific in its domestic politics; again, the record does not bear this out. Until well into the twentieth century, it was common practice to win control of voting places with bands of contending (and armed) musclemen. Rioting has been a typical American response to social and political stress. The use of the police and the army was not unique to Chicago in 1968, but has been resorted to regularly throughout this century to stamp out labor unrest and unpopular political causes.

A realistic interpretation of the pluralist model, then, is that the rules of the game apply only to competition among those who occupy the higher positions on the power curve. For those who attempt to gain a position on the curve, the rules are suspended, except when they are used as rhetorical devices to show how minorities refuse to participate in the system in an orderly fashion.

Multiple Access and Multiple Veto

The pluralist faith that the American system by virtue of its decentralization provides for orderly change and stability through multiple points of access and veto is undercut by the reality of a system that frustrates change by its emphasis on the veto. Repeatedly, progressive legislation is diluted by the baronial committee chairmen. Once passed in watered-down form, it is consigned to a bureaucracy that neither presses issues nor forces compliance from their state and local counterparts. Change may occur, but it is so slow and painful and won at such a cost that often its benefits are outstripped by events. After 16 years or longer, school integration began to gain a foothold in the South; but at that point, the number of blacks in the South was equalled by the number elsewhere in the country, and it became clear that northern schools were less integrated than southern schools. Even when "concessions" to minority interests are granted, they are made so grudgingly that the moral, if not the substantive, effect is lost. The reform of the welfare system was couched in terms calculated to imply that most recipients had been cheating and needed to be flushed out to force them to go to work.

Access is available to those who would exercise a veto; but access for those desiring change is reduced or even prohibited by the existence of the multiplicity of veto points. Incrementalism, as a consequence, becomes a snare. It assumes that the political system *should* accommodate only minor, gradual changes. What it does, however, is guarantee that the political system lags behind the needs and aspirations of important segments of the population, thereby breeding anger, alienation, and pressure to seek means of redress.

Bargaining and Compromise

A good part of the difficulty of the pluralist system lies in the central process of that system, that of bargaining and compromise, which in theory permits change to take place without disrupting or overwhelming the political order. As a process, it is dependent on its central conditions: that interests are willing to bargain, that they have mutually valued objects to exchange, and that they are able to bargain. The pluralist assumes that anyone or any group can find these conditions fulfilled in the political arena. A minority group leader, however, may find that his opponent does not want to deal with the minority and spurns any offer made. Further, the minority group may have nothing to offer that is of value to the opposing party. Consequently, the minority group leader will be excluded from the bargaining process.

Bargaining requires near parity between the protagonists; compromise requires that both can yield something. But minorities are not equal to dominant institutions and groups, and often whatever a minority group must yield is more precious to it than to the group to which it is offered. For a black group, for example, to make concessions on low-income housing projects may be terribly costly, perhaps forcing some people to go without decent shelter or to live in newly created ghettos. These costs may be of little interest to the dominant group to which the concessions are made; this group may even be indifferent, knowing that it can block the projects by other means if necessary.

The central process of the pluralist political system, then, although eminently reasonable to those with power who are seeking to enhance it, is defeating and frustrating to those without power. The latter are asked to participate in a process in which they cannot and then are reviled because they fail to do so.

It is often argued in rebuttal that any grouping that is able to move to group status can act as a swing bloc, or can even form a third party. As a tactic, this is capable of results, but it also has its traps. The tactic depends on a number of circumstances, including the opportunity afforded by divisions within the dominant groups, the willingness of one or more dominant groups to deal with the minority, and the absence of any risk that the minority will be drawn into a battle that is peripheral to its needs and aspirations.

Procedural Versus Substantive Democracy

The pluralist interpretation of American democracy can be criticized for bringing to the world of politics the laissez-faire school of economics. "The invisible hand of self-interest" is expected to motivate men to contend for their respective goals and to create a set of mutually dependent relationships, in which the quest for votes and the process of bargaining and compromise act as the functional equivalents of the pressures of the market place. Both economic and political laissez-faireism suffer from the same problem: differential levels of power. The political monopolist or oligopolist, like his economic equivalent, is less a captive of the marketplace than a shaper of it. The assumption that the needs of the citizen will be satisfied, if the process is preserved and if a kind of political supply and demand is allowed to function unhampered, is based more on hope than on result.

The difficulty, then, with the pluralist model is that it concentrates on process while ignoring the results of the process. If the system is stable, if groups compete with each other for political advantage in an atmosphere of orderliness, and if elections are held periodically, then ultimately all will come out right—so the pluralist believes. The minority viewpoint disagrees with this optimistic assessment of the political system. The basic assumption of pluralism—that all men have equal political opportunity structures or, if they do not, the negative barriers are removed—is incorrect. Substantive democracy is as essential as procedural democracy, and it may be a prerequisite of procedural democracy. That is, minority members lack jobs, capital, and numbers. Faced with discrimination, limited opportunity structures, and a political system geared to the values and attitudes of the affluent members of the dominant segment of society, who are willing to use force to preserve those values, they lack the prerequisites to operate successfully within the system. In effect, the conditions that create deprivation must be corrected before the system can work in the way that the pluralists would have it work; but since it does not work in that way *now,* the conditions of deprivation are improved only slightly on an absolute scale and even less on a relative scale each decade. Procedural democracy is dependent on substantive democracy, but the present conformation of the former is a deterrent to the achievement of the latter.

Certainly, the minority view presented here is a vigorous dissent from the dominant view presented in the preceding chapter, but how widespread this minority view is remains unclear. How accurately does it assess the American political system? There is no satisfactory answer. However, the validity of a viewpoint depends on one's position in the political system. Some Americans have no public power at all and may have very little private power; the very young, those living in such institutions as mental hospitals, prisons, and homes for the aged are obvious examples. They can exert some power, in the sense of imposing their wills on their immediate environments, but it is circumscribed, dependent, and conditional. For those who do possess power, there are obvious differences in kind and amount. The quantification of power is difficult. For example, there seems to be no way of determining who has more power—the president of the United States, the president of the United Auto Workers, or the president of U.S. Steel. Any answer would have to be so qualified as to render it meaningless. But there are significant differences between the power of the president of the United States and that of a file clerk in city hall or between the power of a general commanding a combat division and that of a sanitation worker. An indication of the amount of power held by each may be obtained by focusing on their failures and difficulties. It is even possible to show how the president's goals can be frustrated by a minor bureaucrat; but, on balance, the person having the greatest amount of power, which is indicated by the highest point of the power curve, causes more things to happen or stops more things from happening, according to his wishes, than the person having an amount of power indicated by the lowest point.

Those who occupy positions at the lowest point feel the effects of the power exercised singly or collectively by those at the highest point, with no assurance that they have had any influence on producing those effects. Whether power can be objectively measured or not, subjectively, one has a sense of more or less power.

Minorities fall somewhere at the lower end of the curve; they may have more power than their spokesmen often seem to believe, or they may have less. The reality fluctuates from time to time and from setting to setting, to say nothing of minority to minority. To minorities, however, the system often seems remote, unreachable, and arbitrary. From their relatively powerless positions, they can see only how inaccessible the positions of great power are. To those who occupy those positions, the minority attitude may seem to be perverse or even ignorant.

Bibliography

Baran, Paul A., and Paul M. Sweezey. *Monopoly Capital: An Essay on the American Economic and Social Order*. New York: Monthly Review Press, 1966. A Marxist analysis of American society.

Bazelon, David. *Power in America: The Politics of the New Class*. New York: New American Library, 1967. A thoughtful exploration of changing power relationships in America, with a heavy bias toward the "power elite" perspective.

Galbraith, John Kenneth. *The New Industrial State*. Boston: Houghton Mifflin, 1967.

Gettleman, Marvin E., and David Mermelson, eds. *The Great Society Reader: The Failure of American Liberalism*. New York: Vintage, 1967. A valuable collection of readings that brings together in once place most of the criticisms of American liberalism.

Hayden, Tom. *Rebellion and Repression*. New York: Meridian, 1969.

Jacobs, Paul, and Saul Landau. *The New Radicals: A Report with Documents*. New York: Vintage, 1966. An excellent review of the militant and radical organizations in existence at the time this book was written, with the added advantage of the original manifestos, policy statements, and major writings coming from those groups.

Kariel, Henry S. *The Decline of American Pluralism*. Stanford: Stanford University Press, 1961.

McCoy, Charles A., and John Playford, eds. *Apolitical Politics: A Critique of Behavioralism*. New York: Crowell, 1967. A collection of essays attacking the liberal pluralist view of politics and political science.

Mills, C. Wright. *The Power Elite*. New York: Oxford University Press, 1959. The famous study that has influenced a generation of scholars and activists.

Thirteen
Minorities and the Politics of Access

The pluralist model of American politics outlines what is often called "the politics of access." In the American system, a politics of access assumes that the major institutions of power respond to outside or competing pressures. The president, governors, mayors, legislators, bureaucrats, and even judges are vulnerable to tactics based on organization, numbers, money, and information. Anyone willing to put these tactical necessities together can expect to have his wishes fulfilled through the political process. Homeowners know that to fight the incursion of apartment buildings or public housing into their neighborhoods, they must organize, hire an attorney, hold protest meetings, write petitions, appear at public hearings, and bombard public officials with threats, pleas, telephone calls, and letters. The directors of corporations know that they can best defend their interests through a trade association, campaign contributions, lobbying, institutional advertising, and skillful contacts with policy-makers.

Members of the dominant culture expect to be heard if they are concerned enough to make an effort; and they expect to have the means to make themselves heard and therefore to exert power within the range of their interests. Whether the expectation of being able to wield power is justified is another matter. Certainly, not all dominant groups and institutions always win. They may be defeated by more powerful efforts; their organizations may be split by dissension, out-maneuvered tactically, or even ignored by powerful governmental figures who draw their strength from other power bases.

One of the major differences, however, between dominant groups and minority groups is the degree to which victory can be realistically expected, and this difference in expectation explains the differing perceptions of the political system contained in a dominant view and a minority view. Minority groups do play the "politics of access," but their efforts are attended by severe problems that influence strategic choices and have given birth to a new set of tactics.

Problems in Building an Organization

Roughly speaking, organizations are built from groups. Actually, group and organization may appear simultaneously, and an organization may be a holding company for a number of groups that find it mutually convenient to operate under a single apparatus, either because of historical circumstances or because the groups find themselves drawn together to cope with certain specific problems. Once created, an organization can become the framework for the interactions that produce new groups.

The essential part of an organization, its "apparatus," is a means of continuing the organization's existence through membership recruitment, the keeping of records, planning for the future, and the accumulation of resources for distribution to present and future members. It includes a "secretariat" or a "bureaucracy" for conducting these essential activities, which in turn requires specialization, division of labor, and planning. There are rules, standards, and regulations by which the organization records its experience and guarantees that members fulfill their tasks. There is a means of deciding policy, which includes choosing leadership, allocating benefits within the group, and choosing a posture toward membership expectations and their fulfillment. In all these respects, an organization is an advanced stage of group development, implicit in all groups (even purely social groups), and represents a conscious effort to convert a group into a permanent body capable of undertaking instrumental functions in an efficient fashion. It is this efficiency that makes organizations so important.

Many of the problems associated with minority groups are carried over into the efforts to build minority group organizations. In most cases, these problems are directly associated with and probably stem from the pattern of deprivation the minority has experienced.

Lack of Focal Institutions

A problem that minority groups face in building political organizations is the lack of institutions from which to move into political activity. In the dominant segment of society, corporations, labor unions, stable neighborhoods (and the concurrent identification groups) are focal institutions that can be converted for purposes of political pressure. Since, moreover, the dominant groups have shaped the political institutions of the country, these institutions tend to be responsive to demands and pressures from dominant interests.

Minorities are not so generously endowed, however. Blacks belong to a large number of groups, and the black churches have served well as focal institutions for black political activity. Indian tribal councils are political institutions deliberately designed for governing the reservation Indians through their participation. Student councils, in a weaker form, theoretically serve the same purpose for students.

Women have long had the League of Women Voters and various other reform-oriented groups, together with identification groups, as potential political pressure groups. Mexican-Americans have various social-service organizations, as well as politically oriented groups. The problem is not that of number of groups, therefore, but is more basic.

Minority organizations face two fundamental difficulties as institutions for political action. The first is that of role. Almost all occupy an ambivalent position in relation to their constituencies and to the dominant culture. Is the black church expected to teach the "white man's Christianity," to generate a culturally appropriate black theology, or to use whatever theology is available as a means to political change and action? That Martin Luther King turned to the teachings of Gandhi for much of his political and philosophical inspiration suggests some of the problems associated with "pure" Christianity. And, the problem of a cultural point of reference is more than theoretical. As early as the 1930s, a black researcher discovered disenchantment and cynicism among younger blacks toward their churches and spiritual leaders. The problem is not new: a teaching that emphasizes the postponement of present gratification in order to achieve future salvation can be interpreted as an invitation to political submissiveness. In some cases, whites have found black ministers to be useful means to this end.

Predominantly black universities face the same sort of predicament. Many have been accused of teaching young blacks to be "good niggers," as defined by white organizations and scholarship. Although conceivably serving extremely useful instrumental functions, many may fail to serve functions of identification and, in fact, may help to create identity crises in their students, leaving them confused about their blackness and even ashamed of it.

Other organizations that are potential focal institutions have similar problems. They may serve as safety valves—arenas for "sand box politics" in which minority members feel free to exercise their political muscles on each other but without affecting their environment. Student governing bodies, women's organizations, and tribal councils are all vulnerable to this criticism. The form exists, but the real role is nonexistent. These organizations fill niches left empty by the larger political forces, instead of contesting other power groups. To say that they are useless is too harsh a judgment; but to argue that they are designed to exercise substantial power is certainly unrealistic.

The second problem has been summarized in the statement, "One of the perpetual problems of Mexican-American organizations has been the inadequacy of resources, both money and staff" (Grebler, Moore, and Guzman, 1970, p. 546). Deprivation means inadequate resources and the groups and organizations that act for deprived minorities have terribly limited resources.

The consequences are various. Minority group organizations can attempt to depend on their own group members and the invisible members within the minority for contributions of time and money. The limitations are obvious, however. They can turn to invisible members within the dominant culture, those who sympathize with the group's goals; but the risk is that they must then shape their goals, strategies, and tactics to please their contributors, or at least to avoid frightening them. Or they can attempt to find alternative economic bases, either by establishing minority-owned businesses, seeking governmental grants, or engaging in some form of illegal activity. Building alternative economic bases is valuable because it serves two ends simultaneously: it relieves economic deprivation while providing a resource base for politics. But, of course, to do so requires organization, skill, and economic or political success. Devising a means of broadening an organization's resource base and thereby its opportunity structure is one of the important strategic and tactical tasks that minority groups face.

The problems of role and resources are separable but related. An organization does what it can with the resources it has at hand; and what it does must always be with an eye to how its resource base is affected. Every organization always thinks it needs more resources and struggles to increase its resource pool. Minority organizations feel the pinch more intensely, and, like individuals, they are tempted to be prudent rather than to risk what little they have.

Group Problems

It has already been pointed out that few if any groupings are homogenous; they are structured by geography, age, income levels, occupations, and other salient characteristics. It is, for example, tempting to assume that students as a minority grouping are free from many of these divisive influences; they are all of roughly the same age, are engaged presumably in a common quest, and probably have very similar social and economic backgrounds. However, graduate students can be ten years older than undergraduates; professional or liberal arts majors produce what are in effect occupational divisions; and today actual or available incomes probably vary more than ever before.

These differences can be carried over into groups and organizations. An attempt to reduce the potential for divisions by restricting an organization to a homogeneous membership automatically limits the number of members and thereby further limits the resource base. To build the organization on a broader base, however, is to risk incorporating factionalism, dissension, and differences that can either destroy the organization altogether or reveal it to be so divided that it is unable to act effectively in the political arena.

Circumstances can make minority self-awareness sufficiently salient to override these differences, and a function of the organization's leadership is to emphasize or even to create such circumstances. That task requires skill, however, and the opportunity to act may not readily present itself.

Minority members may recognize their status; they may even feel that "something ought to be done," but there are always some members unwilling to challenge authority to get something done. From fear, past experiences, or simply so-cialization, they have learned the habit of deference, of refusing to make challenges or initiating action. Rather, they would prefer to let the initiative stay with the dominant groups.

From a political standpoint, the habit of deference discourages attempts to create a workable organization. Joining or supporting an organization requires a willingness to court dominant disapproval. Joining or supporting an organization that prospective members *know* will meet with disapproval is even harder, because of the fear that those with power will use it to punish activists. As a result, some minority members will not only refuse to join an activist organization, but will even oppose it, in the hope of either pleasing dominant members or preventing the activists from rocking the boat.

The habit of deference has even more subtle effects, however. One of them is the unconscious desire to imitate those to whom deference is given: the student who tries to match his professors in dignity and erudition, the professional woman who tries to be "mannish," the black or Indian who tries to pass as white. For the minority member, the mimicry is a form of protective coloration and a means of staving off deprivation by flattery. In organizations, imitation can be an expression of collective insecurities and self-hatreds or a hopeful attempt to reproduce the same success that dominant groups have. Minority groups may adopt the forms, constitutions, rules of procedure, and apparatus characteristic of dominant organizations, whether appropriate to the situation and the group goals or not. On its face, there is no problem if the apparatus is in fact appropriate. Often, however, a complicated bureaucracy encumbers a new organization with an unneeded and expensive structure, and it creates an organization that is foreign to those who would normally be its base of support.

Paradoxically, ghettoization both simplifies organization building and complicates it. The concentration of a deprived minority and its isolation and limited opportunity structures simplifies the formation of groups—the basis for contact and interaction exists and may be used. But, because ghettoization is accompanied by a limitation on resources and isolation from information sources, the groups do not necessarily progress to a sufficiently advanced stage of organization to be effective for political action. The often repeated statement: "Our blacks (or students, or Mexican-Americans) were just fine and well-behaved until outside agitators came in," expresses the effectiveness of isolation in dampening political organization. To form groups is a very natural human urge; to convert those groups into political instruments aimed at wielding power requires a conscious effort. People locked into the daily routines of their lives, even with a nagging sense of anxiety, discomfort, and distress, are slow to focus their energies into organizational forms if they must build those forms in the face of opposition, disapproval, and limited resources.

Those minorities, such as Indians, that are ghettoized but spread over wide geographic areas face an even more difficult task in organization-building. Costs, both individual and collective, of communicating, meeting, and interacting are high, and they may so exhaust the resource base of the organization that little remains for political efforts.

Problems in Maintaining an Organization

Once an organization is created, it must be maintained or it will lose most of its political effectiveness. Without a total reconstruction of the American political system, the politics of access requires protracted effort and attention through *time*. Efforts must include not only winning court cases and passing legislation, but also insuring that the decisions are implemented, that year after year money is appropriated, and that programs are not undermined by changes in policy emphases, legislative guerrilla warfare, or bureaucratic indifference and hostility. If the organization that has undertaken the initial effort lapses, the base support of the program erodes as well. One of the primary virtues of organization is that it allows prolonged group action in a single-minded direction. Any organization has problems. In the political arena, an organization may become the captive of the governmental agency it hopes to influence. It may gradually lose its impetus, or its staff members may lose their enthusiasm and come to see their positions as no more than jobs to be done. It may build such a complicated network of alliances and mutual dependencies that it is unable to act alone and, of course, circumstances may change, rendering it obsolete in form and purpose.

All these dangers are more acute for minorities than for dominant organizations. Building an organization requires an initial infusion of resources; maintaining it requires an increasing income if it is to carry out its commitments and meet the expectations of its members. Once set in motion, an organization can hope for early victories in order to obtain the attention, new members, and new resources it needs, but it also must have the capacity to survive defeats. Living through defeat is especially important to minority groups, because they will inevitably encounter the resistance of groups more powerful than they and toward whom some of their members have unconscious habits of deference. They must struggle with their own sense of powerlessness and the feelings of fatalism, resignation, and hopelessness that accompany a sense of powerlessness: why fight against so much resistance, scorn, or even mockery, if the fight is hopeless in the first place?

Successes also create problems. If a group is a single-issue organization, it can suffer the fate of the women's suffrage movement, demise upon winning being the form of the victory. Or others, watching the group and stimulated by its victory, will launch their own competing organizations, perhaps with different tactics and priorities. There will be a struggle for members and for public recognition, and both the public and the decision-makers will see a factional force that can be safely ignored except for its news and entertainment value.

In addition to the problems of resources and competition, however, there are other difficulties that make minority groups vulnerable. These are the problems of group function, leadership, and frustration.

Group Function

It has already been argued that groups serve two functions: instrumental and identification. A political organization is nominally instrumental; its purpose is to win political power accompanied with tangible and intangible rewards for its members. Typically, an American pressure group is heavily instrumental in character; so, to a slightly lesser extent, are political parties. However, even instrumental groups usually function as identification groups for some if not all of their members.

A distinguishing characteristic of many of the groups speaking for the beleaguered minorities is their stress on identification functions. The logic of their position is compelling. A basic need of deprived minority members is to escape subjective deprivation, the sense of their own individual helplessness, and the inadequate sense of self-worth and self-esteem in a society that emphasizes visible success. A minority organization that failed to give its members a sense of being accepted, valued, and capable of effective personal and group relations—in short, a sense of identification—would fail in a task that is probably essential to the group's own survival.

A difficult problem facing a minority group, then, is to move from primarily serving an identification function to primarily serving an instrumental function, that of political action. The shift can be and has been achieved, but often at a cost. Sometimes a group is factioned by those who suspect that its leaders are looking for personal pay-offs; and sometimes adaptation to the characteristics of dominant groups through bureaucratization or concern for its public image generate suspicion. The shift itself may attract members who are less concerned with identification processes than with the instrumental uses of the group, which in turn produces factionalism in the form of conflicts between the "old-timers" and the "young hard-liners." One response to the problem is to attempt to control or even reverse the process. The emphasis in a heavily instrumental group may be shifted toward identification. For example, the Student Nonviolent Coordinating Committee, originally a pragmatic coalition of whites and blacks, was purged of its white ties and moved toward the use of identification symbols rather than appeals to "concrete" political results.

Another response is to try to effect the change by maintaining the essential ingredient of identification while adopting the necessary instrumental apparatus. Student coalitions, formed in the crisis of a campus movement, have attempted this route. Usually the effort to make the groups permanent and instrumental falters. Either the mass membership fades, or the group itself expires. Although it is often argued that the failures stem from the short attention span of most students, it would probably be more accurate to recognize that a very basic group dynamic is at work instead.

A third response is to adopt a frankly instrumental cast; that is, eliminate, by voluntary withdrawal or by purge, those who cannot accept the change and operate on the basis of more tangible rewards in order to retain and attract members. This response invariably has the appeal of "realism," based on the dominant definition of political realism, but it risks the rise of competing groups having a deeper emotional appeal. An instrumental group can claim that it gets things done, but this alone does not serve all the needs of its members. A "bread and butter" organization may find itself more readily accepted by dominant institutions and may even be able to show results, but the very acceptance and success can turn out to be a reason for minority members to distrust it and its ties to the dominant society.

Minority organizations do have other choices, primarily by pursuing politics other than the politics of access. For those groups that hope to rely on the politics of access, however, the question of group function is a persistent one. The longevity and success of the NAACP can be partly explained by its operating as a predominantly instrumental group in a predominantly instrumental political system; but its victories—most of them legal victories—have not saved it from challenges from other groups claiming to represent better the real aspirations and needs of the black American. The same is true for those women's organizations, such as NOW, that concentrate on primarily economic grievances. These organizations are practical and pragmatic; they use the "system" in the way that the system ought to be used in accordance with the politics of access, but they lack the profound emotional thrust that brings minority members to competing groups.

Leadership

Minority group and organization leadership is, of course, important for the same reasons that leadership is always important. Those who are "leaders," either elected, self-designated, or appointed, act as spokesmen for their group, becoming the public image of the group itself. They also acquire intragroup power; they usually have command over the group's apparatus and turn it to the purposes they feel best strengthen their own positions and fulfill members' expectations. For members of the group, the leaders personify and symbolize the group's self-image. They usually deal most directly with the crucial political environment; they present demands, conduct negotiations, write press releases, make tactical and strategic decisions, and attempt to direct and coordinate the group's efforts.

More than any other member, a leader stands to gain the greatest tangible and psychological benefits from the group's activities—whether these benefits are salary, enlarged opportunities, the chance to travel and to associate with the powerful, the ability to feel that what is accomplished is "his," or the joy of exercising power over other people. He pays a price. He must work harder, worry more, and, if defeated, bear the personal humiliation of defeat. The same is true of those who are close to the leader: his friends, assistants, subleaders, lackeys, and supporters. Each stands to benefit more, each takes slightly higher risks than the other members.

The leaders of identification groups tend to be "charismatic," those of instrumental groups to be "bureaucratic," to use Weber's famous typology. A charismatic leader is one whose personal appeal and personification of individual psychological needs is responsive to the group need for a symbol of power, infallibility, identity, and personality. A bureaucratic leader's gifts are those of administrative and organizational skill: coordination, planning, and command of the apparatus of the organization. Each reflects the nature of the group he is leading, and each is a product of the group's expectations. Since every group is some combination of identification and instrumental functions (although one or the other usually predominates), the leader himself must in some fashion combine charismatic and bureaucratic attributes.

Minority group leaders face three problems. Their positions, and the tangible or psychological rewards that accrue to their positions, are desirable objects. The circumstances of deprivation in which minorities are submerged only enhance the desirability of the few rewards available. Therefore, a minority leader is required to sacrifice more, or to seem to, than his counterpart in a dominant group. Even so, he is always the target of challenge, being accused of either benefiting at the cost of his followers or having sold out. A charismatic leader suffers from this vulnerability more than a bureaucratic leader. Because his supporters believe that he is willing to sacrifice himself to set his people free, the revelation that he is living in luxury or that he is prone to pure power urges is more damaging to him (and thus to his base of support) than it would be to a busy and efficient bureaucratic leader.

Since identification groups are built on emotional satisfactions, each member has his own definition of the rewards. A charismatic leader must by instinct and intuition respond to those frequently inarticulate definitions. The relationship of group to leader is intangible and becomes more difficult to assess and manipulate when an increase in group size, increasing organizational complexity, and the demands of program and coordination tend to isolate a leader from his followers. A bureaucratic leader, resting on an instrumental base, is able to evaluate the flow of tangible benefits. As long as he can produce the goods, he can feel assured that his power will continue. The relationship of leader to minority groups is obvious: the pressure for the satisfaction of identification needs requires that every minority leader must have some charismatic qualities, or he will be challenged by those who possess more than he does.

A minority group leader also faces the problems of organizational change. The politics of access tends to thrust groups toward instrumental functions. If a leader cannot move toward the more bureaucratic type of leadership necessary for instrumental groups, he may find himself out of harmony with group expectations. A leader can attempt to control the change, resist it, or adapt to it. In all three efforts, however, he will be challenged by those who feel he is out of step or old-fashioned. And, he may simply lack the ability to adapt. He and his supporters may have risen to power at a time when he was aware of and attuned to member expectations; but, the isolating process of leadership may have caused him to be out of touch. New members and their expectations may introduce new cleavages and demands within the group, and he may no longer be an appropriate leader for it. He may be able to preserve his control, but the price could be a fragmenting of the group into factions or even into competing groups.

Finally, a group leader is vulnerable not only to internal challenge, but also to external challenge. Members of the minority grouping that he professes to represent, who do not belong to his group, may deny his legitimacy and right to speak for the grouping; members of dominant groups may also challenge him and, in extreme cases, may select him for harassment. If he is sufficiently prominent and if the political situation is sufficiently tense, he can become the target of assassins.

Leaders do not make a group or an organization; but when the leadership is under constant threat, problems for the group itself arise. Loyalty to person rather than to identification group may be used as the standard of membership. Resistance to advice or reasoned dissent can begin to characterize the leader; and he can even succumb to political paranoia, resulting in purges, factionalism, divisiveness, intragroup conspiracies, and internecine warfare. Schisms within right-wing organizations, within the Black Panthers in 1971, and within the Students for a Democratic Society had roots in complex reactions and counterreactions to the role of leadership, its need to control the course of organizational change, and threats to it.

Factionalism—or the threat of it—can press a leader to attempt to maintain his pre-eminence by a continuing search for more dramatic and grandiose projects. The projects themselves may bear fruit, but if they are undertaken hastily and are outside the capability of the organization, they can result in defeats that damage the status and strength of the organization itself. At least some observers have argued that the SCLC campaign in Chicago was King's effort to match the challenge of more militant black organizations. Lacking both the base and the planning to carry off the attempt, however, King and the SCLC were dealt a painful setback, casting doubt upon his entire philosophy of nonviolent resistance.

All organizations, whether minority or dominant, are susceptible to leadership problems. However, dominant organizations usually have a greater margin for error; they can make mistakes and survive more readily, partly because of their larger resource base and partly because they exist in a political environment that is less charged with tension.

Frustration

Frustrated goals probably pose the most serious threat to maintaining a minority organization. Minority organizations *are* weaker than their dominant competitors, except in very rare instances. Slight successes demonstrate to the members that victories can be achieved, but major victories stay alluringly just out of reach. Repeated failures show only that an organization, given its leadership and its strategy and tactics, is the wrong one.

For those who have faced a life of frustration, facing it again, after making an effort to overcome deprivation through the group, is a bitter experience. Minority groups find it hard to be patient because that would necessitate a continuation of deprivation and its consequences. Patience is the counsel of those who do not have an organization composed of impatient people. For deprived minorities, it is only another word for continued frustration.

A minority organization that is associated with the frustration of its members' goals will be challenged from within and from the outside. There will be those who believe that they can achieve the results that the leadership has failed to. The pressures, again, are toward factionalism, divisiveness, struggles for leadership control, and the creation of new and competing organizations.

Problems of Political Action

Minorities, then, bring to the political system some serious problems, all of which help to explain why they have trouble moving to higher positions on the power curve. In addition, minority groups face specifically political problems when they attempt to act within the context of the politics of access.

Relative Costs

Political action is costly in any political system. But because power in America is dispersed, effective political action requires prolonged, continuous efforts and attention to multiple layers and branches of government. Both prerequisites for successful access necessitate the acquisition of expertise and the expenditure of time, money, and energy. For anyone engaging in politics, except professional politicians, civil servants, or hired lobbyists, politics is an avocation, requiring time away from other activities. Although it is not a luxury limited to the rich, only those who can afford it or who are dependent upon government and politics to support their other activities can participate.

For minorities, the costs—in relation to their resources—are higher than for dominant groups. Except for the relatively few who gain office, minority members, like other people, must take time away from work and family to pursue political action. Moreover, because they face more intense organizational problems, minorities need more time and energy to build a movement to the point at which it has the political capability necessary to challenge dominant groups and institutions. Those in positions of leadership may be able to get enough money to support themselves and their immediate staff. But for the larger membership the costs are high, especially if political activities entail real inconvenience, such as travelling long distances to vote and to persuade others to vote, to demonstrate, or to go to educational sessions and mass meetings.

Furthermore, to a large extent, members of the dominant groups in society feel reasonably sure that, somewhere, someone is looking after their interests. Their direct or indirect control and representation in the agencies of government and power relieve them from the task of constantly monitoring the political behavior of those agencies. Minorites do not possess that assurance; because they are not well represented in agencies of government and because of the discriminatory patterns already established, their interests are neglected and, consequently, they suffer. Their neighborhoods are vulnerable to urban renewal for middle-class goals; polling places, schools, and other public facilities are located for the convenience of dominant groups rather than theirs; college curricula are designed to suit faculty interests rather than those of the students; men tend to be hired rather than women because personnel directors know that men are more "stable." Without coherent political action, each minority can be reasonably certain that the patterns will continue out of inertia if not out of malice. The advantage of dominance carries the advantage of lower costs for political action, and the lower costs are not only relative, but absolute.

Effective Numbers

Although the "beleaguered minorities" are not minorities because of their numerical strength (women are more than 50 percent of the population, for example), in a political society where majority and plurality votes are the winning votes, sheer numbers count. Benefits, for very logical political reasons, tend to be allocated to the greatest possible numbers of politically active people. If a minority is a numerical minority, it faces a serious handicap.

The crucial statistic is not the total number, but the *effective* number. If all women agreed to elect a woman president of the United States, they would succeed. Like any other grouping, whether dominant or minority, not all women join a single, coherent movement directed at a specific goal. In the early 1970s, the actual participants in the women's liberation movement plus the invisible members added up to only a minority of the population of women itself, to say nothing of the total population. The movement itself is divided regarding commitments, goals, strategies, and tactics. To repeat a point already made, any given minority *group* is always only a small part of a minority *grouping*. The effective political number of every minority group is a minority within a minority.

Every dominant group has exactly the same problem. Its effective numbers invariably represent only a small fraction of the total population. The difference is that those groups generally also possess the advantage of having access to the power system, and, if not, they have a greater resource pool to draw upon in their struggle to gain access. For many minorities, it often seems that their only tangible resources are their numbers and their strategic locations. When they cannot muster the former, and are disadvantaged in the latter, their political problems are only exacerbated.

Organization maximizes the effectiveness of any specific number of people. An organized minority can almost always defeat an unorganized majority, largely because of the efficiencies implicit in organization. But, deprived minorities confront other, not-so-deprived minorities, who have a greater command of organizational resources. The burden facing America's beleaguered minorities is to out-organize groups whose interests and demands either oppose or dilute those of minority groups.

Public Regard

The effective numbers of a group can be geometrically multiplied if the group can enlist the help of its potential invisible members. Minority groups have been very successful in tapping this resource. The accomplishments of the SCLC in its Birmingham and Selma campaigns owed much to publicity through the mass media, helping to reach the potential invisible members of a courageous and charismatic movement. It is probably not unduly naive to argue that most Americans would prefer that their fellow humans live free from poverty, humiliation, and legal injustice. It is, however, probably not unduly pessimistic to say that most people find it difficult to focus their attention on these problems for any great length of time and, although they would be relieved if the circumstances of deprivation were removed, they are not anxious to have them removed in a way that would be costly to them or their interests.

A minority group, then, has a pool of public regard that can be tapped, but under rather narrow constraints. To tap it, the group must have overwhelming publicity and sympathetic treatment in the media. Its objective must be of low cost to dominant individuals or groups and must not threaten the habits, routines, or concepts of potential sympathizers. A violation of these constraints can lead to a reversal of public regard: the so-called "backlash" in which sympathy becomes sharply qualified.

A minority group must answer some hard questions. How much public regard is needed for political success? How can it be won? Can (or should) minority goals and strategies be shaped by anything so fickle as public regard? Implicit in the answers to these questions is the realization that the American public, if not actually prejudiced, has long been indifferent to the plight of most minorities. To wait for change or to nurture it at the cost of more direct action may be to pursue political fool's gold.

The Politics of Minority Access

The picture painted here may seem unnecessarily bleak. Surely, it can be said, minorities have organized successfully, have enlisted public sympathy, have won monumental victories from the political system, have elected officeholders, and have realized other goals. All they had to do was to employ the methods used by other groups and interests in the society. "Old-style politics" has worked and still does. The point here, however, is that old-style pluralistic politics requires and assumes a number of things: first, it requires that minorities accept the political system as is and accept the assumption that they can achieve their goals by working within it. Not all minority groups make that assumption. Second, the politics of access assumes that minorities are willing to accept the costs imposed on them by pluralistic tactics. Minorities are not always willing to accept these costs. Third, pluralistic politics assumes that minorities either will not or cannot search for and produce political goals, strategies, and tactics that are quite different from those of old-style politics. But the difficulties associated with being a beleaguered minority in the United States have already led to just such innovations with possibly far-reaching effects for the American political system.

Bibliography

Bachrach, Peter, and Morton S. Baratz. *Power and Poverty: Theory and Practice.* New York: Oxford University Press, 1970. An excellent examination of the difficulties of deprived groups in using power in an urban setting.

Bell, Wendell, Richard J. Hill, and Charles R. Wright. *Public Leadership.* San Francisco: Chandler, 1961.

Berle, A. A. *Power.* New York: Harcourt, Brace and World, 1969. A valuable study of the preconditions to political power.

Carmichael, Stokeley, and Charles V. Hamilton. *Black Power: the Politics of Liberation in America.* New York: Vintage, 1967.

Dahl, Robert A. *Who Governs? Democracy and Power in an American City.* New Haven: Yale University Press, 1961. Especially valuable for its careful study of the way in which power is put together in a pluralist setting.

Glazer, Nathan, and Daniel P. Moynihan. *Beyond the Melting Pot.* Cambridge, Mass.: The M.I.T. Press, 1963.

Grebler, Leo, Joan W. Moore, and Ralph C. Guzman. *The Mexican-American People.* New York: Free Press, 1970.

Gruberg, Martin. *Women in American Politics.* Oshkosh, Wis.: Academia Press, 1968.

Holloway, Harry. *The Politics of the Southern Negro: From Exclusion to Big City Organization.*

New York: Random House, 1969. A good survey of the successes, and failures, of southern blacks in playing the politics of access.

Wirt, Frederick M. *The Politics of Southern Equality*. Chicago: Aldine, 1970. A careful study of the strengths and weaknesses of blacks in the politics of access.

Fourteen
Minority Goals

Minority groups and members of minorities often win "victories" in the political arena. In 1971, for example, more blacks were serving in the United States Congress, state legislatures, and local governments than ever before. The less than 2,000 blacks in elected office nonetheless fell far short of any proportional representation, since fully 50,000 blacks would have to hold office to reflect the 12 percent black segment of the nation's population. Victories won through the politics of access, however, are better measured by the attention governments devote to the needs and aspirations of minorities. The record would seem impressive on many counts. The cause of the American Indian received concrete attention during the first two years of the Nixon Administration, including the restoration of land to the Taos Indians, commitments of payments to the Aleuts and Eskimos, and sympathetic treatment of Seminole claims against Florida and the United States. Mexican-Americans, blacks, Indians, and other minorities were given National Science Foundation grants to encourage the study of their problems. After a delay, the president did confer with the "Black Caucus" of Congress, though his responses were considered inadequate. The Civil Rights Commission began to undertake a serious effort to protect the rights of women in employment opportunities. Proposals for a modified welfare system, the extension of the food-stamp–food-surplus program, and attention to Operation Breakthrough to produce more and better housing were indications of efforts to provide concrete benefits to minorities.

Two qualifiers are important, however. In the late 1960s a profound awareness of minority problems emerged among dominant institutions, yet the actions stemming from it frequently failed to match either the demands of minorities or the hopes. The viewpoints of minorities conflicted with those expressed by dominant spokesmen who asked, "What do they expect? What do they *really* want?" Simultaneously, minority group spokesmen grew irritated and impatient with the apparent indifference, cruelty, or lack of perceptiveness of dominant leaders. The difficulty was that there were two criteria for measuring minority "gains." From the dominant perspective gains were measured in terms of how far minorities had come; from the minority perspective they were measured in terms of how far the minority had yet to go, which can be determined only by their goals. Often these goals emerge slowly as they are tested in the political arena, as new strategies are evolved, or as new expectations appear.

Minority groups bring three sets of goals into politics. Depending on the group, and the minority from which the group is drawn, the goals themselves will vary, but in general they may be classified as group-survival goals, intermediate goals, and ultimate goals.

Group-Survival Goals

It has already been noted that an immediate demand on any group or organization is its own maintenance; that is, doing what must be done to continue its existence and to satisfy its members. Theoretically, the achievement of other goals serves this purpose, and this is the way in which many groups function, that is, as purely instrumental groups. However, most minority groups also function as identification groups by providing comfort and security, reducing anxiety, and enlarging social opportunity structures that are vital to the group and its members. The group is crucially important to those who have limited identification opportunities, whose families are under severe stress, whose friendship groups are limited by ghettoization and dependency, and who do not have the chance to find new identification groups through wide employment opportunities.

Beyond this, the group itself, if it is a political organization, has a symbolic value. It is the symbol of a mutual effort to achieve something through the political system; it has been created in the face of hostility and fear; it is the embodiment of a hope for the future. The mere formation of a group is a political act of enormous consequence that stands as a symbol of action, courage, and effort. A black in a small rural county observed at a meeting of a newly founded voters league: "Even if we don't do more than this, look what we have done." A student commented at the peak of a campus crisis, "After this [establishment of a student coalition], nothing can ever be the same again." In a memorandum to organizers of women's liberation groups, a key section stresses that the organizer must convince each other woman that she "dares to participate, dares to expose herself. . . ." (Tanner, 1970, p. 156).

The group is not a self-sufficient end in itself, but it is an end. As a source of identification, a statement about the minority member's commitment to the movement, and a symbol of that commitment, it is self-validating. For these reasons it must be maintained and preserved.

Finally, the group is instrumental to other goals of the minority, and as an instrument, it must be kept in working order. Preserving and strengthening the group, then, are basic goals of minority group members.

Intermediate Goals

Beyond the immediate demands of group survival, however, is a set of goals related to the group proper and to the condition of the minority itself. These goals can be labelled "intermediate" because they stand somewhere in time and concept between the basic goal of group survival and the ultimate goals that will affect the future state of society. James Q. Wilson has suggested two of these goals – those of status and welfare. In addition, there are legal and integrity goals.

Legal Goals

Minority groups often attack first the legal barriers between themselves and the dominant culture that mark members of minorities for special treatment. Blacks sought the elimination of Jim Crow and discriminatory voting laws; Indians, the elimination of restrictions on voting and citizenship and of rule by the Bureau of Indian Affairs and congressional legislation; students, the destruction of the concept of *in loco parentis*; women, the elimination of employment "safeguards," abortion prohibitions, and divorce standards. In each case, the attack was against the special barriers or handicaps that the society uses to define the minority through law.

The obliteration of these legal barriers is vital for several reasons. First, they do impose special handicaps on the minority and the handicaps are supported and defended by the power and majesty of government. The minority member is, in his own mind, a second-class citizen, unable to enjoy the privileges reserved for the dominant culture. Should he attempt to do so, he is faced with legal sanctions. He is not only deprived, but deprived by law.

Second, these laws provide for "special treatment," and, in so doing, they are a legal form of cultural marking. Not only does the dominant society informally differentiate, but it does so formally. The legal barriers are not only an enforceable means of differentiation, but a symbol of differentiation – a symbol that has been approved by the political institutions of the society and accepted as good and useful.

Third, legal differentiation is a rationale for other forms of discrimination. Because the law selects a grouping for special treatment, others can justify to themselves and to the society a wider range of special treatment. Historically, the process no doubt works in reverse; the law codifies prior cultural biases, but once they are codified, the law gains its own social and cultural legitimacy. And, so it can be argued that if the law says women are unfit for certain kinds of jobs, it must be because they really are weaker and more unreliable than men.

Fourth, legal standards must be implemented, and the chance to aply discriminatory laws unequally provides political opportunities. Politicians in the South found ways of paying the poll tax for blacks who would vote the "right way." Students who were good, obedient little boys and girls could have their privileges extended. A wealthy woman could always find a cooperative doctor to handle her abortion. Each of these differential applications of discriminatory standards distributes power differentially. The minority member is himself dependent on the administrators of the law and therefore must please them; thus he is drawn away from identifying with his minority grouping by receiving privileges not available to other members.

Finally, there is the highly pragmatic reason of deprivation. The minority that labors under the special handicap of legal barriers suffers not only possible economic and social disadvantages but political disadvantages as well. The cumulative loss of employment opportunities, of self-esteem, and of wider social contacts results in a reduction in substantive democracy and a loss of political resources and information. Where the laws are aimed directly at political opportunities, such as restrictions on the franchise, the political opportunity structure is deliberately limited.

Many of the legal barriers have fallen. For some self-aware minorities, however, they still exist. That which characterizes the minority status of a homosexual, for example, is itself illegal. The abortion laws of most states still impose the burden of bearing and raising children on those women who do not wish to do so. Various laws and guidelines continue to fence in those Indians living on reservations.

It is, of course, not surprising that the laws most difficult to modify tend to be those tied to the cultural universals: age and sex. And, the largest number of rationales for preserving these laws can be found in those two categories. For the same reason, many of the other discriminatory laws were justified on crypto-sexual or -age bases: that blacks, for example, were sexually primitive, or not yet mature enough to participate in governmental affairs. These deep-seated norms are especially frustrating to minority members because they *are* cultural in the sense that they derive from the intellectual values of the society. Logical or empirical arguments are frustrated by the response, "But that's the way it is and always has been."

Minority members feel impelled to attack the cultural values embodied in the law because the law is a vulnerable point at which these values can be removed or weakened. And, even if the cultural values persist, at least minorities are not confronted with a legal reinforcement of them.

Welfare Goals

Welfare goals consist of the economic and tangible benefits of the society. Achieving them requires the removal of the effects of economic deprivation by providing employment, better wages and salaries, decent housing, good health care, and economic security. Because welfare goals figure prominently in the debate concerning minority politics and because in America they can be easily understood and fairly easily measured, they tend to be a major focus of political activity.

For some minorities at least, welfare goals are the most pressing needs. Hunger, poor health, unsafe living conditions for blacks, Mexican-Americans, and Indians take priority over other goals. A minority that faces severe economic deprivation almost "naturally" gives rise to groups whose fundamental purpose is to seek welfare goals. Even nominally economically secure minorities feel impelled to seek welfare goals. The women's organizations that lobby for better employment opportunities for women and the students who seek better housing conditions are in quest of expanding their basic opportunity structures and improving their lot.

Aside from economic and physical well-being, welfare goals have an intangible significance. Economic status is, or is presumed to be, an indicator of an individual's social worth. The person (such as a housewife or a minor) who is dependent on another for his economic sustenance is intrinsically limited psychologically; he or she cannot have the freedom in making personal decisions that others with their own incomes have. And, economic conditions are related to the political opportunity structure. The capacity of organizations made up of impoverished members to undertake political action is limited.

Achievement of welfare goals is demonstrable. Jobs, increased wages, salaries, and fringe benefits, better housing, and better sanitation are concrete gains that a minority group can point to as indicators of success with which to enlist more support as well as satisfy its own members. By achieving these goals, an instrumental group can prove its worth to its members, thereby increasing their commitment to the group.

Welfare goals are, moreover, temptingly achievable. The redistributive powers of government are available to provide jobs, housing, direct subsidies, and an improved physical environment. The powers to tax and to spend are accessible through the political process, and in a stupefyingly wealthy nation, the money must be somewhere at hand and not necessarily at any great sacrifice to anyone. From the standpoint of a deprived minority, a refusal to allocate money for welfare needs is at best miserliness, at worst the greediness of those possessing that which is gained from the misery of others.

The tangible nature of welfare goals makes them politically useful: the public can grasp the conditions of poverty, slums, and unemployment. It is in the "American tradition" to want to improve oneself economically, and, presumably, some measure of guilt can be stirred in the heart of the comfortably placed suburbanite by presentations of the effects of grinding poverty. That other social afflictions—such as crime, drug abuse, increased governmental costs, or social unrest—can be linked to economic deprivation only strengthens the public appeal of welfare goals as a minority group focus.

Status Goals

Whereas welfare goals are aimed primarily at overcoming economic deprivation, status goals are sought to alleviate subjective deprivation. Status goals are the demand for an acceptance of minority members on an equal plane with members of the dominant culture: the elimination of dehumanization. A status goal might be to achieve black and white equality; it might be for women to be regarded as people rather than merely as sexual objects; it might be for students' opinions about their education and the institutions they attend to be as valid as those of faculty and administration. At one level, status goals recognize that self-esteem depends in part on being held in esteem by others; at another level, they are an effort to be accepted by those who have denied acceptance in the past.

As a political target, status goals are harder to translate into concrete aims than either legal or welfare goals. Removing a law from the books by legislative or court action and fighting for a job-training program or a housing project are concrete, visible objectives that can be measured in terms of success or failure. Status goals are more difficult to perceive, however. They require not only governmental action, but reconstruction of individual, private values and preconceptions. There are areas in which action has been taken: employment opportunities may not be listed according to sex or color and applications for employment or admission to college no longer require a photograph or a statement regarding color. Often, to dominant members many efforts to achieve status goals seem petty, even amusing, such as the effort by some women's groups to eliminate the indication of marital status by substituting "Ms" for "Miss" or "Mrs." Often to minority members, however, the dominant attitude seems frustrating. Dominant members fail to grasp the deep-seated subjective deprivation that underlies the effort for change; minority members sense a dominant effort to preserve humiliating distinctions.

The vitality of status goals is that they aim at breaking the habits of thought of dominant groups unaccustomed to reckoning with minorities and of those minority members who need to give up their habits of deference. In other words, the goal of the minority organization is to rebuild behavior patterns to gain a long-denied respect and to encourage minority members to insist that they get that respect, which is a necessary part of their sense of self-esteem.

Integrity Goals

Status goals are the search for respect from dominant groups and institutions; integrity goals are the search for self-esteem and self-respect generated within a minority. The two are in part complementary. Integrity goals are in some respects an extension of status goals, but also are an expression of the inability to attain status goals. Two ends can be achieved by the pursuit of integrity: self-pride and pride in one's membership in the minority and identification with it. Thus, awareness of minority status becomes not only a recognition of deprivation but, and more important, a sense of heritage, communality, fellowship, and being special. Integrity goals reverse the "insider-outsider" category by making minority members feel they are the insiders and the dominant members are really the outsiders.

The psychological benefits of integrity goals are clear. Like the identification functions of the group, they enable minority members to feel needed, wanted members of an important and ego-satisfying grouping. Blacks can take pride in their unique heritage of sensitivity to suffering, their African roots, their music, dance, and political achievements. Students can feel the freshness and promise of their youth, freedom from cant and from bureaucratic habits, and joy in their own special rituals. Minorities thus turn to themselves not only for awareness of minority status but for awareness of the richness, interdependence, and significance of their existence.

From the pragmatic political standpoint, integrity goals are a way of welding a grouping into a cohesive political force. The minority group that expresses and follows integrity goals can hope to extend its actual and invisible membership to encompass a large part of the minority grouping and to bind those new members to the group by identification processes. Further, a strong sense of minority integrity is a shield against efforts to divide the grouping on the basis of other characteristics such as age, income, occupation, or geographic distribution.

Like status goals, however, integrity goals embody intangibles and are thus less easy to formulate or pursue as political programs than either legal or welfare goals. The primary means must be through symbols: "black power," "sisterhood," "community," and specific ways of dress, language, and manner that are unique to the grouping.

Integrity goals serve an identification function because attainment binds a group together. The attainment of instrumental goals, on the other hand, can weaken the bond. But, the goals are less easily expressed and therefore less easily formulated. To the question, "What's in it for me?" there is no answer, because the asking of the question denies the need for identification.

Understanding the pattern of intermediate goals is important because in large measure they determine the kind of leadership, strategies, and tactics that a minority group adopts. Legal and welfare goals tend to require bureaucratic leaders and predominantly instrumental groups. Status and, especially, integrity goals tend to require charismatic leaders and predominantly identification groups.

The real world is never so simple as schemes and definitions might indicate. Often, for example, legal, welfare, status, and integrity goals are not easily separable. As a simple illustration, laws controlling abortions can be regarded as purely legal strictures that place a special burden on women. They also impose welfare handicaps, however, because unwanted pregnancies limit employment opportunities and illegal abortion is expensive. Further, they present a status problem by placing women seeking an abortion in a special category of humans. Finally, they serve as a rallying point, a means of demonstrating to women that they must turn first to an understanding and awareness of themselves in the context of a special piece of social legislation. In short, to ascribe a particular type of goal to a group before seeing how the group is handling and defining the goals it seeks could lead to dangerous oversimplification. A group's choice of goals is determined by a complex relationship between member expectations, leadership decisions, and strategic and tactical choices.

Status goals may be achievable only after welfare goals are met, for it could be argued that dominant institutions will respect a minority member only after he has attained a degree of material success and its corresponding image. Real breakthroughs in achieving other types of goals might not be possible until minority integrity is attained. The emphasis that a group places on any particular type often results from its perception of its circumstances and the most pressing needs of its membership.

At any given point in history two or more groups drawn from the same minority may have stressed different types of goals. But, blacks, women, Indians, Mexican-Americans, and students at least have tended to stress legal goals first, then welfare goals followed by status goals, and finally integrity goals. In each instance the process may be a gradual peeling back of layers of political consciousness. The unfolding realization is, first, that the law is the most obvious target for eliminating discrimination; second, that removing legal barriers does little to better a minority's condition; third, that focusing on welfare goals does not guarantee the full alleviation of economic deprivation if it is accompanied by subjective deprivation; and, finally, that the basic means of achieving change can only be through the pride, awareness, and solidarity that minority integrity and identification can give.

Ultimate Goals

Reaching beyond yet shaping both intermediate goals and the strategies of minority organizations are what can be called ultimate goals. These embrace the kind of society active minority groups need for the minority to be able to exist in a fulfilling, self-respecting way. Often, the ultimate goals of minorities seem the most alarming and confusing to dominant groups because, understandably enough, they are not always very clearly stated or formulated; when they are, they seem foreign or dangerous.

Assimilation

There was perhaps a time when assimilation seemed a desirable goal for minorities in the United States. Although their presence was resisted for a long time and although many families or individuals chose not to be assimilated, this was and continues to be an important process for the "old minorities." Assimilation for them means merging with the dominant segment of society through marriage and economic, social, and political participation so thoroughly that there is no way to distinguish dominant and minority groupings.

As matters stood in the 1960s and early 1970s, however, even large segments of the old minorities had apparently resisted assimilation. Although they adopted the language and certain aspects of the life styles of the dominant Anglo-Saxon society, although they became far more like "Americans" than like people from the "old country," many members of ethnic groupings continued to preserve their cultural patterns.

As already noted, the old minorities are separated from the beleaguered minorities by two major factors. First, assimilation seems more easily attainable for the Italian-American, Polish-American, German-American, or Greek-American than for the black, Mexican-American, or Indian. If a member of an ethnic minority elects to speak another language, to shed his cultural heritage, and (perhaps) to change his name, he can "pass." Blacks, Indians, women, and the young can do nothing to alter their skin color, sex, or age.

Second, awareness of ethnic identification is not as deeply embedded in the dominant culture as awareness of color, age, and sex. Accompanying that awareness is deprivation, either objective or subjective, or both. The old minorities apparently can be in situations in which their ethnic backgrounds are the least important characteristic that marks them; the beleaguered minorities do not seem to have that chance.

The important point is that although assimilation has occurred, it has not occurred to the extent that was once expected, even for the old minorities. The reasons seem to lie in the need for identification groups having a common cultural tradition. What is true for the old minorities is even more true for the new, because it is to some degree forced upon the latter. Although assimilation continues to be an expectation of a few minority group members, it is not an expectation of all.

Cultural Pluralism

Cultural pluralism is perhaps closer to the "Great American Dream." Minority groupings would be integrated into the economic, political, and social spheres of the society but would retain their cultural differences without discrimination or deprivation. The heterogeneity of American society would be preserved. Many members of the society would perhaps continue to speak more than one language, yet political divisions, social differentiation, and cultural values would not be based on an "insider-outsider," "we-they" set of categories.

A problem with cultural pluralism is that it speaks primarily to ethnic groups, less so to color groups, and not at all to the categories based on sex or age. Presumably, this omission is amenable to correction. Homosexuals, for example, could be openly accepted without facing criminal prosecution. Women and men could be considered equals. The "youth culture" could be regarded not as a deviation, a threat, or a passing phase, but as a basic and legitimate life style in a pluralistic society.

But, cultural pluralism assumes that society can stop attaching discriminatory values to those who preserve a minority cultural tradition or who are culturally or biologically marked. Apparently, for many ethnic groupings, it can. But there are two possible explanations for the gradual decline in ethnic tensions: one is that Americans have become more tolerant; the other is that actual differences between ethnic groupings and the dominant culture have declined. A man may be nominally Italian-American, and even may on occasion think of himself in those terms, but he no longer speaks the old tongue, as often as not eats American food, dresses in the same clothes as everyone else, and, as he prospers, moves into a suburb that is culturally mixed. Whichever explanation is correct (and probably both are), it is also true that ethnic identification persists and that belonging to an ethnic grouping does not necessarily cause one to be denied the benefits of the society.

To what extent is cultural pluralism a desirable, or even an attainable, goal for the beleaguered minorities? For "moderate" minority groups, cultural pluralism has been the persistent goal. Their aim has been a society in which black and white, Indian and Anglo, male and female, young and old, would regard each other as self-respecting and mutually respectful. Differentiation would certainly continue, but without discrimination. School integration, equal employment opportunities, integrated housing, income maintenance plans are all status or welfare strategies aimed principally at the achievement of cultural pluralism. The dilemma of the moderates, however, has been that of power relationships. Can a minority be accepted by dominant groups and institutions without having to become a mirror image of the dominant culture? Is the price of nondiscrimination the rejection of one's identity to become like those who are in control of most of society's resources and power?

The answer to either question is not necessarily yes, but the dominant assumption often is that it will be. That is, cultural pluralism for the new minorities may translate into deculturation. For women, it will remain a man's world, and women will have to adopt those schedules, habits, and practices already established to be accepted into it. Blacks must become like whites in manner and style; Indians must forget their tribal origins and heritage; the young must become "mature and responsible"; and homosexuals must offer themselves for psychotherapy. How generalized this dominant expectation really is is difficult to say, but even traditionally moderate groups like the NAACP, the Urban League, student governing bodies, and various Indian groups are rethinking the concept of cultural pluralism, especially since it seems possible only on terms set by dominant groups and institutions.

The idea of cultural pluralism is not at fault. From the minority standpoint the question is whether the idea can be made to work, and whether the dominant culture is capable of modifying its cultural values sufficiently to accept difference without discrimination.

The burden becomes that of the minorities. They must prove themselves to the dominant institutions and, at the same time, attempt to change their values while they struggle to achieve their own intermediate goals. As blacks have said, "There is no *black* problem, there's only a white problem."

Although the statement is an exaggeration, there is also an element of truth in it. A minority member may be willing to exercise tolerance toward dominant members; but how is he to achieve the same level of tolerance in return? Must he bear the responsibility of teaching dominant members of society as well as his fellow minority members?

Of all the ultimate visions of American society, however, cultural pluralism continues to offer the greatest attractions. It is the vision of "black and white together," the hoped-for reality of the dream that Martin Luther King revealed on the steps of the Washington Monument. It is the vision of the present American society, with its wealth, its economic and social security, and its capacity for doing so much good extended to all groupings while preserving the humane values of difference and pluralism.

Structural Pluralism

One step further along the road to diversity is structural pluralism. The basic difference between cultural and structural pluralism is that under cultural pluralism a minority shares the opportunity structures of dominant institutions; under structural pluralism the opportunity structures of a given minority are largely (but not entirely) confined to that minority. Instrumental and identification functions would be served primarily by minority groups under structural pluralism. Although members of a minority may choose to participate in some economic and political activities outside their own grouping, the emphasis would be on those within the grouping. Although cultural pluralism assumes that members of minorities will continue to identify with their own groupings, structural pluralism contemplates not only identification but economic, social, and possibly political dependence on a minority grouping. Under cultural pluralism, primary participation would be in the dominant segment of society and its institutions; being a member of a minority is only secondary. Under structural pluralism, the reverse is true.

With the passage of time, minority groups have been finding structural pluralism an increasingly more attractive ultimate goal. This attitude stems from the resistance of the dominant culture—or segments of it—to minority efforts to gain access. Black students, as a consequence, are willing to attend predominantly white institutions, but they wish to participate in their own programs on black culture, which become the core and focus of their educations. Some blacks have also given up attempting to gain access to the white corporate world and instead choose to establish their own business firms, using white capital and selling to white customers, if necessary, but essentially creating activities that are black in purpose.

Structural pluralism conforms to integrity goals. The emphasis is on a minority member's own grouping, on brotherhood or sisterhood within the grouping, and on group pride and accomplishment. As a goal, structural pluralism can be rationalized as a matter of looking after one's own first, behavior that has certainly characterized both ethnic minorities and dominant groupings throughout the history of the country.

The risks for a minority are almost self-evident. "[Structural pluralism] could very well foster a strong 'we' and 'they' feeling, leading to less communication, more misunderstanding, more prejudiced attitudes and higher levels of discrimination." (Kitano, 1969, p. 145). Beleaguered minorities are vulnerable, having limited resources, in many cases being the targets of sporadic violence, and in every case being the objects of prolonged deprivation. Structural pluralism would possibly only emphasize that vulnerability. It could be argued that America's one great venture in structural pluralism has been the Indian reservation, at a catastrophic cost to the Indian.

Several of the beleaguered minorities have little choice about being in favor of structural pluralism as a goal. As long as education is dominated by the values of faculty and administrators, students may feel that they must rely upon experimental universities for a complementary and "relevant" education; as long as corporations and unions are willing to admit only a token number of blacks, the only alternative may seem to be black businesses hiring black employees. That the Japanese-American pursued a modified form of structural pluralism for a long period is evidence that the goal is not impossible.

Moreover, structural pluralism requires relatively little modification of the values of the dominant culture. It requires no more than a willingness to let minorities try to "do their own thing." The cost to dominant groups in terms of value changes, money, and effort is low, as long as they can grant minorities freedom to work out their own destinies.

Separatism

A question haunting the concept of structural pluralism is whether the dominant institutions are willing or ever would be willing to allow minorities to pursue their own interests and values in their own ways. For those who fear that structural pluralism would merely become another form of colonial indirect rule, the answer is complete separatism. Although the concept of separatism is troubling to many, it is not new to the country. The American Revolution was more a separatist movement than a revolution in the political, economic, or social sense. Various utopian communities have been established in this country, usually on the basis of religion or philosophy, but occasionally on the basis of race or age. The "hippie communes" that dot the nation are primarily separatist in impulse and purpose. And the Republic of New Africa movement to establish self-sufficient black political entities is patterned on the Prosser Rebellion of 1800.

Separatism has the special advantage of total independence from a dominant society that to the minority group seems hostile and exploitative. To a beleaguered minority, surrounded by prejudice, discrimination, and threats, the creation of an independent "nation" must be tempting. The minority would have not only the symbols but the forms of identification and integrity: its own economy, society, politics, and government. To the argument that separatism must inevitably fail because no minority can be self-sufficient, the response is that the newly independent nation would be willing to accept foreign aid—on its own terms. Moreover, if Israel was able to build a new nation while surrounded by enemies, there is little reason to believe that blacks, Indians, Mexican-Americans, or others could not do the same.

Obviously, the principal practical difficulty with separatism is that of the geographic location of the new nation or nations. Thus far, no state has shown any inclination to surrender all or part of its territory to a new nation, and it could be expected that dominant members of the society would violently resist giving up their homes and property. The principal alternative for blacks is the central city, where they will become more and more predominant if the present trends continue. Since whites are voluntarily surrendering ownership of the cities, black political jurisdictions will automatically come into being, and it is not entirely facetious to think that the day may come when some states will consider letting their "problem-child" cities secede.

Separatism obviously assumes that minority and dominant groupings cannot coexist on any level that is tolerable to the minority. The only hope for the beleaguered minorities is total independence; perhaps dominant groups would be equally happy to rid themselves of a people they dislike anyhow. Then the relationship between the two would be a matter of diplomacy, not a matter of sharing power.

Reconstitution

Aside from the fairly explicit ultimate goals described in this section, there is the general concept of a "reconstituted" society. Often this takes a Marxist form, but it may also embrace more generalized ideas such as "rule by the people," anarchistic elimination of all forms of authority, a total recasting of values to eliminate materialism and discrimination, or the reconstruction of the political and economic system along community or syndicalist lines.

To the extent that it is possible to generalize about the wide variety of possibilities included in reconstitution, two major themes appear. First, owing to the suffering inflicted on them and the sensitivity they have gained thereby, minorities are the basic agents for reconstitution. Second, reconstitution is not necessarily a question of forms and procedures or institutions and processes, but of values. That society's present values are in fact not only hateful to minorities but even to those who hold and defend them is evidenced by the high rate of alcoholism, mental illness, suicide, crime, and violence against other nations. The middle class itself is not happy with these values, but it lacks the knowledge, courage, consciousness, and flexibility to seek a different set of values and style of living.

In a reconstituted society, men and women would not pursue their selfish urges, attempting to find gratification by exploiting their fellow humans and the natural environment, but would recognize the continuity and mutuality of all living things. The problem is not that of formally designing such a society but of producing the change in values from which such a society would naturally evolve, since social forms are an expression of social values.

For the hard-headed pragmatist, such a utopian concept belongs in the category of childish fantasies. Two points must be restressed, however. The first is that however "objectively" valid or invalid an idea is, if people are willing to act on the basis of the idea, the consequent behavior *is* a reality. Second, the quest for a reconstituted society has motivated some people toward challenging the existing political institutions and the values on which they are based. And, the act of challenge produces political behavior that is itself new, or at least different from that which is tailored to fit the existing political order. In short, the search for a reconstituted society can build political responses and counterresponses that produce a change in the political system.

The leap from maintaining an organization to the ultimate design of a society is large, and often the three types of goals are not logically connected or systematically worked out. Even the Bolsheviks had to evolve goals while coping with day-to-day organizational details, and each modified the other.

Further, the selection of goals is profoundly related to the minority group's interpretation of the political system. Those who share the pluralist view must inevitably tend to select goals that are compatible with that view; those who accept a power-elite or a Marxist view tend to select goals that are compatible with their views. For all, political and social goals serve a variety of purposes. They can be symbols and images around which followers may be organized; they can be guides to action; they can be comforts in times of failure and rationalizations for both success and failure. As a result, they are both means and ends of political action and rarely exist in any pure form except for very fleeting periods of time.

As tempting as it is to dismiss any discussion of the ultimate goals as an exercise in futility, it must be remembered that America's beleaguered minorities have chosen to or been forced to think long and seriously about the nature of their country. Unlike dominant groups, they cannot and do not make the assumption that the system is fundamentally right; they therefore consciously or unconsciously must choose an alternative view of what the system should be like. In doing so, a minority group, its choice of intermediate goals, and its strategies and tactics will be influenced by its selection of ultimate goals. The more "militant" groups move toward integrity goals and structural pluralism; the "radical" groups tend to move directly toward separatism and reconstitution.

Although any given group may modify its aims on the testing ground of political action, these aims will affect its purposes and performance and the way that it chooses to seek power.

Bibliography

Barbour, Floyd B. *The Black Power Revolt.* Boston: Expanding Horizons, 1968.

Bird, Caroline. *Born Female: The High Cost of Keeping Women Down.* New York: David McKay, 1968. A powerful statement of the welfare goals of women.

DeLoria, Vine. *Custer Died for Your Sins: An Indian Manifesto.* New York: Macmillan, 1969.

Foster, Julian, and Durward Long, eds. *Protest: Student Activism in America.* New York: Murrow, 1970. Contains several essays that outline the goals of students.

King, Martin Luther, *Why We Can't Wait.* New York: New American Library, 1964.

Kitano, Harry H. L. *Japanese Americans.* Englewood Cliffs, N.J.: Prentice-Hall, 1969. A good study of one minority that tried structural pluralism.

Millett, Kate. *Sexual Politics.* Garden City, N.Y.: Doubleday, 1970.

Scott, Anne F., ed. *What is Happening to American Women.* Atlanta: Southern Newspaper Publishers Association Foundation, 1971. A valuable collection of essays spanning most of the goals possible to a minority.

Steiner, Stan. *La Raza: The Mexican-Americans.* New York: Harper & Row, 1968. The place of integrity goals in building a set of ultimate goals for the society.

Tanner, Leslie B., ed. *Voices from Women's Liberation.* New York: New American Library, 1970.

Young, Whitney M., Jr. *Beyond Racism.* New York: McGraw-Hill, 1969. One of the better statements of the necessity for assimilation and cultural pluralism.

Fifteen
Strategies

A political strategy is a general course of action by which power can be increased or gained. Tactics are the means by which strategies are executed. For dominant-group organizations in American society, the strategies and tactics of gaining and exercising power are so familiar as to be embedded in a description of the political system (see Chapter 11). For the beleaguered minorities, however, the approaches are not so clear-cut. Because of their inability to gain positions in the political structure, minority groups are forced to reexamine strategic and tactical possibilities. In effect, if the political opportunity structure as constituted is disadvantageous to a group, the group will seek some way to enlarge it; in fact, it must do so, or it will be doomed to failure.

There are risks in political innovation, however. New strategies may not work as well as hoped; they may be more costly than ever imagined, or they can provoke a counterresponse powerful enough to destroy a group's political effectiveness. Strategies and tactics are, moreover, shaped by a group's goals, but logical consistency is rarely perfect because there are multiple strategic routes to a given goal and a variety of tactics available for any given situation. Just as important, strategies and tactics are affected by a group's circumstances and resources. Some are simply too ambitious for a group's capabilities (which does not mean they will not be tried anyway). Any generalization, then, must be tempered by the context of specific situations.

Minority groups have an array of strategies available to them. The more "moderate" approaches—integration and access—assume that the political system itself is sufficiently flexible and has enough built-in slack to allow minorities to find a useful niche, a degree of power commensurate with their numbers and needs. Moreover, the moderate approaches would ultimately lead to cultural pluralism as the final construct of the society. The more militant and radical approaches require societal change in the sense of moving away from the present trends of political and governmental action and approaches.

Strategies of Moderation

The basic "moderate" strategies accept most of the premises of the American society. They rest on the assumption that dominant groups and institutions, given the opportunity to work with minorities and to recognize minority problems, will accept minority groups into the political structure. If confronted with minority power, they will at least cooperate in fulfilling welfare and legal goals. In this respect, dominant groups can be considered to be as deprived, in their own way, as minority groupings. Outmoded social arrangements, habits of thought, and sheer ignorance have perpetuated conditions that are satisfactory to neither dominant nor minority groups, but the former have allowed those conditions to continue because they are so much less deprived than minorities. Thus, whites are profoundly troubled by the condition of the cities, and expend vast sums of money on ineffective programs; they live in fear of racial violence without trying to understand what causes that violence; they stifle intellectual freedom in their universities and for themselves without understanding what they are doing; and they deprive themselves of the diversity and the richness of life that could be the products of minority-dominant equality.

Integration

Integration, along with its somewhat elderly uncle, desegregation, is the most direct route to cultural pluralism. It is also a clear-cut strategy for attaining welfare and status goals. Desegregation was aimed at eliminating the barriers that created ghettoization; integration is the affirmative action to eliminate ghettoization. Its application to blacks is the most familiar, but it has relevance to other minorities as well. Were women to occupy a proportional number of both public and private leadership posts, men would learn that women are as fully qualified and competent as men, thereby gaining for the women the welfare and status goals they seek and teaching men that the two sexes can work together as equals. Were students fully integrated into the teaching and administrative structures of the colleges and universities, they, too, would demonstrate their capacity and their commitment to the institutions, and, equally important, they would gain the opportunity to shape the practices and performances that affect them.

Two results can be expected from integration. The first has already been emphasized. Dominant groups and minority groups would learn to understand, respect, and cooperate with each other. In place of fear, resentment, and tension, mutual respect would arise. The old "we-they" category would be replaced with a universal "we."

Second, full integration would have a practical effect. So that governments could distribute benefits to dominant groupings they would also have to distribute them to minorities. As one black mother said, "I don't care about numbers; I just want to see enough white faces in that classroom to know my kids are getting the same quality education." The same would apply in housing; no longer could minority neighborhoods be left to languish with inadequate services since all neighborhoods would be both dominant and minority neighborhoods. To under-service one grouping would be to under-service the other. From a pragmatic political stand-point, politicians could not afford to ignore the wishes of minorities because of the chance that minority and dominant interests were congruent.

Integration has now been doggedly pursued for decades. As a strategy, it con-tinues to remain the enunciated policy of the federal government and, willingly or unwillingly, of state and local governments as well. As a strategy, however, it has encountered severe practical and conceptual problems.

The most serious practical problems are those of deprivation, the effects of generations of discrimination. Whether blacks, Indians, Mexican-Americans, and Puerto Ricans are socially sorted according to income or according to race and culture, society does sort them out from other groupings. Unemployment is higher; functional illiteracy is higher; disease is more prevalent; reported crime rates are higher; drug abuse is more frequent; and attitudes toward sexual mores are different from the "middle-class, Anglo-Saxon" standards if not practices. The sorting process produces two concrete results. First, minorities can rarely afford homes in expensive suburbs; second, even if they can afford them, they may be denied access to them.

Schools—the primary targets of integration efforts—are still based principally on residential patterns. Although integration can be attained, at great cost in effort and energy, through the pairing of schools, busing, and building new schools on the edges of ghettos rather than in the centers, these are still considered "extraordinary" policy and administrative measures. They frequently produce a certain amount of ill will between minority and dominant groups: the minority because of the resistance it must overcome; the dominant because it is their resistance that is being over-come.

The same pattern holds true in employment and in attaining access to union membership. As of 1971, it seemed that the "Philadelphia Plan" was at best partly successful; the "Chicago Plan" was deemed a failure; the "New Orleans Plan" had never gotten started. Each was an effort to bring a certain minimum percentage of blacks into union training and apprenticeship positions. The failures were less a consequence of concept than of execution and a lack of will to make them succeed. At higher levels of employment, recruitment of minorities continued, but the economic recession of the early 1970s clearly demonstrated that the traditional pattern of "last hired, first fired" still applied.

This is, however, a pessimistic view. It was clear that for blacks and Indians, especially, and to an extent for Mexican-Americans, Puerto Ricans, and women, economic conditions were improving. There were larger opportunities for those having the education, faith in their opportunities, and the right geographic location to move into positions that had been previously held only by dominant members of the society. But, a decade of effort underscored another of the major practical problems. Integration was not to come about by either private efforts or by governmental policy statements and suasion. If it was to be a workable strategy, it would require decades of persistent lobbying, monitoring, court proceedings, administrative actions, and organizational effort. At the same time, ghettoization, especially in the large urban centers, continued.

From the conceptual standpoint, the first, and perhaps the most difficult, question concerning integration was: Is it worth it as a strategy? Considering the effort required, would the results validate the costs? Integration as a strategy assumes that cultural pluralism is both desirable and attainable as an ultimate goal for minorities. Questions about cultural pluralism also cast doubts on the usefulness of integration as a strategy to pursue that goal. Conceded that public opinion polls indicated a diminution in personal prejudice toward blacks, little concrete achievement could be seen as a result of that lessening. That is, individuals might dislike minorities less *in absentia,* but, when confronted with the tangible costs of integration in the form of busing children to schools, "invasion" of their neighborhoods, higher tax costs for training and social-welfare programs, and competition for limited employment opportunities, would they continue to be tolerant?

Second, integration requires a degree of self-denial on the part of minorities themselves. Since dominant groups clearly possess a monopoly of welfare resources, real integration requires that minorities seek welfare goals in the context of dominant institutions and behavior. In effect, to gain the status and welfare goals controlled by dominant groups, a minority must sacrifice at least a few integrity goals. And to a number of blacks, especially the younger generation, the bargain looks like a poor one. For black colleges to accept white applicants, for blacks to be scattered according to income throughout now predominantly white residential areas, for blacks to become relatively isolated junior executives in white-controlled firms is to surrender integrity goals in exchange for achieving strictly personal instrumental goals (on the white man's terms). Integration also dilutes the political power of a potentially cohesive bloc. As one youthful black political leader argued, "If I were whitey, and had any vision at all, I'd push open housing like crazy. What kind of political power would 23 million blacks have if they were scattered over 180 million whites? They'd vanish, they could be discriminated against, pushed around—and forgotten. And there's not a thing a one of them could do about it."

But, because cultural pluralism still contains the greatest promise of the least tension among minority and dominant groups, integration as a strategy continues to have appeal. The costs in time, energy, and money are obviously high, but, for some minority members, the costs would be well worth the fulfillment of the goal.

Access

Although much has already been said about the politics of access, a few additional points need to be made. First, as a strategy for political action, the politics of access assumes that the dominant political system is open enough so that leverage can be gained. Second, it is a multipurpose strategy. It can be directly used as a means to accomplish legal and welfare goals, or it can be the first of several strategies. Thus, almost every goal and therefore almost every associated strategy requires initially extracting concessions or benefits from the political system, whether these are the removal of Jim Crow laws, funds for busing, or statutory changes permitting community control. Except for revolution, all strategies depend upon some degree of access.

Third, the politics of access is the politics of direct power. Unlike integration, the success of which does require a measure of good will on the part of dominant members of society, the politics of access assumes that dominant politicians will respond to power in their accustomed manner. Their primary goal is to maintain their own power; if to do so they must deal with minorities whom they have ignored in the past, they will. Mills Godwin, democratic governor of Virginia, who was a leader of the massive resistance movement of the 1950s, openly appealed to the rising black vote in his campaign for governor in 1965; Moon Landrieu, mayor of New Orleans, did the same; governors of Alabama, Georgia, and South Carolina made public and open appeals for racial tolerance; all of these were repetitions of patterns that had been established earlier in the northern industrial states. The reasons, it could be argued, lie simply in the growth of a black electorate, the election of blacks to state and local offices, and the recognition by white politicians that to reduce their costs and risks they must appeal to black political groups and bargain with them.

Nor are the results of the politics of access limited only to blacks. Students have gained admittance to faculty and administrative committees, university boards of trustees, and curriculum review boards. They have even seen the establishment of state commissions on youth problems. Women have won increasing recognition of their employment demands, the desegregation of previously all-male public and private facilities, and the formation of courses of study on the problems and needs of women in colleges. Chicanos, under the leadership of Cesar Chavez, won a major battle with the California produce industry and achieved union recognition and bargaining rights. The politics of access, as a means of finding positions of power within the political system, has shown results and has simultaneously shown that the political system does conform to its own standards of power.

Three major concerns dampen the obvious successes of the politics of access. The first is simply the basic limits of power for a numerical minority within a system that stresses numerical majorities. Because minority groupings have been deprived for so long, it can be argued that their needs are in excess of their voting strength.

The legacy of deprivation cannot be removed by proportional representation because the legacy has been cumulative.

Second, the politics of access assumes that the basic standards and values of the system are good and that minorities can satisfy their needs by conforming to those values. The rules of the game were written by dominant groups, but minorities are expected to play by them even though they had no share in writing them. In spite of limited resources, fewer numbers, greater vulnerability, and the pressing costs of deprivation, minorities are expected to follow the rigorous demands of a political system that requires money, numbers, staff, time, and patience. Institutions such as seniority systems, extraordinary voting majorities, multiple veto points, frequent elections, and shared powers mean that the relative costs for minorities are higher. The pay-offs are smaller in relation to costs, and the results are slow in coming for groups that require fast action so that people who live in poverty, misery, illness, and hopelessness may be relieved of their deprivations before another generation has passed on. In short, the politics of access, although a necessary adjunct to other strategies, may have inherent limitations as the sole strategy for minority groups.

Third, the politics of access may ask more of minority groups than they, as political organizations, can deliver. The necessity for bargaining and compromise may be intolerable (see Chapter 12). For dominant groups, free of economic deprivation and socially and psychologically secure, to give a little in return for a little is no serious matter. But, if a minority makes concessions on housing programs, some people may have to live in substandard housing; if it surrenders a point on a food stamp program, hundreds, perhaps thousands, of children may go hungry; if it tolerates a delay in educational reform, young people will graduate before they can benefit from the change; or if it compromises on employment programs, blacks, women, or Mexican-Americans may be frustrated, desperate, and dependent. The realities of the two positions are in conflict: dominant groups emphasize process; minority groups, substance.

A minority leader who accepts the process of bargaining and compromise risks losing the support of his own group. He leaves himself open to being accused of having sold out to the power structure, of having forgotten those who helped put him in a position of power and who depended on him to obtain benefits for them. Because the politics of access is fundamentally a politics of instrumental ends and means, to pursue it devotedly is to risk destroying the identification base of a minority group. Factionalization, every-man-for-himself, or disillusion and frustration can be the prices paid.

Nonetheless, the politics of access, whatever its weaknesses as a single strategy (and not all would agree that these weaknesses are controlling), remains the strategic means to other strategies. It is a set of maneuvers that can be used to pursue other methods. As such, most minority groups at some point are forced to rely on it.

Militant Strategies

The "militant" strategies can be so called because they involve the pressing of claims on dominant institutions, based on the assumptions that what can be gained will be only at great resistance, that the power structure cannot be dealt with except from a position of great internal strength, and that, basically, only self-interest and naked power shape political relationships. The militant strategists contemplate changes in the "normal" processes of American politics and in the present power structure. Both changes demand more than the usual give-and-take of pluralistic politics and a greater degree of minority identification and self-awareness than are required by the moderate approaches.

Compensatory Equality

The concept of compensatory equality is directly related to the idea of substantive democracy. The flaw in the politics of access as a strategy for a deprived minority confronting an affluent dominant society can be overcome only if the dominant institutions provide the resources. Militants argue that the resources are owed to the minority as retroactive compensation for generations of slavery, domestic servitude, inadequate pay, poor education, humiliation, and degradation. They insist that those who built the nation (or who owned it in the first place) should be paid what the dominant society owes them, as a moral and practical matter.

The payment can take a number of forms: a guaranteed annual income that would insure a decent standard of living; a massive lump-sum payment ("reparations"); the reservation of specific political and economic positions for members of minorities; the guarantee of a minority veto power over various programs and policies; or a combination of two or more forms. In one step, short-cutting the tedious negotiations and evolutionary processes of integration and the politics of access, minorities would have the resources they need to meet their welfare and status goals and the capacity to pursue their ultimate goals and to do battle with dominant groups on an even footing.

The costs in dollars and in power would be high to dominant groups, but militants argue that the alternatives (such as revolution) might be far more costly. Moreover, the strategy of compensatory equality has the advantage of establishing a firm objective, one that would fulfill the most pressing intermediate goals and that would enormously widen minority opportunity structures.

In this respect, compensatory equality has other applications: minority members whose qualifications do not meet admissions standards could be accepted by colleges and universities; minority members could participate in special training programs not available to others; or private enterprise priorities could be reversed so that minority members might be employed even if it would mean operating at a loss for a period of time. Common to all of these is an effort to compensate for past deprivation.

The greatest advantage that compensatory equality offers minorities is the rapid satisfaction of welfare goals. Group leaders can focus the attention of group members on a tangible target, explain it in terms of identification and self-awareness, and, if it is achieved, claim credit for the victory. Further, if compensatory equality were attained either generally or in specific instances, the minority group itself would be in a strengthened political position in relation to dominant groups and institutions. Power relations would no longer consist of the affluent versus the deprived.

The greatest theoretical disadvantage of compensatory equality is its dependency on the forced or voluntary generosity of dominant groups. Whereas minority groups may feel that their history and their present efforts have earned them the benefits, payment must come from dominant groups. Moreover, how can a price tag—whether in dollars or in quotas—be put on the minority experience? In effect, dominant groups can make the payment and feel they have washed their hands of guilt or responsibility. If the price turns out to have been low, minorities may well be left with little bargaining leverage.

Deferred Pluralism

An important variant of the politics of access is the strategy of deferred pluralism. To follow this strategy, a minority would withdraw into itself, fulfill its integrity goals, build its own political resource base through independent efforts, and, once strong enough, return to the general political arena ready to claim its place in the power structure. The purpose is to be able to deal from a position of strength, which the dominant system could ignore only at its own risk. In this sense, deferred pluralism reverses the "normal" sequence in which the politics of access leads to another strategy; deferred pluralism could lead to eventual participation in the politics of access on a stronger basis.

In its milder forms, deferred pluralism is, of course, no more than the preliminary tactical organization required for political action. In its more militant forms, however, it requires a degree of separatism, a willingness to adopt aggressive political tactics, a deliberate shunning of premature cooperation and bargaining, and a willingness to make exceptional, short-term sacrifices to achieve internal strength.

The strategy of deferred pluralism defines both integration and premature participation in the politics of access as traps to be avoided. Dominant groups cannot be trusted; they will exploit weakness, use minorities for their own ends, and then reject them. To those who advocate the use of this strategy, the only alternative is group cohesion, uniting the entire minority, and an avoidance of fraternization with the "enemy." Black colleges should remain black and should develop their own cultural perspective in complete freedom from the pressures of the dominant society. Women should avoid association with males until a full consciousness of sisterhood has been developed. Students should avoid the paternalistic concessions of "liberal" faculty members and administrators and concentrate on developing their own institutions. When the minority is assured of its own strength and identity, it can deal with dominant groups on a power basis, and, at that time, political cohesion and organization will make itself felt.

It would seem that one possible ultimate goal of deferred pluralism is as likely to be structural pluralism as it is to be cultural pluralism. Certainly, once a minority had developed its own internal resources, a pattern of identification, and a strong sense of cohesion, it would be reluctant to surrender the pragmatic and psychological benefits derived from them. Thus deferred pluralism could very well lead not to a politics of access but to a politics of community control.

Radical Strategies

The radical strategies require a fundamental shift in power. The power to influence governmental and political decisions regarding a particular minority should belong to that minority—not to a dominant monopoly or a minority-dominant coalition. To achieve a shift in power, a minority must obviously force a degree of political reconstruction. Because they require the rearrangement of the present society, such strategies as community control and various forms of revolution are necessarily "radical." Further, they assume that minority and dominant institutions, as presently constituted, are incompatible; neither can survive as a dependent or an adjunct of the other—or even as a partner.

Community Control

Although community control is not a new idea, it began to attract serious attention in the late 1960s. In part, it grew out of the frustrations of powerlessness—the feeling that the basic apparatus of government was so remote from minority control that it needed to be brought back to "the people." In part also, the idea of community control stemmed from the concept of participatory democracy—that those affected by decisions should make the decisions. The Community Action program, with its emphasis on "maximum feasible participation," and the Model Cities program, with the same proviso, were experiments in limited community control. In New York City's educational system, however, community control became the battle cry. And it was there that the basic theory was developed.

In brief, community control is a strategy of shifting legislative and administrative control from the traditional jurisdictions (cities and counties) and their networks of intergovernmental relations to local areas, specifically to neighborhoods made up primarily or entirely of minority populations. The local citizens would determine program content and priorities, select officials and administrative personnel, and evaluate results, whether in education, health, law enforcement, poverty programs, physical planning, or public works.

In its more moderate forms, community control can be considered a means of making bureaucracy more responsive to its clientele. In its more militant forms, it is a means of placing program design and implementation in the hands of those affected, so that programs are not designed and run to benefit dominant groups. It can be argued that educational curricula are designed for white, middle-class people and taught by them; law enforcement is aimed principally at protecting the middle class by repressing the poor; and physical planning (housing, urban renewal, and parks and playgrounds) is aimed at the economic and social benefit of the power structure. The only way to correct the imbalance is to transfer control of the political opportunity structure from dominant groups to minority groups.

There are practical problems associated with community control. What defines a "community?" Where will the resources for implementing programs come from? What if various elements within the community itself disagree? In addition, the concept of community control is not consistent with many of the contemporary norms of administrative and policy practice: the efforts to achieve coordination, uniformity of quality, and economies of scale.

As demonstrated in New York City, teachers are reluctant to surrender their hard-won collective bargaining privileges to community boards. Police share that attitude. Even sympathizers fear that parochial politics will become the standard in place of judgments based on equity and professional competence. The advocates of community control argue that many of these criticisms are rationalizations or screens and, in fact, are symptomatic of the problem. To worry about administrative neatness is to stress procedural democracy. That teachers and policemen are anxious about their unions is indicative of a standard of performance that places bureaucratic and selfish goals ahead of good and effective education and law enforcement.

Community control can be a strategy leading to structural pluralism, or it can be a route to separatism. Its most serious problem is that of resources, for to depend on dominant funding might be to have the form of control but to lack the substance. Community control requires the development of a community's economic base that is fairly independent of the larger society.

There are, of course, less radical alternatives. Dominant governmental institutions could conceivably be persuaded to provide bloc grants with no strings attached, but the amounts of money and the ways in which it is spent are bound to be tension-producing issues. The tradition of accounting for the use of public funds would die hard, and such accounting implies control from a higher level.

The appeal of community control is obvious, however. In its early stages, at least, it combines many of the virtues of separatism without making the final break. It allows a minority to govern that which affects it most directly without requiring the minority to take on functions that are better and more economically handled by the larger jurisdiction. And as important, it gives real power to those who feel powerless.

Revolution

Revolution is aimed at the ultimate goal of reconstituting society. Its basic purpose is to transfer power from one set of hands to another, taking power from "them" and gaining it for "us." Revolution can be considered necessary for two reasons. First, those who possess power are unwilling to give it up. They possess it for their own satisfaction; the small amount they are willing to share is insignificant and easily taken away if not used to the liking of those in power. The only way to get power is to wrest it from those who hold it. Second, as seen from the minority perspective, the holders of power use it to deliberately or indifferently crush minorities. The power structure creates a system in which powerholders cooperate with one another to strengthen their own positions while allowing just enough benefits to dribble down to the little people so that they must compete endlessly and desperately with each other for them. To survive, the average citizen must please the powerholders and reject the powerless.

The grip of the power structure on society leads to a pervasive corruptness and a state of anxiety. Even the "successful" who have been denied access to the power structure fear that their success will be taken away from them unless they adopt the postures and values of those in power. This fear finds expression in racism, the subjugation of women, the "programming" of students, the persecution of the young for daring to dress and behave differently, and direct exploitation of the blue- and lower-paid white-collar workers, as well as indirect exploitation of the middle classes.

The situation can be changed not through piecemeal efforts at reform by means of community control or strategies of access, but through a full-scale dismantling of the corporate, bureaucratic structure of society. The revolution could take the form of the classic Jacobin-Bolshevik method, that is, through the intense efforts of a dedicated band of professional revolutionaries whose function is to establish revolutionary cadres, to raise the awareness of the oppressed to the point that they will take action when the opportunity presents itself, and to help create that opportunity through revolutionary guerrilla tactics.

Or, the revolution could come about by exposing the "internal contradictions" in the system. These contradictions include a stability that rests on individual insecurity, the affluence of a few based on the economic deprivation of many, the wars against colored peoples fought by drafted colored peoples, and education paid for by students who have no control over its content nor its purpose which is alien and hateful to the student. They are expressed in the dilemmas of the middle-class worker who competes frantically all day to earn enough money for alcohol and tobacco to relieve the effects of such competition, of the teacher who fills the minds of children with material that the teacher knows to be useless but does so in order to keep his job, and of a governmental system that pollutes the surface of the moon with expensive bundles of metal, plastic, and wire but cannot find the money to eliminate air pollution in its own cities. Because Americans are fundamentally no more foolish or cruel than other peoples, when they recognize the extent to which their humanity and self-respect is destroyed by the system they are forced to support, they will revolt against it and produce a system more consonant with their own values.

These two approaches to the same strategy are not mutually exclusive or even separate. One may be necessary for the final effort; the other is essential to convince the mass population that revolution would serve their economic and cultural interests and would only be resisted by the members of the power structure.

The major problems with revolution as a strategy are empirical. First, it is by no means certain that a revolution is possible in a modern, post-industrial society. All other revolutions have occurred in semi-industrial or agrarian societies, and it may be that the concentration of technological power that resides in the hands of government forecloses an effective challenge to that power. Second, it is by no means certain that "the people" are sufficiently unhappy with their lot to disrupt it for the uncertainty of an unknown regime, a period of civic strife, and a probable loss of amenities. Some minorities might be actively miserable, but the vast body of the American populace may be sufficiently content with their physical circumstances that they prefer palliative to reconstitution. In fact, the existing power structure may be in power simply because it possesses a little more of what most Americans want for themselves. Finally, it is not certain that revolution would produce a real reconstitution of American values. Racism, sexism, or opposition to social deviance may not come from a particular political and economic relationship; rather, the political and economic relationship may be a product of cultural values. Although it can be hoped that values can be changed by consciousness-raising efforts, it is not certain that cultural norms can be changed in less than several generations.

Revolution is a desperate measure—a last resort—involving great risks not only for the revolutionaries but for the society they are trying to change. If the goal is reconstitution, however, a minority group has little choice. Revolution may not require the use of machine guns and molotov cocktails, but it obviously requires challenging the whole system with the intent of reducing that system to such a state of ineffectiveness that something else must emerge from it. There is no reason that such an effort will not meet with dogged and violent resistance.

Which Goal? Which Strategy?

What are the best goals? Which is the most logical strategy? It is tempting to try to answer those questions. But, if the purpose here is to understand rather than prescribe, it is more useful to recognize that each goal and each strategy involves an interpretation of American politics and the American system upon which people are willing to act.

The minority situation is complex. The difficulties confronting a minority in selecting goals and strategies was vividly illustrated in March, 1972. During that month, over 3,000 delegates met in Gary, Indiana, in the first National Black Political Convention. The hope of the convention was to create a unified national organization through which all blacks could pursue their demands.

Severe stresses became apparent in the course of the convention, however. Delegates from several states walked out; others took conflicting positions on the same issues. The consensus of the delegates was to oppose busing as a means of achieving integration in schools. At the same time, however, the NAACP was attacking President Nixon for his opposition to busing.

Although the issue of busing was only one of many, it illustrated an important point. Not only was there disagreement about strategies (integration versus community control), but there was a more fundamental disagreement among black leaders about goals (cultural pluralism, structural pluralism, or separatism). Nor was the black experience unique. Mexican-American groups, Indian organizations, and women's organizations were locked in the same debate, although rarely as publicly or as intensely as were the blacks.

In short, that groups drawn from the same minority and sharing the same mark can differ on goals and strategies indicates that the minority condition is far from homogeneous. Within the women's liberation movement, NOW hopes to attain only legal and welfare goals while certain chapters of WITCH and other groups advocate separatism based on sex; the NAACP and the Black Panthers subscribe to drastically divergent views of American society. Both examples indicate that, even with minority self-awareness, the groups that are formed on the basis of that self-awareness understand their circumstances, opportunities, and mandates very differently. Militants would argue that these differences are a result of differing levels of self-awareness: the failure of the moderates to face up to the real intransigence of the dominant system. Others would argue that the more militant and radical approaches are expressions of individual psychopathology: fantasies of possessing power, paranoia, and the working out of childish aggressive urges. But the multiplicity of strategies and goals is indicative of the different levels of objective and subjective deprivation within each minority and the different means of expressing minority self-awareness.

Very few minority goals and strategies coincide with a pluralist view of American politics. They incorporate approaches to the American political system that rest on three important assumptions:

1. The "standard" view of the American political system is incorrect from the minority perspective.

2. The political system is morally wrong.
3. The political system must be changed.

Although some goals and strategies may be more palatable to dominant groups than others, all are statements of discontent and statements of political intention. And, the discontent and intentions find expression in political tactics that seem frightening and threatening to many Americans.

Bibliography

Altshuler, Alan A. *Community Control: The Black Demand for Participation in Large American Cities.* New York: Pegasus, 1970. The best single discussion of the concept and practice of community control.

Carmichael, Stokeley, and Charles V. Hamilton. *Black Power: The Politics of Liberation in America.* New York: Vintage, 1967. A closely reasoned and well-documented argument for the strategy of "deferred pluralism."

Clark, Kenneth B., and Jeannette Hopkins. *A Relevant War Against Poverty.* New York: Harper & Row, 1969.

Glenn, Norval D., and Charles M. Bonjean, eds. *Blacks in the United States.* San Francisco: Chandler, 1969. Many of the essays in this collection cover the various goals available to the black minority.

Howard, John R., ed. *Awakening Minorities.* New York: Aldine, 1970.

Kenniston, Kenneth. *Young Radicals.* New York: Harcourt, Brace and World, 1965. This work examines carefully both the nature of young people in revolt against "the system" and their aims.

Litt, Edgar. *Ethnic Politics in America.* Glenview, Ill.: Scott Foresman, 1970. A very useful review of various minority strategies, with special reference to how these strategies apply to ultimate goals.

Morgan, Robin, ed. *Sisterhood is Powerful.* New York: Vintage, 1970. An excellent collection of readings that lays out the more militant strategies available to women.

Wallerstein, Immanuel, and Paul Starr, eds. *The University Crisis Reader: The Liberal University Under Attack.* New York: Vintage, 1971. An outstanding collection of essays and readings that describe, among other things, the strategies available to students in rebellion.

Sixteen
Tactics

Political tactics are the means to gain specific ends, the way in which strategies are carried out: applied power. Whereas most strategies tend toward intermediate and ultimate goals, tactics are more expedient and pragmatic. Revolutionaries, for example, might well adopt for a time tactical forms that seem better suited to a politics of access; and those pursuing integration might well seem to be using "radical" tactics. Virtually all minority group tactics have one thing in common: they are aimed at "destabilizing the system." Their purpose is to produce a new stability; for those seeking moderate goals, a stability in which minority groups would be included in the existing power curve; for those seeking more radical or militant goals, a stability that would be represented by an entirely new curve.

The Importance of Stability

Although the American political system is—justly or unjustly—proud of its ability to adapt to change, its ability to maintain its own stability and that of society is equally important. Stability in social and political affairs incorporates a number of important—perhaps necessary—conditions of contemporary life. In the collective sphere, stability provides an assurance that the economy will not be disrupted, with investments devalued, capital equipment rusting, supplies cut off, and production unmarketable, that, in short, demand and supply and the forces underlying them will roughly coincide. It means that although population shifts will occur, each shift will be partly compensated by another and thus changes will be gradual rather than abrupt, continuous rather than discontinuous.

Stability in political affairs assumes that although voters may realign themselves in relation to the two great political parties, the realignment will take place over generations rather than as an abrupt restructuring of values and perceptions.

Collective stability does not mean that all changes are either scientifically predictable or controllable, or even that it is possible to prepare for them were they known in advance, but it does mean that the impact of change is limited. In effect, a kind of dialectic occurs, a tension between past patterns and emerging ones, and the result is gradual change rather than sudden change. Americans do not, all of them at once, stop driving large American automobiles in preference for small foreign ones; they do not suddenly abandon single-family housing for apartment complexes; they do not give up smoking; and, even though many may be disgusted with either political party or both, a large percentage continues to vote, many for the party they have always supported.

Individual stability means psychological security. If a person works, goes to college, and puts savings into insurance, the stock market, or the bank, the future is assumed to be a more or less known quantity. Illness, accident, divorce, or other personal crises may radically alter that future, but within limits an individual handles only a few anxieties at a time. His job will not disappear overnight (he expects) and his home will be there when he returns from work. Although his life may be somewhat unstable economically, he believes it to be physically secure. Unlike his ancestors, he does not need to examine every tree, shadow, or corner to anticipate an ambush. He cannot claim to be free of "fear and trembling," but his social, political, and economic systems reduce the number of objects upon which he must focus his attention at any one time. Collective stability is a means to individual stability; institutions act as surrogate worriers for an individual's anxieties.

Stability produces a degree of predictability. In government political candidates know that the office they have won will be there when they go to claim it. They may be faced with innovation once in office, but the demands on them to cope with change will be limited by past commitments as well as by present conditions and future circumstances. Administrators can rely on past precedents as reasonably safe guides to present action and can look forward to a level of forthcoming operations that approximates that of the past.

Political stability is largely guaranteed by bargaining and compromise under the present political system. Negotiations are almost invariably between change and the status quo (and the various proponents of each). The compromise is *some* change. Whether it is weighted in favor of the status quo or major innovation depends on the power of the participants, but rarely does one side win everything that it demands. The unspoken assumption is that "the system" can always tolerate some adjustment, but it cannot tolerate discontinuity.

Stability, then (or, if preferred, incremental change), becomes an end in itself. It is not only a value, but a necessary condition. As a value, it shapes the preconceptions of those in politics, the preferences that influence them in selecting strategies and tactics. As a condition, it determines which strategies and tactics are "legitimate," which goals are proper, what can be bargained, what can be compromised, and what the final outcome of the negotiations will probably be.

One of the vital functions of a political leader is the preservation of stability and the handling of situations that could produce drastic instability, what are commonly called "crises." The "crisis of the cities" concerns the ability of municipal governments to continue the services that populations have come to depend upon, to keep racial tensions nonviolent, and, in short, to function as they have pretty much always functioned. The "welfare crisis" concerns the possibility that the pyramiding of demands placed on a bureaucratic system will lead either to violent rebellion by welfare recipients or to a taxpayers' rebellion against the costs, which could precipitate conflict between the recipients and bureaucracy. A political leader attempts to control the destabilizing directions of these problems, to channel them into familiar patterns and categories, and to find solutions that incorporate enough of the past to be in harmony with a pattern of continuity but enough of the future to anticipate new conditions.

For a minority group, the thrust toward stability in the social system provides a tactical opportunity. Dominant groups tend to define stability as a condition that excludes minorities from positions of power; as a consequence, few minorities have a vested interest in political stability, since it means preserving the power curve as presently constituted. A principal goal of a minority political organization's tactical scenarios is to interfere with the pattern of stability; and, there are major differences in the approaches of moderate, militant, and radical groups. Moderate groups may use radical tactics, but their goals and strategies are primarily an effort to rearrange the pattern of political stability so that minorities can be a part of the existing pattern; militant groups go one step further, having as their goals and strategies sufficient disruption of the pattern that it must be rebuilt—with their active participation in the rebuilding process; radical groups have as their goals the total destruction of the existing pattern and the ultimate substitution of a new one.

Although tactics may sometimes overlap, these differing approaches to goals and strategies do tend to separate preferences for tactics. Moderates and militants are reluctant to destroy "the system," to force it to the point at which it becomes totally inoperable. Their goals, rather, are to play on its weaknesses; that is, on its basic tendency toward stability to the point that any concession becomes palatable to dominant groups and institutions. Radicals, however, are not seeking concessions except to the extent that these further emphasize the internal contradictions of the system. They seek total destabilization from which reconstitution eventually must come.

As important as these differences are, both to the groups themselves and to dominant institutions, minority political tactics are not as easily categorized into moderate, militant or radical types as either goals or strategies. A group will use the tactics at hand; it will pursue its intermediate and ultimate goals and strategies using the tactics that the situation calls for. As a result, seemingly "radical" tactics will be pursued by a moderate group, and what defines its moderation are its goals and its unwillingness to push its tactical advantages to the point of total destabilization. Tactics are the use of power. And, although in Martin Luther King's phrase, the "means are the ends becoming," many if not most minority organizations feel they cannot indulge in the philosophical restraint the dictum requires. Minority groups are relatively powerless; they must use the tactics of the powerless.

Coalition Tactics

Every minority group has one resource: its own numbers. If the ties of identification are strong enough, those numbers can be counted upon to influence political decisions, *if someone else needs them.* The logic of coalition politics is to find someone who needs a minority group's resources and who will "pay" for the use of them. Some other political group seeking to gain a higher position on the power curve, to create a stability in which it will be more powerful, may need to add to its own resources, and the minority can hope to become a part of the process, thus advancing its own cause. The theory is one of simple arithmetic: a given group's numbers are multiplied by a mutually useful alliance. Coalitions work not only for pressure-group politics, but also for elections, for legislative politics, and for pressing cases through the judicial system.

Obviously, coalition politics appears to be no more than a form of the politics of access, and, in fact, the two are literally the same. Coalitions are built on a system of bargains, promises of mutual support, and shared benefits and rewards in case of victory. The tactical scenarios for pluralistic politics apply for a coalition once it is built.

The only major variant is the hoped-for coalition of minorities: blacks, Indians, students, women, Mexican-Americans, poor whites, Puerto Ricans, homosexuals, and the invisible members of each grouping. Presumably, if these groupings were mustered into one coalition, it would be of sufficient strength to control a large part of American politics. As a plan it is appealing; as a reality it is no doubt capable of local success, but as a general tactical scheme it would seem to suffer from the difficulties of divisions within each grouping, divisions that seem to be a long way from uniting. Further, there is a tactical inconsistency in attempting to create strong intraminority identification and integrity while coalescing with other minorities. Only by accepting the class interpretation of politics, arguing that it is the underclass banding against the bourgeoisie, can this inconsistency be overcome.

The basic requirements of coalition tactics are as follows:

First, to determine which other group or groups need the minority group and its support. The determination requires cold-blooded realism. It is pointless for a minority group to ally with another group if even together the two would stand no chance of success. In an urban political setting, for example, a minority that allied with a feeble reform movement might simply hamper its opportunities. The choice has to be based on an instrumental estimate of the value of the other group or groups. If a winning coalition means tying in with the "bosses," then that is what must be done; if it requires allying with political leaders who may have personally racist or sexist attitudes, that is what must be done.

Second, to establish contact, preferably covertly and in privacy initially to avoid countertactics. Contact must be with the real leaders of the group in question, rather than with factional leaders. Contact can be made through an intermediary (if that person can be trusted); it can be made after a series of conciliatory public statements (which help to create a "constructive" climate); or it can be made directly.

Third, to establish the terms on which the coalition can be built. If the coalition intends to move into electoral politics, it must decide which offices are to be targets and how they will be apportioned among the participants in the coalition, what programs will be the special preserve of each participant, and what will be the respective share of resources to be committed and responsibilities for action. If the goal is to win program concessions, the participants need to agree on what maximum and minimum concessions will be satisfactory. The prearrangement is to avoid future quarreling about who was to receive what and who was to do what, which can lead to a breakup of the coalition should it be under severe stress.

Fourth, to combine group efforts by means of an organizational form, either public and formal, or private and informal. The organizational form provides a means of working out details as tactical problems arise and as resources need to be reallocated. It also allows each participant to monitor the behavior of the other.

Fifth, to carry out the commitments and ensure that the other participants do likewise.

The leader of a women's organization illustrated some of these points in a letter to me in the summer of 1970:

> The situation we faced was like this. There was – – Company which was about the biggest hirer of the sisterhood around, but you can't imagine the kind of exploitation and repression the working sisters suffered under. We pushed, but you know we just didn't have it going for us. I think we could have made a case under the Civil Rights Act but, no money and no cheap legal talent.
>
> So, one of the sisters was into this ecology group. They were a pretty sad bunch, MCP,[1] messing around with speaker's forums, news letters–all that scene, but no action. But this – – Company was like an easy mark for them, it was screwing up the environment with herbicides, stuff in the streams, I don't know what stuff. What we did was through this sister we talked to the ecology nuts a couple of times over coffee and all to see if we could put our gigs together.
>
> Well, the way it worked out was we could throw them some bodies for picket lines and house-to-house canvassing and stuff, stuff they were too uptight to do. And they had a couple of big deal attorneys in their group who were game to help put together a

[1] Male chauvinist pig.

complaint for our oppressed sisters. Well, to make a long story short, we had those business execs coming and going. They didn't know who'd hit them next or with what. So they agreed before the [State Pollution Control Board] to lay off. . . . Then came Catch 22. That funky legal talent from the eco-group really faded fast. . . . Tactically speaking, if we had to go that route again, and I mean *if,* we'll nail down the other stud's support a lot harder than we did, but you learn by doing. . . .

Obviously, coalition tactics establish a mutual dependency; they also establish conditions under which mutual suspicion and distrust can be high. For a coalition to last, and therefore to be successful in the politics of access, it must bargain for specific objectives that can be specifically met. Repeatedly, coalitions involving minority groups have fallen to pieces. They do so because in a minority-dominant group coalition, the minority may not be able to provide the resources it promised or the dominant group may fail to deliver what the minority believes it has coming, either correctly or not. Minority-minority coalitions, whether different minorities (such as blacks and Puerto Ricans or black and white students) or two or more groups belonging to the same minority have fallen to pieces for the same reasons, plus those associated with minority groups in general, that is, internal divisions and differing goals.

For minority groups, then, a general tactical rule is that groups can establish a working coalition if differences among them are minimal, if they have the same general strategies and goals in common, and if they can, as a result, deal with each other with the least possible distrust. It is clear that minority self-awareness alone is not sufficient; minority groups hoping to work together must also be pointed in similar directions and along similar paths.

The major effect of coalitions in which minority groups are a part is that the system is faced with a new power bloc. Through a coalition a minority group overcomes its isolation; it has not only increased its effective numbers, but also established outside contacts to be used in seeking power. The degree of de-stabilization produced is limited, since the coalition itself requires a bargaining process and will also have to bargain with other powerholders, but the simple emergence of the minority as a part of a newly formed power bloc introduces a novel element into the system. Until a new coalition makes its aims public and clear, until its targets are openly acknowledged, those in positions of power cannot be sure of what directions it may take. It possesses, at least briefly, the tactical element of surprise.

Bloc Tactics

An increasingly important modification of coalition tactics is "bloc tactics" or "selective participation." A primary difficulty with coalition politics is that the minority group places itself in a dependent position; it shares in tactical decisions and results, but it needs its partner as much as the partner needs it. Once the coalition is built, the participants become captives of each other. The arrangement is tolerable (especially if it brings tangible results) until one partner finds a better alternative. What ties a coalition together are instrumental functions. Minorities are vulnerable to broken commitments; they risk being abandoned once the other coalition partners have won what they sought. Theoretically, the converse is true as well, that is, minority groups could abandon their partners; but at least in dominant-minority coalitions, the needs of the minority are vaster and more pressing, and the relative costs of politics are higher. Because their political opportunity structure is narrower, they are apt to be more dependent on their partners than the reverse. Further, there are times and places when there are no potential partners for a coalition. The need, then, is for a tactical alternative. Bloc tactics are one such alternative.

Bloc Voting

The classic minority strategy is the bloc vote, that is, casting its votes cohesively for a designated candidate. Ethnic groupings pursued it for generations and it is still the basis of the "balanced ticket" in ethnically heterogeneous communities. As a technique, however, its usefulness has been limited for the new minorities, because except in a few places minority candidates have not been offered.

Chuck Stone (1968, p. 43), however, suggests further dimensions. The black vote should "oscillate" between the two major parties, so that neither party could take it for granted. This would be selective bloc voting, in which a minority electorate commits its votes not according to party label or party loyalty, but to achieve leverage. Each party would have to bid for the minority vote, which would go to the highest bidder. The advantages are obvious. Instead of being the captive of a coalition, the minority group could demand an attractive offer, and, if the offer were unsatisfactory, it could shift its allegiances to the opposing party. Neither party could assume the stability of the bloc vote; each would attempt to insure that stability by making concessions to the minority.

A number of prior conditions are necessary to make this tactic workable. First, the two parties must be sufficiently competitive to warrant their both seeking the minority vote. Although this may be the case in a national election (and it may not be, too), in state and, especially, local elections one-party dominance is frequent enough that even a minority swing vote cannot affect the smaller party's chances.

Second, the minority vote itself has to be "deliverable." To seek commitments, receive them, and then be unable to deliver the promised vote would eliminate the minority as a necessary calculation for either of the two parties in the future.

Third, a deliverable vote requires a high degree of organization, leadership, and identification.

And, finally, the structural opportunity must exist. That is, if the vote is not available to a minority (e.g., minors or students in a university system), or if a party refuses to deal with a minority regardless of its objective "need" for the vote (which occurred in the South after Reconstruction), then bloc voting is meaningless as a tactic.

A variation on the bloc vote oscillating between the two parties is "single shot" voting, or a vote focused on one office although a number of offices are to be filled in the same election. The single-shot vote serves, first, to demonstrate the potential power of the minority. And, second, if only one candidate is attractive to the minority group, the single-shot vote not only shows the group's strength, but also lets the candidate know to whom he owes his election (if he wins). Even if he has a hunch that he could have won without minority support, he can never be sure. He is thus made dependent on the minority to reduce his future risks; and, of course, if he himself is a member of the minority, all the better.

Single-shot voting can also be applied to minor political offices. One of the great vulnerabilities peculiar to local government is the large number of minor political offices that must be regularly filled. They include such positions as treasurer, member of the school board, tax assessor, sheriff, clerk, auditor, and attorney. The parties find these offices a rich source of patronage, and since few voters care about the offices or who fills them, they are easily controlled by the party organizations with a small handful of loyal voters. Although these offices lack the glamor of other, more salient positions, they often present a valuable opportunity to minority groups for obtaining welfare and status goals. A minority can run a candidate for one of these offices and be fairly assured that the mass electorate will be indifferent. It becomes a straight fight between the core loyalists of the local parties and the minority organization, and it is possible for the latter to outnumber the former, especially if the two parties are competing for the office, thereby splitting the dominant vote. If the minority candidate wins, the minority gains an office that provides tangible benefits in the form of jobs and salaries, which can then be used to further strengthen the minority political organization.

Bloc voting is destabilizing, although easily compatible with the rules of the politics of access. Party loyalists tend to rail against the bloc vote when exercised by the new minorities, simply because it is destabilizing and therefore inconvenient to them. It reduces the predictability of the party contest. Dominant preference is for minorities to attach their loyalties to the two parties and having once done so become an assessable factor in the party struggle. For any segment of voters to respond to internally generated leadership, goals, and strategies increases the unpredictability of their behavior and the costs to party organizations to woo and win them. To restabilize the system, the party organizations must readjust their patterns of behavior to accommodate what they consider an unstable power element. This requires altering the power curve to include the minority group and its invisible membership, with all the anxiety, disruption, and confusion that accompanies changes in the power curve.

A somewhat more subtle version of bloc voting is "in and out" voting. Since elections in the United States are frequent, a minority can choose to turn out massively for a given election, perhaps exercising the single-shot vote, and, in the next, to abstain from voting at all. As a tactic, it demonstrates the power of the bloc vote and is directly destabilizing since the parties and their candidates cannot depend on or even anticipate minority voting behavior. The only way in which they can hope to "control" it is by making substantial commitments to the minority group.

As a tactic, however, in-and-out voting is both risky and difficult to use. Organization largely depends upon having something for the group's members to do; abstention is nonaction, and the group members can feel that not doing anything tangible to influence political decisions is a senseless procedure. They may tend to drift to more activist groups. In-and-out voting may be too subtle for any but those groups having the highest level of identification, which are apt to be groups with small memberships and thus little voting strength. Voting is a habit; to establish a pattern of behavior in which it is deliberately not a habit is to risk that the bloc vote will not be there when the time to vote comes.

The Strike and the Boycott

Bloc voting is useful only in electoral situations that are sufficiently competitive to give a minority group leverage. Moreover, bloc voting requires masses of people, and sometimes a minority group cannot satisfy that requirement except in local elections. A group simply may find that the electoral system effectively forecloses the possibility of using voting tactics with any hope of success.

There are, however, more specific tactics that can have a far-reaching impact. In addition to the resource of its numbers, however small they may be, every minority possesses a minimum of economic and political power. The tactical problem is to apply this power at those points at which minority participation is needed by the dominant society: where the money from minority members is vital to the conduct of business and their presence is essential to the functioning of institutions. To withdraw their patronage and support is to threaten the existence of the businesses and institutions that depend upon them. This was, of course, the purpose of the Montgomery, Alabama, bus boycott; it is the purpose of tenant strikes, boycotts of stores, student strikes, and boycotts by the clients of governmental agencies. In each case, the particular institution is destabilized, often with wider emotional and practical consequences for the society. The merchant, the landlord, the university, or the bureaucracy needs the minority members in order to function.

Much planning and organizing is required for a successful strike or boycott. The target must be selected carefully; it must be vulnerable. To boycott a store, for example, that does not depend on minority patronage for its existence is to court a disappointing and group-destroying defeat. Moreover, the group must be cohesive enough that the strike will be inclusive. The refusal of a small number of students to go to class may be a nuisance, but it does not necessarily create a destabilizing crisis. Finally, the members of the group must be able and willing to tolerate inconvenience and sacrifice: in a tenant strike, the risk of eviction (alternative housing must be available); in a strike against a retail store, travelling to some other place to shop (transportation must be available); in student strikes, the deferment of receiving a degree; and in strikes by workers or agency clientele, such as welfare recipients, economic losses (other sources of income must be available).

All of this stresses that a minority group must have the identification base and resources for a bitter and protracted struggle. If it is unable to carry out a boycott or strike once it has been launched because of overestimating its capabilities or underestimating the endurance of its opposition, the group itself will emerge from the struggle in a battered condition and those who depended upon it are left more deprived than before the effort was undertaken.

The purpose of a strike or boycott, however, is not only to destabilize the system but to equalize the costs of political action. The sacrifices made by a minority group can be matched by the costs suffered by its target. A shopowner or landlord can face bankruptcy, and an institution can continue to have overhead costs without the ability to perform its job, often with its sources of revenue being cut off. The test becomes that of staying power, which is why the target must be carefully chosen.

The problems associated with using the strike or boycott are those associated with the need for overriding group identification. The social and economic sacrifices can be accepted if the psychological rewards (identification functions) and eventual tangible rewards make the effort worth it. A famous boycott of the retail stores owned by whites in Port Gibson, Mississippi, in 1969, was built on strong identification (precipitated by the slaying of a black) in a small community. It also demanded intense organizational effort to preserve the integrity of the boycott.

The necessary ingredients for success in the use of the boycott or strike, then, are:

1. A vulnerable target—one that will be clearly and quickly damaged by the withdrawal of the minority's presence.

2. Group identification.

3. Alternative sources to fulfill the physical or psychological needs of the strikers or boycotters. Group identification can go a long way toward overriding fear and anxiety about the future, but if housing, food, or money is required the group must have the necessary resources or be able to obtain them.

4. Strong organization to handle the logistics and monitoring of the effort.

5. Sufficient tangible and intangible resources for staying power.

6. Realistic estimates of group capability and of the duration and intensity of the struggle.

Because a strike or a boycott is a dramatic effort, it can receive public attention through the media, which can help to enlist the support of potential invisible members of the group, but which can also help the opposition to enlist the support of its potential invisible members. In certain parts of the country, especially, such as the South and the West, the strike is considered to be "illegitimate" and "Communist-inspired." If a strike receives publicity through the media, the group must be ready to try to present its position in a way that will elicit support.

Flooding

Another, and now familiar, bloc tactic is that of "flooding" an institution with unwanted bodies. It was one of the bases of the civil rights movement of the early 1960s when public facilities and then jails were saturated with passive resisters. The National Welfare Rights Organization undertook a similar campaign in the late 1960s and early 1970s by swamping local welfare organizations with previously "undiscovered" clients and thereby contributing to a breakdown in local welfare systems.

Flooding destabilizes institutions because all operate on implicit or explicit anticipations of need for their facilities or services. If there is an increase of such magnitude that it is discontinuous with past trends, the institution cannot cope with the "crisis." Flooding, moreover, does not quite require the organizational sophistication that a strike or boycott does. Often a one-time appearance on the part of an individual is sufficient, rather than a continuous presence or effort. Flooding, however, is not applicable in all situations. Public rather than private institutions are more vulnerable to flooding. Students can, for example, register and reregister for classes, thereby swamping the college registration system.

Flooding, like all bloc tactics, is based on the realization that a complex economic and social system is a product of mutual dependencies, which in turn are predicated on the predicted future behavior of individuals and collectivities. If these expectations are not borne out, the institutions that make the system function face crises. The crises can be purely psychological, or they may be both psychological and practical, involving the loss of money, confusion over the allocation and use of manpower and resources, uncertainty about future needs, and the fear of institutional failure. Under enough stress, any concession can seem preferable to a continuation of the anxiety of a crisis.

Bloc tactics serve another purpose. They stress identification: the capacity of "us" to do something to "them." Even a minor victory can demonstrate that the powerful are not as invulnerable as they seem and the powerless are not as helpless as they thought. To see the system in confusion, its leaders flustered and frustrated, shows that the system is vulnerable to cohesive groups working with a purpose in mind. Members of minorities can break their habits of deference, thereby enlarging their capacity for self-awareness, group identification, and personal confidence. Those who have believed themselves to be powerless can begin to believe that they have power, and the belief is the first step toward creating the reality.

Street Tactics

Street tactics are actually a form of bloc tactics carried one step further; their emphasis is on publicness. Publicness enlarges a group's audience, which, it is hoped, will expand its invisible membership and perhaps even its actual membership. Publicness also highlights the responses of dominant groups and institutions. Neither action nor response can be ignored, and the commitments made or stances taken thus become public issues.

To a great extent, also, street tactics are demonstrative. They present the numbers, the concern, and the effort of the minority in a tangible form to a wide audience. They also provide some sort of crude measure of how dominant institutions respond. Finally, they may modify the attitudes of important parts of the public, and the modification of attitudes toward minorities is a destabilizing result in itself.

Street tactics carry an implied threat as well. A system that is dependent on stability is fearful of mobs, of intense bursts of emotion, and of disregard for the normal patterns of public behavior. Even though a street meeting or demonstration may be nonviolent, it produces anxiety—especially if a minority is participating, because of the common assumption that minorities are less mature, less responsible, and less in control of their emotions than members of the dominant society.

To summarize, street tactics serve four purposes: (1) like all bloc tactics, they destabilize the system; (2) they appeal to a larger audience by a public demonstration; (3) they call attention to a concern and the response to that concern; and (4) they pose a threat.

Demonstration and Protest

A demonstration, or mass rally or march, is no more than a public petition carried to a public place. The psychological persuasiveness of the act ("I was there, why not you? I took the risk, showed the interest and concern, why not you?") is its primary function. Coupled with that is the hoped-for persuasiveness of public concern directed at public officials who might feel their political opportunities endangered, their political and personal commitments challenged.

As a tactical exercise, a demonstration requires an enormous logistical effort. A time and place must be selected; meeting permits must be obtained; arrangements must be made for speakers, musicians, and other entertainers, for crowd control marshals, for emergency facilities for those who become ill, and for sanitary facilities; and contingency plans must be made in case the unexpected occurs. Moreover, there must be sufficient advance publicity and organizing effort to guarantee a good turnout, because a pathetically small demonstration does more damage to the participating group or groups than no demonstration at all.

A demonstration requires mass participation, and this is its greatest asset as a political tactic. Participation is accompanied by a sense of long-term commitment. It involves a break with the habits of deference and nonaction, and, to some extent, those who have been in a demonstration have a stronger identification with the organizing group.

In the 1960s, demonstrations became commonplace, thus weakening their effectiveness. Because of their frequency, their dramatic impact declined, as well as their appeal to the mass media, other onlookers, and remote participants. Each successive demonstration's capacity to reach a large audience, beyond the immediate participants, and to produce a large turnout had a tendency to decline. Constant demonstration threatens to become "normal" politics and, with normality, to lose its impact.

Nevertheless, demonstration and protest continue to be valuable tactical devices, still capable of drawing large audiences, as proven by the "May Day" demonstrations of 1971. In sum, demonstrations are useful to minority groups because:

1. They can help to produce identification with a particular cause in the minds of the onlookers as well as the participants and to convert identification with the cause into identification with the group, thereby increasing its invisible membership and its active membership.

2. They can help to destabilize the political system by changing the minds of political decision-makers who recognize that their political fortunes may be at stake.

3. They can help to destabilize the system by changing the attitudes of those who constitute the base of support of the powerholders.

4. They form a politics of release, an opportunity to vent frustrations and express opinions in a collective form.

As a destabilizing device, however, demonstrations remain a moderate tactic. They underscore grievances, make frustrations and concern public, and perhaps enlist new recruits, but fundamentally they are limited to the expression of feelings rather than changing political behavior.

Disruption

A large number of people are required to keep an institution running but it takes only a few to disrupt it. Disruption as a political tactic poses a direct threat to the system's stability. Interference with traffic, communications, or university classes create psychological and physical crises. When disruption is massive, it is almost impossible to control, except by a massive law enforcement effort.

Those engaging in the tactics of disruption need not undertake the complex logistical operations of those relying on demonstrations, but the tasks of planning, timing, and selecting targets are even more important. Since the goal is less that of maximizing participation than of stressing the vulnerability of the system—of placing it in a position of responding with excessive force and thus eliciting the sympathies and loyalties of others—the targets selected should be both reasonably impersonal and crucial. They should be impersonal because disruption aimed at an individual may actually evoke sympathy for the target. Students, for example, have been especially prone to violate this principle, thereby alienating potential sympathizers. The targets must be crucial enough to force the dominant institutions to defend them and, in the process of defending them, to make it appear that impersonal forces or processes are being brought to bear against self-sacrificing individuals. The "perfect" scenario is disruption aimed at a corporate entity that will defend itself with lines of uniformed policemen made faceless by their riot-protection gear, who resort to using police dogs and armored vehicles. Human beings (the disrupters) are then confronting the inhuman symbols of a bureaucratic system, which, even if it performs with restraint, nevertheless appears depersonalized and depersonalizing.

People at the margins of the disruption—onlookers or television viewers—will be susceptible to identifying with the minority group undertaking the disruption *even if they do not agree with the strategies or goals of the group.* In a word, they can be "radicalized" or activated because they can identify with the humanness of the disrupters and are repelled by the impersonality of the institutional defenders.

The principal risks of disruption are that it can be costly, resulting in jailings, beatings, and even deaths. Although there may be an initial romantic attraction in confronting the police, a group that is imprisoned is reduced in terms of its political opportunity structure and few individuals have a taste for repeated beatings. The financial costs of bail, attorneys, and appeals are also high. Since group members cannot be abandoned to languish in jail, the costs are necessary costs, but they drain the resources of the group.

Street tactics carry bloc tactics into a more intense and public arena. They create specific pressures on the system, but their potential cost and demands often require more organizational resources, skills, and information than are immediately apparent to the casual observer. Further, they are tactics that must be applied with restraint, because repeated use robs them of their vitality. People become bored with an endless stream of demonstrations, and the core members of a group can be jailed for repeated attempts at disruption, or they can simply become exhausted.

Street tactics do create an atmosphere of crisis for group members, onlookers, and institutional defenders. They sense that "something is about to happen," that the system is facing new dilemmas, and that people are doing something. The psychological effect is double-pronged: they can help strengthen identification bonds within a group, and they force rash and hysterical reactions from dominant groups, thus destabilizing the political and social system.

Guerrilla Tactics

The rise of guerrilla warfare in the United States took place at the end of the 1960s albeit on a small scale. Between July, 1970, and June, 1971, for example, there were over eighteen hundred bombings. In their pure forms, guerrilla tactics are the deliberate, violent destabilizing of the system, with reconstitution being the ultimate goal. In theory, they are one stage prior to the open clash of organized bodies of troops in set-piece battles. In less pure forms, they may be no more than the release of frustrations and aggressions or a rationalized life of crime.

When guerrilla tactics are pursued with a concrete minority strategy in mind, however, they pose a serious threat to the system. The advantages to the users are numerous. First, guerrilla tactics are by nature covert and thus difficult to detect and counter. Second, because they are covert, they give the guerrillas themselves the emotional satisfaction of close identification. Third, they require only small numbers and thus do not create the problems associated with massive organizations. Fourth, they create a climate of fear in dominant groups and institutions, often leading to paranoid and irrational attempts at self-protection, which further radicalizes the minority and its invisible members.

Guerrilla tactics have disadvantages, too. Most importantly, a guerrilla places himself outside the law, which means that the modern technology of law enforcement is brought to bear against him. If caught, he will probably be imprisoned. Further, a guerrilla is dependent on those around him for protection from the law. As a result he is highly vulnerable to informers, and, thus far, no conspiratorial network seems to be invulnerable to informers. He thus lives a life of suspicion, fear, and constant mobility. Although the conspirator's life has been endowed with glamor by movies and novels, it is emotionally draining and physically wearing. From a political standpoint, the guerrilla limits his own political opportunity structure. Covertness and violence are the only means available to him; he has at his command only one tactical scenario.

His power to destroy and escape, however, is an effective means of demonstrating the power of a small, cohesive group. And the use of violence has a dramatic appeal that few other tactics possess. It writes in italics the intensity of commitment and the risks the group is willing to take for its cause.

Fundamental to the success of a group employing guerrilla tactics are: (1) a cohesive identification group; (2) the skills and determination to perform violent tasks; (3) a secure refuge; (4) an environment that allows the group to exist without exposure to the police; and (5) a willingness to accept unlimited personal sacrifices. If any of these ingredients are missing, the group is pathetically vulnerable.

Organizing Tactics

It is clear that the strength of minority group tactics comes from the group-as-organization. Without successful organization all tactical plans and efforts are exercises in pointlessness. Further, a group must be able to reach those outside its core membership; it must be able to attract invisible members, in addition to enlarging its active membership. This expanded membership will increase its resources and manpower, and will help to create the sympathetic human environment necessary for attracting attention and providing leverage. If the tactical aim is to destabilize the system, the more who participate the more rapid and effective the effort will be.

Every group, however large or small, functions in an environment of potential new members. The problem is to tap that potential and thereby increase the group's basic resource: its own numbers.

The basic tool of organizing tactics is the organizer, the much-feared "outside agitator." His task is neither glamorous nor especially exciting, but for a politically active minority group it is crucial. The organizer acts as the personal contact with potential members of the group, and, when possible, converts the potential into reality. At the very minimum, the organizer aims to create an invisible membership that can be rallied in times of maximum political effort or need.

The organizer's task is difficult but not complicated. His function is to create minority self-awareness (consciousness-raising) and to channel the newly acquired or intensified self-awareness toward the group itself. To do so, he must:

1. Locate minority members and meet with them. His most efficient route is often through existing institutions, such as schools, churches, clubs, neighborhood organizations, gangs, or fraternities.

2. Generate minority awareness by stressing minority status as the common bond among those being organized. He may be able to interpret "incidents" that show that the dominant groups and institutions treat the minority as a single category, even if the members of the minority fail to think of themselves in those terms. He may be able to conduct educational sessions in black history, women's history, or student problems. He may use variants of sensitivity training and encounter groups, in which minority members unveil their emotional stresses, which can then be explained in a minority politics framework.

3. Produce awareness of the deprivation resulting from minority status—initially in individual terms, which can then gradually be expanded to show that all members of the minority share the same problems and needs.

4. Emphasize the futility of solitary, individual efforts at relieving the deprivation, while stressing the potential power available through collective action.

5. Provide a channel for collective action (the group).

6. Provide a general target at which "we-ness" and "they-ness" can be focused.

7. Educate group members with regard to organizational and tactical skills.

Preferably, the organizer should not overtly lead the group members-to-be. They should act of their own accord and by so doing commit themselves and reap the psychological rewards of their courage. The organizer hopes that once set in motion, group processes will bind potential members to the group. His job is to provide them with new information. He lets them know that what they are considering has been done elsewhere and therefore can safely be attempted by them. He is also their parliamentary advisor, providing information on forms and procedures and laying out alternatives that will produce the desired effect.

Not all organizing efforts work. Some fail because the organizer lacks the competence or energy to do the job. Unless he is a person of enormous patience and self-restraint, he can spoil a good beginning or abort any beginning at all. Some efforts fail because the potential members cannot accept group goals, their backgrounds are too diversified, or they are too fearful. Some are stifled by counteractions or competition from other groups. But, the organizer is the crucial means by which a group expands; if it fails to do so, it is often because its organizing campaign was neglected or unsuccessful.

An "organizer" of some importance is the mass media. To a great extent, minority group tactics are designed to attract the attention of the media and thereby to communicate to invisible members and potential members what is happening, why, and what further can be done. Television made the SCLC civil rights campaigns successful; it helped the student revolts of the late 1960s and early 1970s to reach every campus in the country. It guarantees that group goals and strategies are communicated to an enormous audience.

Because the media need news, to the extent that minority groups can make news means that they have the media at their disposal. But "making news" requires that the media, first, know of the event in advance; second, find it possible to report it; and third, find it newsworthy, that is, visual, comprehensible, and dramatic, as well as "different." The media's needs require that to an extent tactics be shaped to fit them. If not, the reportage that emerges (if any) may be hostile and distorted. If handled correctly, the media can be an invaluable supplementary organizer by attracting people who may be potentially organizable either as group members or as invisible members.

The Unilateral Bargain

The unilateral bargain, or nonnegotiable demand, underlies many tactics of minority groups. There are two dimensions to such a demand. First, the nonnegotiable demand, which dominant groups refuse to meet, is a means by which the minority can show potential members the intransigence of the "power structure." In this sense, it becomes a communications device and a means by which dominant groups are forced to overreact to a tactical maneuver. Second, it *is* a bargain. It is a statement that the minority group is offering to forego disrupting the stability of the system in exchange for a complete concession to its power (rather than to its specific demands). In effect, the unilateral bargain says: If you want stability, you must revise your definition of it to include us in the power curve.

Dominant groups faced with a unilateral bargaining situation have a difficult, if not impossible, choice to make. To refuse is to face further destabilizing tactics. To accept is to face a new pattern of stability that would include the minority. Compromise will not work, because the list of "demands" are not the *real* demand; they merely symbolize the real thing, which is a revision of the power system.

Thus, the question, "What is it that they *really* want?" can be answered as follows:

1. A means by which members and potential members can be convinced that the group is not powerless.

2. A symbol around which the group can fulfill its identification needs.

3. Destabilization.

4. A revision of the power curve.

Dominant groups tend to deal with the content of minority demands in the belief that they constitute a bargaining and compromise situation. Often these demands have little significance, other than symbolic significance, to the minority group itself. The minority leader or spokesman is dealing principally with identification needs and these are not subject to bargaining.

Thus, the unilateral bargain is itself a destabilizing device, since it confuses dominant groups, creating stress, inappropriate responses, and misinterpretations of the real political situation.

Uses of Minority Tactics

To many, the minority group tactics described in this chapter must seem appalling. Those tactics seem to contemplate chaos, confusion, and even anarchy. They seem to lie outside the American traditions of orderliness and reasonable negotiation among reasonable leaders and seem to invite a politics of ruthlessness. Whether defending or attacking these tactics, one must acknowledge that they are engendered by the perception (correct or not) that the power curve of American society provides no other choice for some minority groups.

Although demonstrations, riots, rebellions, and system destabilization are by no means new to the United States, conscious theorizing about them and testing of them are. Many observers would call it extreme to argue that these tactics were born out of desperation. More to the point, they exist, and, because they do, some minority groups at some times will use them.

Bibliography

Alinsky, Saul. *Rules for Radicals: A Pragmatic Primer for Realistic Radicals.* New York: Random House, 1971. A compendium of the wisdom of one of America's most successful tactical organizers.

Chatfield, Jack. "Port Gibson, Mississippi: A Profile of the Future?" *New South,* 24 (Summer 1969), pp. 45–55.

Meier, August, ed. *The Transformation of Activism.* Chicago: Aldine, 1970. Contains useful essays on the new tactics of minorities.

O. M. Collective. *The Organizer's Manual.* New York: Bantam, 1971. One of the very best collections of information on minority groups and the tactics appropriate to each.

Schwartz, Edward, ed. *Student Power: Philosophy, Program, Tactics.* Washington, D.C.: National Student Association, 1968.

Stone, Chuck. *Black Political Power in America.* Indianapolis: Bobbs-Merrill, 1968.

Walker, Jack L. *Sit-Ins in Atlanta: A Study of the Negro Revolt.* New York: McGraw-Hill, 1964. A study of the strengths and failings of various minority tactics, including coalition tactics.

Wright, William E. *Memphis Politics: A Study in Racial Bloc Voting.* New York: McGraw-Hill, 1962.

Seventeen
Response and Counterresponse

Historically, dominant institutions have made the decisions, leaving the minority to react to them—to follow or to resist, to benefit or to suffer. As indicated earlier, the balance has turned, and one reason for the shift has been the rise of a set of strategies and tactics that are minority group oriented. The political system must now respond to initiatives from minority groups, or resort to counterresponses aimed at vitiating the minority group assault.

But has the thrust of this interpretation been fair? Is it correct to set up a political model in which a minority is pitted against a dominant group? Assuming that their interests diverge is emphasizing the darker side of American politics, is it not? Certainly, the story of the black movement is also a history of courageous whites, risking their fortunes, community respect, and even their lives to obtain for the black his rights. The list would include Quakers, Abolitionists, white civil-rights workers, and countless others who quietly sacrificed themselves for blacks without benefiting greatly themselves, except for the emotional rewards of doing what they believed to be right. Indians, Mexican-Americans, women, Puerto Ricans, Japanese, and homosexuals have had devoted allies outside their minority groupings who have been some of the more important components of the invisible membership of minority groups.

As easy as it is to say that they could have done more, a fairer judgment perhaps would be to say that what they did was far more than what was done by those who did nothing. To arrive at a balanced judgment requires making a difficult decision. A society can be measured by its "central tendency," which for many minorities has been that of indifference and too little too late. It can be measured by one extreme tendency: the bigotry and brutality of slavery, Indian massacres, and years of discrimination. Or it can be measured by the other extreme tendency: the tens of thousands who died to eliminate slavery and the men and women now forgotten who struggled for civil rights, Indian rights, women's rights, and students' rights. Is the pattern of America that of repression and exploitation or is it that of groping toward humanity and mutual dependence, a dependence that requires neither an individual nor a group to sacrifice integrity and identity? An answer, like all answers to political and social questions, would be a mixture of hope, idealism and ideology, personal experience, both short- and long-term political aims, personal ambitions, and popular rhetoric.

The answer given by any group or individual is apt to reflect self-serving political ends: to convince, to persuade, to commit one's followers and potential followers. As is so often the case, political answers become self-executing prophecies. Those who believe in the power structure can always find it willing to oppress them if provoked enough; those who believe in pluralism can always find generous evidence of the progress of minorities over the decades. Probably the answers can be found only in a detailed examination of every action and nonaction, of every example of conflict and cooperation, and if such a task were possible, it has not yet been undertaken.

Ultimately, relations between dominant groups and minority groups are the product of a range of actions and reactions, differently interpreted by each participating group. The interpretations are shaped by the degree to which one group understands the motives and aims of the other. And, the picture is complicated because the responses and counterresponses available to dominant groups are not one-dimensional, nor are the groups monolithic.

Expediency Responses

A reputed reality of the American political system is that it "oils the wheel that squeaks." Any interest that makes a sufficiently strong demand, which is to say, that goes through the process of forming groups and organizing, amassing resources, using publicity and the media, and applying pressure, is going to get attention and be rewarded in the political system by acquiring a foothold on the power curve.

The basic assumption of the "expediency responses" is that politics responds to realities. The concept of pluralism rests on that assumption. In the constant shuffling and confusion of innumerable centers of power, those who remain silent will be forgotten, which is unfortunate—perhaps even undesirable—but is nonetheless a reality that should be recognized. And, so it could be argued, the mistake made by the new minorities is to have been late in accepting this very simple truth. The old minorities did not make the same error, and, although they suffered discrimination and deprivation, they overcame the effects by clamoring for admission and earning it by shrewd political bargaining and the realistic use of the politics of access.

The process is not easy, as the pluralists would concede. It requires struggle, effort, commitment, and a willingness to accept defeats as well as to learn how to handle victory, but it is the one thing to which the political system responds.

Implicitly, it requires an acceptance of the political system itself, because no system can allow admission to those whose aim is its destruction.

The lesson, it can be argued, is modest but vital. Politicians, being human, do no more than they must. They do not unnecessarily risk their careers if they can avoid it, especially if they would derive no real benefits. But if matters that they cannot ignore are called to their attention, if the risks of inaction are higher than those of action, if problems are presented to them so that they can use the power they have without surrendering it, they will respond.

It can be argued that it is because of these simple precepts that blacks find themselves in elective and appointive positions all over the nation; that women find the federal government taking action to upgrade their employment opportunities; and that students have been placed on faculty and administrative committees. Perhaps the gains fall short of minority aspirations, but, it could be argued, this is the nature of the human condition. No one gets all he wants all at once, perhaps because aspirations are unlimited and realities are limiting.

The two principles governing expediency responses are, first, that the political system makes change possible. The minority goals, strategies, and tactics that contemplate disrupting or destroying that system only invite counterresponses. To those who have worked within the system and in their turn made it work to their benefit and the benefit of those they represent, radical change is not only difficult but immoral. For, as much as minorities press their demands, there are others whose demands are pressed equally hard, and it is neither good politics nor moral behavior for the politician to ignore one segment of his constituency in favor of another. Interests must be balanced; each wheel that squeaks must be oiled, and although no single wheel gets all the oil, every wheel gets some.

The second governing principle is that the political system is built on power, on the desire of every individual (or interest) to impose his will on as much of the environment as possible. Every man thinks his position is right; he can justify his behavior with research, argument, and rhetoric. He points to others who would benefit from the total satisfaction of his needs and to those who stand to lose if a competing interest is benefited. The politician who works within the framework of pluralistic politics, however, knows that underneath all the research and rhetoric is the more basic urge: "I want to run things around here." Those who go into politics want power, to state the proposition in its simplest terms. Those who are seeking power may say they want it for a variety of reasons—to do good, to save the nation, to redress wrongs, to get theirs, to protect the helpless, or to make money. But all of it boils down to the same thing: a desire for power.

Since all men who go into politics want power, few are willing to give it up once they have it. Conceded that minorities may believe that they could do a better job of running things than the people who are running them now, they are no different from anyone who reads a newspaper or watches the news on television. The acid test of the ability to use power is to gain and keep it. To say what one might do is no substitute for setting to work to do it.

For minorities to ask or demand that power be surrendered to them is not only childish but unrealistic. When, through their own organizational skill, they prove that they are essential to politicians, they will not need to be "given" power, they will already have it.

Minorities who grumble about lacking self-government do not realize that the pluralistic system gives them just that. It is their choice to organize politically or not. They are the initiators, the only people who can recognize their own interests and pursue the political process in an effort to bring about the changes they desire.

From the standpoint of a minority group, the expediency response can seem to shift the blame for deprivation to the minority and by so doing can ignore past and present failures of the political system. Also, it can seem like a false invitation: you will be admitted if you fight your way in, but you must conform to our rules in the struggle.

It is difficult to appraise how many Americans would fundamentally ascribe to the expediency response, but it is safe to guess that the number would be large if not a majority. The expediency response is the most pragmatic interpretation of the politics of access. It is in keeping with the American concept that a person gets what he wants by hard work, by earning it, and by not depending on others to do what he can do for himself. There are, however, built-in limits to the permissiveness incorporated in the expediency response. Deliberate destabilizing tactics, separatism or reconstitution, and even integrity goals are of dubious legitimacy. It is probably safe to generalize that the basic assumption of expediency responses is that minorities are no different from any other political animals and should therefore behave like the others.

The Coalition Response

Many members of the dominant society accept the legitimacy of minority goals and aspirations and, in fact, consider them to be congruent with their own goals. Robert Kennedy, for example, shared the anger and anguish of deprived minorities and sought to bring them into the political system. His response was that the only alternative to a bitterly divided society is one in which dominant groups join forces to pursue common aims—a response that is now characteristically "liberal." These aims, moreover, do exist. The elimination of poverty is a benefit not only to those who suffer directly from it, but also to those who must pay the bills through taxes to eradicate the ills springing from poverty. Achieving minority status goals not only raises minority self-esteem but improves the quality of human relations among dominant members of the society. That is, although members of dominant and minority groups may differ on specific techniques of accomplishing fundamental aims, reasonable people cannot differ on the aims themselves.

Responsibility for achieving these aims is a joint responsibility. Minority groups certainly must struggle on their own, but to leave them to struggle alone against the weight of hundreds of years of deprivation is to renounce the responsibilities of political leadership. An inevitable result is that minority groups will turn to violent tactics, benefiting no one.

Basically, the dominant coalition response is similar—if not equivalent—to the integration and cultural pluralism strategies and goals of minority groups. The fundamental assumption is that social progress occurs through cooperation, even though there may be conflict concerning specific applications and timing.

The coalition response does limit its support of minority aspirations. It asks that both minority and dominant groups agree that the political system is workable; the system may require reform, but it does not need reconstitution. It also asks that both minority and dominant groups understand each other. As pressing as minority needs are, progressive-minded members of dominant institutions also face problems, most significantly the limits imposed by the political system. Success will come, but only in stages, through bargaining, compromise, and a recognition that one must accept what can be gotten today and use it to build toward tomorrow. The liberal politician straddles two worlds: one comprising the politics of access, the other the politics of minorities. His hope is to bring the two into congruence, as a matter of conviction and as a shrewd assessment of his power bases. Presumably, both worlds must yield something. The dominant groups will have to make major strides in meeting the welfare and status goals of minorities; minority groups will have to be willing to forego some of their more militant and radical strategies, accept the politics of access (and the delays implicit in it), and probably sacrifice at least some of their integrity goals.

The coalition response has produced minority gains. It has also generated a general distrust of "liberalism." As is so often the case, the politician who attempts to build bridges often fails to satisfy those standing on either shore. He is distrusted by his more conservative colleagues and supporters for "giving in to unrealistic demands"; he is regarded with hostility by minorities who suspect him of using them for his own gain while counselling patience. Minority group leaders are apt to feel that the coalition response to their demands is an enormous legitimizing influence, providing rich opportunities, especially for attaining welfare goals. On the other hand, there is the risk of becoming dependent on a partner that does not need you as much as you need him. The question is, How far down the road is the liberal willing to travel with his minority allies? Too often, the answer is, Not very far.

Acceptance Responses

Some members of the dominant society in fact accept the basic premises of the more militant and radical minority groups. They agree that the minorities alone can judge what is needed and that the strategies and tactics that they pursue are the right ones. Often, the acceptance-oriented members of the dominant society assist by offering money, advice, and comfort where it is denied and by actively seeking to help destabilize the system themselves.

They agree that the political power structure is unbalanced and may become more radical than the minority groups with which they identify. There is some suspicion, even among the minority groups that are receiving aid, that dominant members of society who are radicals are following a fad and that their behavior is really a subtle form of patronizing those who are disadvantaged. Adopting Indian dress, pretending to be younger, using the jargon of the streets and of revolution do not turn people into a minority; it only allows them to play a role and perhaps avoid the more basic duty of trying to convince other dominant members to think sympathetically about minority problems.

The distrust is not universal. In one study, only about 20 percent of the blacks interviewed expressed their distrust of whites who try to help them, and only 30 percent felt that the whites who took part in civil-rights demonstrations were insincere in their motives (Marx, 1967, pp. 171–173). But the percentages are high enough to indicate a solid core of distrust toward white assistance. Of course, the distrust that exists may be unjust. Certainly, some members of the dominant society are engaged in make-believe, adopting the latest fad only to shed it when a new one comes along. Others, however, are profoundly committed and sincere, sharing with the minorities a sense of subjective deprivation.

From the minority perspective, however, such friends are not always useful. Many observers can understand the struggles of minority groups to improve their own lot, but what are the motives of dominant members who identify with the minority? Are they "Communist agents?" Are they legitimate spokesmen for the minority? Or are they only trying to cash in on the misery of others? The minority group can end by looking like the pawn of its dominant sympathizers, seemingly unable to speak for itself, too incompetent to do its own work, and turning to outsiders for leadership and control.

Every minority group must inevitably be dependent on an invisible membership drawn from the dominant members of society who favor either the coalition response or the acceptance response. A minority group may regard these invisible members with skepticism and even cynicism, considering them useful tools for obtaining financial contributions, favorable press releases, and support, which helps to fragment the strength of dominant groups and institutions in times of political crisis. Few if any minority groups can survive without a dominant-based invisible membership, however. The arithmetic of minority numbers and resources and the strategic location of dominant members in courts, legislatures, executive offices, and the bureaucracy means that without some sympathizers the minority group will be unable to gain sufficient leverage to pursue any strategy except revolution.

The crucial question for a minority group is what price must be paid to gain that support. If it can be achieved through tactics that do not require binding commitments on the part of the minority group, but nonetheless evoke sympathy from members of dominant groups, the situation is ideal. If the price of support, however, is that the minority has to mold its strategies and tactics to please its dominant supporters, it will have been locked into a coalition situation, but perhaps without the assurance of success that good coalition tactics demand. Thus, protest, demonstration, and street tactics in general must be aimed at winning sympathizers from the potential dominant invisible membership as well as from the potential minority membership. The political realities stress tactical skills, information, and an ability to think through the complexities of the minority condition.

Counterresponses

Dominant groups may not accept in any degree the efforts of minorities to assert claims on the political system. They can, in fact, resort to counterresponses, that is, efforts to vitiate, disrupt, and render impotent minority groups and their political supporters. Counterresponses are not necessarily the result of conscious planning; they may be the reaction of a political system and its leaders to a destabilizing threat. Naturally, when the counterresponses are the product of careful planning, logistics, and organization, they will probably be more successful. Basically, all counterresponses are aimed at maintaining stability by crippling those who are or might be destabilizing influences.

Concessions

The most direct counterresponse is, "We'll go so far but no farther." Some minority group demands are granted–those that are the most "realistic, feasible, and responsible." The minority group in question does gain something and cannot claim to have been met with indifference. Dominant group members can feel they have dealt in good faith with the minority and thus can assuage any doubt they may have had about refusing to acknowledge the justness of its claims.

Concessions place a strain on the cohesiveness of the minority group. Members not anxious to pursue more militant goals, who are readily satisfied by the symbols of victory or by directly benefiting from the concessions made, are less anxious to insist on the terms of a unilateral bargain, especially if the situation is shaping up to be an all-or-nothing proposition. In short, concessions can help fray the identification commitments within the target group.

At the same time, concessions reduce the appeal of the group to its invisible membership, especially those drawn from dominant members of the society. Because the group has "won," its need for further support seems less; and if it makes "unreasonable" demands after having received concessions, it seems ungrateful, irrational, and greedy.

Concessions, moreover, can be a public-relations tactic, a device by which the dominant group attempts to maintain its solidarity and appeal to its own invisible membership and that of the minority at the same time. Concessions often shift the burdens of blame, reason, and orderly behavior from the dominant group to the minority. They present the minority with the troubling task of proving to its own members and its audience that the concessions should be rejected because they are inadequate. And, shifting the blame (if successful) means that minority leadership must as a consequence concentrate some of its energies on renewed organizational problems rather than on tactics aimed at the dominant society.

Because concessions can take a variety of forms—ranging from substantive concessions to study commissions, joint commissions, appointments to positions, the announcement of new programs yet to be implemented, and high-level conferences between minority and dominant leaders—they can create the appearance, if not the actuality, of progress. There are, however, basic problems associated with concessions as a tactic.

First, members of dominant groups may reject the granting of concessions. They argue (often correctly) that minority demands are only a ploy, a foot-in-the-door tactic calculated by the minority group leadership to prove the group's power and to appeal to the invisible and potential membership of the group. Those opposed to granting concessions argue that the demands are unlimited, sensing, if not overtly recognizing, the nature of the unilateral bargain in which the question of relative power positions is at stake rather than the demands themselves. University administrators and faculty, thus, often resist permitting students to be observers on key committees because they expect the next demand to be for voting membership. Resistance of this kind creates problems for dominant group leaders; they must face the question of how far they can go without splitting their own members into warring factions.

Second, concessions must be carefully timed. If concessions have been granted too grudgingly and too late, a minority group will have already united its members and rallied its invisible members. It will have had a chance to establish a "we-they" situation in which identification bonds are strong enough to provide a basis for moving beyond any concessions that are made. Minority leaders will have been given the chance to explain that it is the principle rather than the substance of the demands that is at stake; and the apparent unwillingness of the dominant group to make those concessions proves their point.

Therefore, the ideal position of dominant leadership is to be able to move swiftly, forcing the minority leadership to make concrete demands and then giving in somewhat on each. Whether the dominant leadership can do so usually depends on the internal dynamics of the dominant group or institution.

Cooptation

Cooptation is a classic tactic for dealing with dissidents. By being incorporated into the existing political system, by being assured of some of the benefits of the system, and also, it is hoped, by being educated in the "responsibilities" of decision-making, the dissenter is converted from opponent to participant, from minority group leader to liaison between the dominant system and the minority. Cooptation is an adjunct to or a part of the tactics of concession and is a potent means of picking off minority group leaders or potential leaders.

The success of cooptation depends on a number of conditions. The dominant group itself must be willing to allow the coopted person or group to participate in affairs. To fail to do so is to risk creating an even more embittered, cynical—and knowledgeable—adversary. Further, the opportunity must exist. A group that is too distrustful may resist cooptation, or may even accept the forms of cooptation but use the positions gained for militant tactics against the system. VISTA (Volunteers in Service to America), the Teachers Corps, and the Community Action Program were all cooptive, yet in a number of cases local programs became radical training grounds and centers for destabilizing political tactics.

Cooptation is most effective against groups in which identification bonds are less significant than instrumental ties. As a payoff in benefits, status, and some measure of power, cooptation is tempting to the members of an instrumental group and in fact may be equivalent to its goals. Used against a group that predominantly serves identification functions, however, it will be resisted strenuously.

Instrumentalism

The relatively greater resources possessed by dominant groups and institutions provides them with the opportunity to "buy off" minority groups, to undermine or prevent the development of identification as the primary group function. This costs something, perhaps in terms of welfare benefits and even status concessions, but in the American political system instrumentalism is both a familiar and long-proven political tactic.

Some minority groups or some members of every minority group participate in political activities primarily to achieve instrumental goals. Even though they may have strong identification ties, when faced with the tangible benefits they could gain, they are cross-pressured. And, a cross-pressured individual is predisposed toward indecision and inaction.

Others will gladly reap the instrumental benefits of the system and accept political conventionality as the reasonable and legitimate price to pay. To a great extent, this has been the assumed, and perhaps the actual, functioning of the American political system. For many ethnic groupings and such movements as the labor movement, the exchange has been a fair bargain and a workable one.

For the new minorities, however, instrumentalism as a counterresponse has been either too inadequate, too late, or inappropriate. This is not to say that it cannot work, but it works only if dominant groups are willing to pay the price; and, as the identification functions of minority groups gain in importance and strength, instrumentalism, however vigorously pursued, simply may not work. A minority group that has progressed to the stage of fulfilling its integrity goals will scornfully reject the idea that it can be bought off by mere welfare rewards. And, if the group's leaders suggested it, they might find themselves replaced by more charismatic leaders.

Instrumentalism is, however, a basis for concession tactics and it can serve to short-cut a group's appeal to invisible and potential members not yet reached by its organizers. As a tactic, then, it limits the potential power base of the target minority group. On the other hand, it can turn a minority group into another economically based pressure group that is only incidentally composed of minority members.

The Invalidation of Leadership

An old, if ugly, technique is to strike at an opposing group by invalidating its leadership, demonstrating that those who lead are corrupt, insincere, stooges for a covert movement, or morally repulsive. Because at least some minority groups use their leaders as symbols of identification and rely on their charismatic appeal to provide the bond for group cohesion, presumably these leaders, and their groups, are vulnerable to invalidating tactics. A result is to throw the group into disarray, frustrate and embitter members, and probably hopelessly fragment the group.

Often proof is not required to achieve invalidation. All that is needed are sufficiently persuasive rumors and quasi-evidence to cast suspicion on a leader, leave him facing distrust within his group, and place him on the defensive.

Leadership invalidation through rumors, press reports, or planted accusations from compliant group members is far from simple, however. Knowledge of the group itself, its processes and bases, and its relations with its leaders is mandatory. For example, for some groups, proof that a leader had once used narcotics or had committed a crime may do no more than show that he has shared "the people's" experiences. Divorce—a major political stigma in the world of conventional politics—could well be a badge of honor in a women's liberation group.

Invalidating a group's leadership can have another effect, however. Even if it fails to strike at the leader's position within his group, it can harm the group's relations with its dominant sympathizers. They may be fearful of being linked with criminal or communist elements, reluctant to support a group that "authoritative" sources show to be led by unscrupulous men or women. Thus, the group's resource base is at least limited if not eroded.

As a tactic, however, it must be well executed. An invalidation attempt that fails can cause a group and its sympathizers to align even more closely with its leaders.

Counterorganization

Another long-standing tactic is the creation, usually through covert sponsorship, of a counterorganization. Ideally, the counterorganization is vocal enough and sincere enough to compete for the membership of the target group. Because rewards and concessions can be channelled to the counterorganization so that it receives the bulk of the welfare and status benefits, three ends are achieved. First, the dominant group can point out that a minority group is making progress, primarily because it is "sensible" and "responsible" in its tactics and strategies. Second, the target minority group is beleaguered by the counterorganization. Its present and future membership base is being sought by another group; its own approaches are being invalidated by its competitor's successes; and it must devote much of its effort to doing battle with its competitor. Third, the minority itself will be speaking with a divided voice, since at least two groups will be claiming to represent the minority's true interests. Dominant groups, then, will be in a position of relative security, knowing that the minority's internal divisions provide them with the freedom to respond as they see fit.

Creating an effective counterorganization is not an easy task, however. It requires access to the minority grouping through reliable agents. It requires knowing enough about the target group to create a counterorganization that will challenge its position. And it requires constant nourishment of the counterorganization once created. If the minority group already has sufficient hold over its membership, the counterorganization may never be able to fulfill its role. Exposure of the effort can lead to a strong reaction of sympathy for the target minority group. And, there is always the possibility that the counterorganization may, sooner or later, choose to go its own way, free of its dominant sponsor, to become an activist minority group.

Suppression

Minority group tactics can be met with deliberate attempts to squash the group through arrests, harassment, beatings, and even murder. Although murder is hardly sanctioned by law, it has been used extensively to suppress black and Indian political efforts.

Suppression, however, is a difficult tactic to use. It invites group counteraction, it risks evoking widespread sympathy for the target group, and it can lead to the creation of martyrs who act as symbols for group identification. Further, suppression is expensive. Even with the advantages of modern technology, it requires enormous research and surveillance efforts and often lengthy legal proceedings. Widely feared by minority groups, however, the very threat of suppression may be effective enough to impose moderation on more cautious minority members.

Generated by the belief that nothing short of the most extreme methods will work, suppression tactics are the equivalent of minority guerrilla tactics. And, of course, revolutionary groups hope to force dominant groups to rely on suppression, because it helps to reveal the internal contradictions of a system that professes equality and peace but uses selective law enforcement and violence.

Probably, in any given situation dominant groups and institutions possess the means to overwhelm minority efforts at system destabilization. Such a generalization, however, is based on a number of purely theoretical considerations. The dominant groups themselves must be cohesive and undivided; they must rationally and logically select the counterresponses that will work for the situation they are facing; and dominant leadership must be willing to resort to whatever method is required to overcome a challenge to its power.

Rarely do any of these conditions exist in real life. The reasons are largely unexplored, probably because social scientists often tend to assume that politically motivated persons operate within a rational framework. It would seem, however, that as strong as the urge toward power may be, very few individuals are motivated solely by power urges. Psychologically, forces at work within them make them recoil from the use of absolute means to meet a threat. These forces include a belief in the traditions of the system, which argue that machine guns are not a reasonable solution to political problems (at least domestically), a personal revulsion at taking the responsibility of jailing or ordering the harassment of other human beings, and, probably more often than is conceded, a recognition that many of the goals of minority groups are just and proper.

Even those people lacking significant internal controls face the consciences of others. Few possess so much power in America that they can order anyone to do anything. Few can avoid being criticized, attacked, or challenged by other powerholders in dominant groups if the measures they take appear to be "excessive." And, given the state of the art, no political leader can be absolutely sure of what his supporters think is appropriate or of what they feel to be excessive. In choosing from the alternatives available for dealing with minority group demands, every dominant group leader must operate in a haze of uncertainty, and the uncertainty is itself a moderating and controlling influence.

In the "real world" rather than the world of lists of alternatives, both minority group and dominant group are interacting with each other, each searching for a responsive note, hoping to avoid precipitating a situation in which its base of support is suddenly threatened or eroded, and hoping to gain the greatest advantage at the least cost. Each leader is tied to his cause and his interests by pragmatic considerations and emotional involvements, and neither can accurately predict the future effects of his actions. Each leader knows that his own power is a function of his organization, the support of his group and its invisible members, and the degree of cohesiveness that exists within his group. He must meet a complex network of expectations, express them through his own behavior, and often anticipate changes in them. He can move neither so fast nor so slowly that he risks setting into motion the forces that render a group impotent.

There are clearly no simple formulas or assessments. In many instances, the situations are so new that they have no precedents. All that can be said with real confidence is that the beleaguered minorities raise basic questions about the American political system for which neither they nor the dominant groups of society have workable answers. Thus the new minority group politics has become a new form of politics for the rest of society as well.

Bibliography

Etzkowitz, Henry, and Gerald M. Schaflander. *Ghetto Crisis: Riots or Reconciliation?* Boston: Little, Brown, 1969.

Janowitz, Morris. *The Social Control of Escalated Riots.* Chicago: University of Chicago Press, 1968. A fascinating study of the responses available to one form of minority revolt.

Marx, Gary T. *Protest and Prejudice: A Study of Belief in the Black Community.* New York: Harper, 1967.

Moynihan, Daniel P. *Maximum Feasible Misunderstanding: Community Action in the War on Poverty.* New York: The Free Press, 1969. An analysis of the failure of liberalism as a response to minority conditions.

Powledge, Fred. *Black Power White Resistance.* Cleveland: World, 1967.

Skolnick, Jerome H. *The Politics of Protest.* New York: Ballantine, 1969. A useful analysis of the interaction between minority and dominant groups in protest situations.

Urban American, Inc. and the Urban Coalition. *One Year Later: An Assessment of the Nation's Response to the Crisis Described by the National Advisory Commission on Civil Disorders.* Washington, D.C.: 1969.

Wallerstein, Immanuel, and Paul Starr, eds. *The University Crisis Reader: Confrontation and Counterattack.* New York: Vintage, 1971.

Eighteen
The Coming Legacy

Can American politics ever be the same again? There are those who devoutly hope so; others who devoutly hope not. The answer would seem to be that even though the American system may never be totally reconstituted, it cannot return to the days of the pristine politics of access, if those days ever really existed. The reasons are numerous, and important, because they constitute what will become the permanent legacy of minority group politics to the American political style.

Widening Politicization

Perhaps one of the most crucial changes is the widening of "politicization," increasing the number of objects that are considered to be political. For a long time it was argued and perhaps generally believed that "you can't legislate morality," despite innumerable efforts to do just that. But it was considered appropriate that certain objects and certain human behaviors were outside the realm of politics, including individual prejudices and preferences, various economic activities, and an enormous variety of social practices. The increase in the number of political objects has not been sudden. The union movement, the Depression, two world wars, and the "Cold War," as well as the growing pressures of minority groups—all helped to increase the number of political objects to include the relationships of corporations to minorities and of public schools to minorities, housing patterns, private clubs, advertising and the media, and even the arts.

Yet, until the 1960s, even the widening politicization had a basic relationship to government and its traditional activities. Governmental intervention in corporate and union recruitment and personnel practices was justified by government expenditures through contracts. Concern about housing could be rationally justified by federally supported housing programs and state-supported and locally supported land-control policies. Courts and bureaucratic agencies moved slowly to desegregate private clubs and associations, and pressures to improve the presentation of minority members in the arts, movies, and the mass media were as much a private response as a public one.

But the beleaguered minorities have expanded the number of political objects far beyond the confines of government *qua* government. Without necessarily adopting Marxist theory in its entirety, minority groups have accepted the proposition that government is an extension of something else: a society's economics, social structure, and cultural values. Government can influence those other "spheres" to effect change. It is vulnerable to political action, but it is not the sole arena. And real changes in government may have to come about through changes in the other spheres. The laws governing sexual deviance, sexual crimes, abortion, divorce, and domestic responsibility are necessary targets of the women's liberation movement and of "Gay Power," but as targets they are not sufficient means to the ends sought. The relationship between individuals is just as important, because the values that determine the roles within this relationship, which can be regarded as a power relationship, also shape governmental behavior. Arranging a household, assigning duties to respective members of that household, and training children are not only "private" and "domestic" matters, but political matters as well; matters of power and power politics that require changes in organization, group identification, and political tactics. That these personal relationships are reflected in the political system only emphasizes the deeper cultural problem.

The same extension of politicization has occurred in universities, colleges, and increasingly in high schools. Institutions of higher learning have long been "political" in some fashion, since they are publicly supported either directly or indirectly and are places in which political values are examined. Until very recently, however, the concept of power politics was not applied *within* an institution itself. Although parietal rules, honor systems, grading standards, and the quality of education have long been subjects of dispute, the basic power structure of an institution was not disputed. Now it is. And the issues encompass not only moral or educational philosophy, but political goals, strategies, and tactics.

The "problem" concerning blacks, Indians, and Mexican-Americans has been traditionally interpreted as being a problem of objective deprivation. To eliminate poverty and to enlarge the opportunity structure would solve the problem. The realization that subjective deprivation can be as important as objective deprivation is fairly new. The only solution to a sense of powerlessness is a sense of power. For some groups and some individuals, at least, adequate housing, good jobs, effective schools, and integration do not produce that sense of power.

The politics of the beleaguered minorities then is not only an alternative to the politics of access but a challenge to it. Once the conflict is stated in unequivocal terms, once the issues are enunciated, once the old tacit assumptions are faulted, the questions raised do not disappear through benign neglect.

Minority group politics, in short, has politicized and is continuing to politicize objects that were long considered outside the political realm and therefore not amenable to either political solution or political analysis. Some observers decry the extension of power politics to include family life, educational systems, age categories, and identification groups. They make a persuasive argument that it is the first step, and a long one at that, toward totalitarianism. The practical problem, however, is that some minorities have what is to them a very good reason for extending politics into these spheres. And once they have done it, decrying the extension will not halt it.

The effects of the extension may not be great, of course. For one thing, the politicized objects themselves may not bear the weight of power politics. A man and a woman, for example, perhaps will agree that they are indeed engaged in a power struggle in their marital relationship; yet, they continue to resolve their differences in the same old ways. Universities may be the scenes of conflict for a period of years but continue to be basically places where young people get degrees and older people teach and do research, or supervise and support those who do the teaching and research.

Blacks, Puerto Ricans, Mexican-Americans, and Indians may experience economic improvements but find, as Jews have found, that a society will relinquish only some of its prejudices and is willing to accept a people only on its own terms. Like Jews, they may choose to preserve some of their minority self-awareness but surrender the hope of real structural pluralism. This alternative—which is really a reassertion of system stability—depends on a great deal. It assumes that the system will find ways of substantially reducing the objective and subjective deprivation of the beleaguered minorities and soon. It assumes that minority groups serving identification functions rather than instrumental functions will be willing to surrender the benefits of group integrity. It assumes that somehow the politics of access will prove to be workable for the beleaguered minorities, and that the tactics adapted to minority group politics will prove themselves useless. It assumes that marked groups will, after all, find that they live in a society in which the mark is less important than, say, occupation, ability, tact, energy, and income and that in this regard society's treatment of people is independent of the cultural mark.

These are large assumptions, and for the "old system" to reassert itself, every assumption must be borne out. If not, the struggle will be over the whole range of economic, social, and political values of the society. The real "new politics" is a politics of cultural values.

The Rise of Conscious Theory

Fifty years ago an interpretation like this would not have been possible. There would have been no way to attempt to discuss systematically alternative views of society, of strategies and goals, and of tactical applications. There were, granted, various Marxist, syndicalist, utopian, and capitalist progressive constructs of the society, some of which had been built by minority groups themselves. They were the preserves of people like Eugene Debs or a Marcus Garvey and commanded the attention of a substantial group membership and an even larger invisible membership. There is no question that the new minorities have a significant if often unconscious debt to the "old radicals." But time has wrought change. Today the social sciences are far more sophisticated. Analyses of society that depend on vulgar Marxism need no longer be the mainstay of minority-group thought. Understanding the dynamics of their own groups allows leaders and would-be leaders to apply tactics that simultaneously serve multiple ends, such as system destabilization, group identification, public relations, and instrumental goals. It is possible to think—and theorize—about cultural interrelationships because the "knowledge explosion" has now provided the information that makes it possible to think about them.

The suffragettes, of course, pondered these matters, as did the Marxists and the progressives. The ideas they developed are often used today. The major difference, however, is that those ideas were foreign, esoteric, and even frightening to a large number of Americans. Today, the situation is remarkably changed. Americans can and do make a best-seller out of a book that deals with contemporary social analysis in layman's language. What they may do with the knowledge gained thereby is a different matter, but the opportunity to affect an ever larger segment of the population now exists. The potential invisible membership of any group is both absolutely and relatively larger.

The mass media, mass literacy, and increasing mass higher education mean that conscious theorizing can find an audience that is able to grasp the implications of the theory. It has long been argued that Americans are not ideologically inclined. Although it is still too soon to say, the inclination may be changing or may have changed already. If so, minority group politics have played an important role in making ideology and ideological politics a part of American politics. Minorities have helped to build the theories, and they have pioneered the strategies and tactics for putting theory into application. Americans can expect to be doing battle not about the distribution of specific benefits within the system, but about the nature of the system itself.

Destabilizing Tactics

Even if minorities ceased their efforts, even if their theories vanished into historical footnotes, the tactics that have been developed by minority groups would have become a permanent fixture in the American political arena. To say that they have become permanent is not to say that the politics of access will wither away. Like minority groups, other groups will use the politics of access either as a sole strategy or as a first step in other strategies. Elections will continue to be hard fought, politicians will continue to bargain and compromise, patronage will continue to be allocated, and administrators will continue to expedite or delay. Further, as has been pointed out, minority groups did not invent their tactics. The tactics came from the labor movement, the peace movement, and even from the old minorities.

But minority groups have begun to change the focus and the context. The strike, the boycott, the bloc vote, the disruptive demonstration were previously calculated to obtain a short-term goal at a minimum cost. Minority groups have found that destabilizing tactics do produce confusion and inconsistent and irrational responses from the "system." Those in power feel that they must respond, or counterrespond, but they do not know how to do it without producing the effect they seek to avoid—instability in the system.

The uncertainty creates opportunities for gaining power. Political leaders confronted with a unilateral bargain face an impossible set of choices. They can make an endless stream of concessions that will eventually lead to a revision of the power curve, creating dissension within the ranks of dominant group members, or they can make no concessions at all, thereby alienating those dominant members who are sympathetic to the minority's aspirations and solidifying the minority group by proving how intractable the dominant institutions are. By making no concessions they encourage the use of destabilizing tactics to force another decision. Or, they can make a counterresponse that solidifies the minority, alienates an ever-increasing number of those in dominant groups, and consequently destabilizes the system. The unilateral bargain is not a fool-proof tactic, but it presents agonizing and therefore destabilizing choices for dominant group leaders. Ironically, the more sympathetic dominant leadership is toward a minority's aims, the more agonizing the decision will be. So far, no one has managed to respond or counterrespond satisfactorily to a minority that is willing to take a unilateral bargain through its entire course.

Not all groups, dominant or minority, are willing to use destabilizing tactics. They hope, instead, to benefit from the system and want to maintain it relatively intact; or they shrink from the possible effects, one of which could be the rise of an authoritarian regime. But others, both minority and dominant, will recognize that the unilateral bargain is a means by which the power structure can be altered, which could lead to at least a temporary widening of political opportunity structures.

College faculty members, high-school teachers, right-wing groups, blue-collar workers, white-collar workers, civil servants, the aged, and ecology advocates, if under sufficient stress, may find that the tactics of minority groups have their uses. Thus far, the principal limitation has been that self-awareness and the group identification that provides the necessary organizational base for developing those tactics have not yet occurred among other groups and groupings, except occasionally.

Since few weapons of war are allowed to rust for long, however, it seems unlikely that other groups will ignore the possibilities for attaining power inherent in the tactics of minority groups, whatever the strategic aims may be. The political system faces the prospect that, however the power curve is constituted, there may always be some group or groups using minority tactics to destabilize it.

The Minorities

A central argument in this book has been that the beleaguered minorities are culturally marked in a way that makes assimilation and cultural pluralism more difficult for them to attain, should they be desired, than they were for the "old" minorities. The new minorities have been regarded as "different" and as "outsiders" by dominant members of society, who have been responsible for their deprivation. It is conceivable that members of the new minorities could continue to be regarded as different without the patterned deprivation, which has largely happened to ethnic minorities. This is, of course, the dream of cultural pluralism, and would be the best of both worlds. Three phenomena cast doubt upon the possibility. First, the cultural marking and the associated deprivation has existed throughout the history of the country. History does not make an imperative for future conditions; progress is possible and even likely, for economic welfare and power has increased for each of the minorities examined herein. Second, however, what had been *groupings* have been converted into *groups*. If the term "minority group" is used—as it so often is—to refer to a collection of fairly discrete individuals, then it is only a collection of individuals whose progress is measured by statistics. If however, the term "group" is used to designate a collectivity of interacting people who are seeking to satisfy identification and instrumental needs, the situation is much different. A group has its own requirements; its individual members are aware of themselves and measure their progress and achievement through the group. Certainly, any minority group is concerned with the minority as a whole, is pleased and made hopeful by the progress of the minority as a whole, but it must deal with the current expectations of its members. Group dynamics—the expectations of the group members and the group's dependence on its members—impose their own demands. To fail to understand that principle is to miss the force that makes minority group politics what it is. The existence of minority groups explains why it is unresponsive to say to a minority group, "Look at all the gains you people have made in the last ten years." The point need not be belabored, but many dominant members of society are beguiled into believing statistical progress is equivalent to satisfying group needs.

Third, as has been argued, the important political data are subjective. To use a simple analogy, the objectively wealthy man who *feels* impoverished will behave as though he is impoverished. Certainly, objective circumstances establish conditions that shape subjective attitudes. It is less likely for wealthy people to feel poor than it is for the poor to feel so. But some poor men feel poorer than others. The same is true for the members of minorities. Their perception of their deprivation is not measured solely by objective standards. It is also a product of the experiences they have and the extent to which their deprivation is forced upon their consciousness. Their perceptions are also affected by their sense of power, their capacity to control their lives and the world around them, and their ability to do something about conditions that they find unpleasant or intolerable. To say to blacks, "Look at the progress you've made," may only provoke them to anger, because the progress is relatively minuscule in relation to need, aspirations, and the benefits enjoyed by dominant groups. Further, the progress may apply to all blacks but not a particular black. A thousand job openings in industry would still leave tens of thousands without jobs. And, finally, statistical progress may not be progress that has actually been achieved. A minority member may still feel that he is a helpless pawn of economic, social, and political forces. The helplessness guarantees him only that what has been arbitrarily given can as arbitrarily be taken away. It is, in essence, a matter of opportunity structure, and the broader the structure, the greater the chance an individual or group has to exercise some power. The narrower the structure, the greater the dependence on a single opportunity or situation. A woman having only domestic skills, who is dependent on her personality, charm, and body for security, is a vulnerable person when she becomes middle-aged. Her world is restricted to her marriage; if that fails, as so many marriages do, and her body and her face have lost the youthful attractiveness that society stresses, she can be economically and socially helpless. A man's marital status rarely affects his economic opportunities; a woman's marital status may summarize her economic opportunities.

The beleaguered minorities struggle against a set of cultural categories that limits their opportunity structures. They have found that dominant institutions are reluctant to expand those opportunities. They have also found that group membership partly compensates for their deprivation and aids them in attacking the sources of deprivation. Whether group action was forced upon the beleaguered minorities by an unresponsive society, evolved naturally, or was the product of "outside agitators" is a moot question. The groups exist, are increasing in number, and are evolving their own approaches to meeting the problems they face.

The Reinterpretation of Politics

American politics is being reinterpreted, and minority groups are the primary agents for that reinterpretation. They have either forced their condition upon the attention of political participants and observers or themselves laid down the outlines of the reinterpretation. The precise nature of the new interpretation is still obscure. To some it will seem horrifying: a nation engaged in perennial strife with its own people constituting the warring factions. To others it may hold a promise, a restatement of the position of man as an individual and as a member of society. It is tempting to adopt an apocalyptic viewpoint. The stresses are great. Struggles over cultural values are never easy because the values are acquired without questioning and imbedded into our unconsciousness. With the exception of a handful of successful revolutions, there have been few deliberate efforts to modify an entire nation's cultural categories, and those efforts would lead an observer to believe that the process can only be a bitter and angry one.

It is possible, of course, that the interpretation set forth here is wrong or, if correct, mistaken in its emphases. The information available is scanty, and another person might examine the same material and come forward with a far different analysis. It may well be that the politics of access will, perhaps grudgingly, reassert itself and gradually absorb the beleaguered minorities as effectively as it did the ethnic minorities. The reasons that this seems unlikely have been argued at length, but reasons do not remove possibilities.

It seems true, however, that American politics must take on a different shape. The insistence on new opportunities, opportunities not presently available, is too clamorous and has lasted too long to have no effect. The distribution of power in American society can never again be quite the same.

Index